RSTATE AND DEFENSE HIGHWAYS

AS OF JUNE 30, 1969

SUPERHIGHWAY—SUPERHOAX

Helen Leavitt

SUPERHIGHWAY—
SUPERHOAX

DOUBLEDAY & COMPANY, INC., GARDEN CITY, NEW YORK 1970

Library of Congress Catalog Card Number 70–86890
Copyright © 1970 by Helen Leavitt
All Rights Reserved
Printed in the United States of America

*This book is dedicated
to urban dwellers everywhere*

I wish to thank the scores of people who knowingly or unknowingly contributed comments, ideas, and efforts to the preparation of this book. I am particularly indebted to the members of the staff of the Bureau of Public Roads library who were so helpful and generous of their time and material. Henry Bain deserves special thanks for his unflagging support and crucial critique of the manuscript during the two and one half years it was in preparation. My husband, Bill, deserves kudos for his patience, enthusiasm, and input of fine editorial talent, while Tony and Nick merit an award for helping in roles only five- and six-year-old sons can play.

Contents

SUPERHIGHWAY—SUPERHOAX

1. Highways in the Urban Scene

*"These are the joys of the open road—For him who travels
without a load"*
—Bliss Carman, 1861–1929

The red, white, and blue shield, patriotic emblem of the National
System of Interstate and Defense Highways, is a familiar highway
guidepost to American motorists. It is now posted along more than
26,000 miles of superhighways on a network that has been taking
shape across the continental United States for more than a decade.

The Interstate Highway System is the largest single public works
project ever undertaken by man. As originally projected in 1944,
it was to contain 40,000 miles of highways. As approved by a law
enacted in 1956, its mileage was boosted to 41,000 miles and its
cost was estimated at $27 billion. The system was to be financed by
federal and state funds on a 90–10 ratio—Uncle Sam would contribute nearly $25 billion, the states $2.7 billion. The highway network
would cross and, in effect, link every state and pass near all major
metropolitan areas. It was to be completed by June 1971.

Today, interstate highways extend across open country and mountains, traverse rivers, follow our coastlines, and not only pass near
our cities, but actually enter them. Two thirds of the Interstate System has been completed at a cost of $33.3 billion, a figure already
$6 billion greater than the original estimate. The ultimate cost has

been estimated at twice the original figure, total mileage has been increased again to 42,500 miles, and the last links are likely to be completed no sooner than 1975—if ever.

Those sections of the system already completed in and around our urban areas are the most heavily used, particularly for suburban commuter trips, rather than for interstate travel. Critics who have questioned the wisdom of extending sections of the superhighway system into the cores of our cities, which fill up with commuter-trip automobiles, have been told by highway officials and highway boosters that these urban sections of interstate highways are essential to the economy, national defense, and safety of our transportation system. Persistent critics, those who question these premises, are dismissed by officials as fanatics, unpatriotic (since the highway boosters claim the highways serve national defense), or simply uninformed. Those who argue that the cities are being engulfed with commuter automobiles are told this is all the more proof that even more such highways are needed to alleviate congestion.

This urban congestion was not the result of the original nationwide network of highways contemplated in 1944, however. That plan called for bypassing cities in an effort to provide long-haul travel between cities and states. It was not planned for the local commuter traffic we see today. By the time the plan was implemented in 1956, however, there were some beltways and arterials, forerunners of the Interstate System, already built around the perimeters of some of our cities, which in turn encouraged suburban development. The lure of 90 percent federal funding provided the short step which led politicians and highway officials to the conclusion that highways should actually enter our cities. Shortly thereafter, automobile congestion and urban "sprawl" began in earnest, nurtured by our federal highway program.

The superhighways held great promise for the future when the project was still on the drawing board. An article in the December 1956 issue of *Automotive Industries* commented:

In laying out the general pattern of the 41,000 mile chain of national express routes the planners have steered away from the heavily built-up industrial and residential cores of the cities. Belt lines and bypasses are to allow through traffic on the new system to remain free of urban bottlenecks. Those drivers with destinations downtown will be able to reach them via access thoroughfares, but there is to be no dumping of Interstate traffic in front of city hall.

Another article in the same issue predicted that

. . . the pressure toward more and more decentralization will become irresistible. The downtown commercial and industrial sites will become things of the past . . . in their place neighborhood units will spring up—pleasant residential areas, made up mostly of medium-sized apartment buildings located close to modern factories and office buildings, thus eliminating the need for a great deal of commuting. . . . Transportation no longer will be a problem. Most people will be able to walk to work. Pedestrian and vehicle traffic ways will be separated, perhaps on different levels, and walking will once more be safe and pleasant. . . . The city would become a pleasant place to work in and to live in; instead of asphalt jungles, the verdant city without suburbs; instead of obsolete street patterns, an efficient, well integrated network of expressways and arterials. In such an environment, the automobile would vastly increase its mobility and therefore become a more valuable part of urban living.

It didn't work out this way in the cities, where 5000 miles of the Interstate System have already been opened and where 2500 more miles are scheduled to open by 1974. Our great urban centers have been subjected to the busy concrete mixers and asphalt rollers in the guise of progress, where the ribbons of highway they create are further strangling automobile traffic, adding to the already dangerous air pollution levels and displacing the city's residents with still more cars while transportation daily becomes more difficult.

According to the Bureau of Public Roads, federal overseer for the project, the Interstate shield represents the best engineering and design, maximum safety standards, and, ultimately, a transportation system vital to our country's economy and defense. American motorists, says the Bureau, can expect to wheel onto any portion of this gigantic highway system, confident in the knowledge that it represents technological, economical, and social progress. Each completed link adds to the system's emerging form and hastens fulfillment of the highway engineer's ultimate dream—to be able to drive from one corner of the country at high speed to another without stopping for a traffic light.

This view of our highway program is supported by a vast lobby consisting of state highway officials, contractors, auto manufacturers, engineers, congressmen, state legislators, newspaper publishers, and representatives of road users groups. They all know better.

Instead of fulfilling the Bureau's claims, the Interstate System has in effect forced our society to scuttle all forms of transportation except the automobile (and, for long-distance trips, the airplane), a serious mistake. The Interstate System, with its multilane roadways, elaborate interchanges, bridges and tunnels, is not the only villain, however. The federal government also helps the states to finance (at a 50–50 ratio) several hundred thousand miles of primary and secondary roads, both urban and rural. These highways can be just as destructive of cities and countryside as the interstate routes.

City dwellers and homeowners in the path of proposed freeways or adjacent to already constructed highways are not impressed with the economic or social "progress" peddled by highway boosters. They are concerned with the cost in terms of human values, for which there is no price tag. No one has yet devised a method for putting a dollar value on space to live, work, play, and breathe. This concern for human values is especially felt among residents of older cities, which were built long before the advent of the automobile. Freeways do the most damage to these cities. And the Bureau of Public Roads and state highway departments have a long record of ignoring just such concerns, especially when they are expressed at public hearings which are supposed to tell public officials what the community thinks of their proposals. Four-, six-, and eight-lane highways that stretch across the open country providing a link between cities are one thing. But when the same kind of freeway blasts its way into the heart of cities where people live and want to continue to live, the effect is not progress and speed, but destruction.

Freeways isolate nonauto owners, as happened in the Watts district of Los Angeles, where the ghetto area was sealed off by highways. Freeways take living quarters, tightening up an already overburdened housing supply and eating up valuable land, destroying established neighborhoods. Untrammeled freeway construction in urban areas is exacerbating the very crisis in our cities we are hoping to allay. Nowhere has the connection between freeway construction and crisis been more poignantly expressed than in a letter, postmarked Newark, New Jersey, to Daniel Moynihan, then director of the MIT-Harvard Joint Center on Urban Affairs, now Special Assistant to President Nixon on Urban Affairs with cabinet rank, shortly after that city's 1967 riot. Its author pleaded, in part, that "They are tearing down our homes and building up medical collages (sic) and motor clubs and parking lots and we need decent private homes to live in. They are tearing down our best schools and churches to build a highway. . . ." The evidence is on public record. Michigan Governor George Romney told a Senate committee shortly before his appointment as Secretary of Housing and Urban Development that freeway construction in Detroit was a major cause of that city's 1967 riot.

Besides gobbling up precious land, freeways simply attract more cars into the city, thereby clogging streets so that public transportation, particularly buses, cannot operate efficiently, which in turn results in a decline in passengers, rise in fares and fiscal crises. Urban freeways can only bring automobiles, trucks, and buses into cities. They cannot provide parking spaces for the vehicles they attract, which leads to still another depredation: More and more downtown land is converted to parking space. Nor do freeways stimulate the "dying downtown economy" as Chamber of Commerce and Board of Trade officials would have us believe. Despite massive freeway construction in central business districts of urban areas, retail sales there continue to lose ground to suburban stores, which attract the mushrooming suburban populations. Boston, for instance, lost 9 percent of its total retail sales between 1958 and 1963, despite considerable freeway construction. San Francisco, on the other hand, increased its sales 9 percent during the same period, then halted all freeway construction in 1966. By 1967, sales increased 16 percent over 1963 sales.

At peak hours, the typical urban freeway is clogged with automobiles competing for the same road space, and often, as in the case of the most celebrated Long Island Expressway, cars move bumper to bumper at five miles an hour. Yet an important ingredient in the rationale and justification for building urban freeways is time saved for the commuter. Actually, at peak hours 7:30 to 9:00 A.M. and 4:30 to 6:30 P.M., drivers are likely to be whizzing home on urban expressways at from six to twelve miles per hour. The horse and buggy did as well.

Highway planners respond to such congestion with plans for more lanes of the same or more access or exit ramps. They talk of double-decking lanes of expressways, more tunnels, and bridges. But these new facilities fill up as fast as the concrete hardens. Then the congestion builds up again as more cars are enticed onto the system by the added facilities. More cars enter congested areas, demanding more parking spaces and operating services, all of which take precious and expensive urban land.

In 1966, the Bureau of Public Roads estimated that the federal government was financing to some degree 51,000 miles of highways in our cities alone, and more are planned, to alleviate "urban congestion." Yet, a helicopter trip over any of our major cities quickly demonstrates that our auto traffic problem is not the result of a shortage of streets, but rather, the result of already having too many.

While 5000 miles of interstate freeways have been completed in urban areas, there are 2500 more still to be imbedded in our cities and plans to construct these last miles are meeting stiff opposition from the public. Ironically, these roads are being promoted at the very time 30 percent of the land use in fifty-three central cities in the United States has already been converted to street use. If these cities must continue to absorb more freeway construction, it will mean that their tax bases will be diminished further at the very time our cities are starved for revenue to cope with staggering demands for services. Moreover, these are the most expensive and least economical segments of the Interstate System. New York's most recently proposed Lower Manhattan Expressway was estimated to cost $100 million a *mile*.

While the city resident is slowly squeezed into smaller dwellings, and space for strolling, playing, and shopping diminishes or is carved up by freeways, his counterpart, the commuting suburbanite, trapped in the monopoly of auto transportation, has to maintain two or more cars with the same care and financial commitment he provides his offspring. Furthermore, even suburban commuters are discovering that their cherished quarter acres can be swallowed up by freeway planners. Their land is being taken for widened streets or spurs as the thirst for space to build roads increases. Where once commuters looked on in bewilderment at pickets protesting a freeway through city homes and neighborhoods, today many are inclined to sympathize and even join the protesters because they too are threatened when the highway reaches into their neighborhoods. Suburban housing no longer escapes the path of the freeway any more than central city dwellings. As the burgeoning metropolitan population spreads out—the consequence of beltway and expressway construction—more roads are built to link suburban communities and connect them with the core cities. As a result, suburban Americans spend a great deal of time aimlessly driving around on freeways.

Still, it is the urban portions of the mileage that cause the most serious repercussions, and it is this portion of the Interstate System which was not supposed to be and never should have been built. The standards for the Interstate System are too demanding of land within large cities. The highways are at least four lanes wide. Some are eight and ten lanes wide. This means wide swaths of concrete from 48 to 144 feet, not including footage for dividers, median strips, signs, light poles, and shoulders. A highway this massive can only serve to disrupt the neighborhoods it dissects.

As originally conceived in 1944, the Interstate System was to serve intercity traffic only. It was to serve long-haul traffic and defense purposes. There were to be only spurs from within the cities to connect to the Interstate System, and few of them, not the massive highway construction cities such as Cleveland, Washington, New York, and Chicago have witnessed.

Our motor vehicle traffic was supposed to consist of trucks, buses, and a few interurban private cars. The volumes of automobile traffic we see today were not going to materialize because they were not supposed to be accommodated with all the highways they would need.

But by the end of World War II, highway boosters had decided to make the private automobile the dominant form of urban transportation, and overemphasis on superhighways, particularly Interstate and primary highways, and lack of attention to public transportation left the public with no choice except to drive cars. This multibillion-dollar highway program, so damaging to our cities, is the only means of transportation for most people who drive the same trip in and out of the city each day. Our highway program has, in effect, made it possible for every automobile owner to have his own private transportation system. That meant 86.5 million separate automobile transportation systems in 1969. The average automobile trip is nine miles in length, and most trips occur within a twenty-five-mile radius of metropolitan areas. For such a small area, any other commuting system would have proven more beneficial to the public than our present system of highways which long ago passed the point of efficiency.

The man who promoted the means for financing highways is Representative George Fallon, Democrat, from Maryland. He favored attaching a special purpose tax on gasoline and oil to pay for the system. Unlike other tax revenue, which goes into the general treasury, this tax money goes into a special fund for highway construction only. This elevated the proposal to a self-perpetuating building program and demonstrates how a special purpose tax eternalizes its own use. Critics of the Highway Trust Fund like to point out that if it is justifiable to use gasoline taxes exclusively for highway construction, the federal tax on alcohol should be spent to promote and expand the liquor industry.

At the very time highways were being promoted, public transportation should have been beefed up to provide a more economical means of moving people while demanding less land, money, and waste than expressways, with alternate methods of commuting, such as rapid rail, subways, and improved and express bus service, systems which move large numbers of passengers. The car mania we see around us today would never have developed if people had been provided the sort of public transportation that could have competed successfully with autos and offered our cities truly "balanced" transportation. Instead, by the mid-seventies, the public will have spent more than $50 billion for highways and less than $1 billion for mass transportation. How did we get on this course in the first place?

In 1956, the Federal Highway Act specified that the Interstate System "may be located both in rural and urban areas." It also provided for 90 percent federal financing, an irresistible lure for the politicians, contractors, and state highway officials who wanted as much of the federal pie as possible. Thus it was that expansive freeways through open country were extended into the heart of our major cities. As each new segment of a city's freeway system is completed, it fills up with cars, justifying to highway officials the need for even more of the same. Ironically, the rural portions of the Interstate System cross open land and have little traffic and few lanes. As they approach metropolitan areas, more lanes are added at the very point where land becomes scarce and densely populated.

On the other hand, today's public transportation suffers from freeway construction in several ways that makes it difficult to provide the public with good service that will draw people away from their cars. Bus service is slow because streets are clogged with auto traffic. Then, too the number of transit riders and revenue have traditionally declined in areas where bridges, tunnels, expressways, and parking lots are provided for automobiles, which auto and highway boosters say are the most comfortable and flexible means of transportation. Thus, as profits on public transit nose-dive, equipment deteriorates and service is continually cut back to reduce operating costs. Even such conservative revenue-generating measures as fare increases backfire by reducing still further the number of daily riders. Public transportation is in the doldrums while automobile transporta-

tion dominates. The outlook for the future is more of the same—
only worse.

It is clear that if every commuter to New York City drove in by
car, or if the population of Manhattan attempted to travel around
town by car, the city would long ago have perished. Yet this has been
and is exactly what is being planned in cities across the country.
Bureau of Public Roads, state highway officials, and congressmen intend to provide each automobile driver with enough highway facilities to enable him to drive by car anywhere he may wish to go.
After the completion date of the present Interstate System, state
highway officials have yet another imposing plan waiting in the wings.
Among other items, it calls for beefing up the present freeway system
in urban areas by building more of them to "relieve" the traffic
congestion of the cities!

And they can do it. The federal Highway Trust Fund collected
$5 billion from taxes on gasoline, tires, and auto accessories in 1969.
This money, combined with taxes collected by the states, amounts
to a $15-billion-a-year-road-building operation. That large an in-
ducement is hard to resist. Add a dash of the strong lobbying from
trucking and auto interests on Congress and the public ends up with
a massive road-building program.

To appreciate the magnitude of the U.S. road-building and automobile complex, one need only study Detroit's own figures. In 1966,
according to statistics issued by the Automobile Manufacturers Association, automotive retail sales, including passenger car, bus, truck,
tire, battery, gasoline, and accessories, totaled $81 billion. This
amount, coupled with the $15 billion road-building operation, plus
the cost for insurance, driver education, and parking expenses, brings
the total bill for motor vehicle transportation to $100 billion each
year.

We spent $28.5 billion in 1966 for grades kindergarten through
twelve in our public school system and $48.8 billion for *all* educa-
tion in the United States. Thus, we are spending twice as much on
automobile transportation as on all forms of education. Education,
however, must vie among the country's list of priorities for its funds,
while highways are assured a steady inflow of cash to the Trust Fund.

Detroit's figures ensure a rosy future for auto manufacturers. From their point of view, a $15-billion-annual-road-building project, financed by the taxpayer himself, provides the system so necessary for the increased use of their products. Detroit's optimism is well reflected in a 1966 statement by Lynn Townsend, chairman of the Chrysler Corporation, in which he said:

> The same powerful forces that have created the steadily growing demand for cars over the past five years will continue to operate in the years ahead. These forces include the steady growth of the population and the addition each year of millions of potential new customers, the rise in personal income, and the increasing reliance upon the automobile for personal transportation. In the early 1970's we expect these forces to create a yearly demand ranging between 9 and 12 million new cars.

Mr. Townsend might have mentioned forces more powerful than the population growth or rising personal income (auto prices increase each year too) which operate to "increase reliance upon the automobile for personal transportation." These forces are the auto manufacturers themselves, labor unions, engineers, road contractors, truckers, steel, rubber and petroleum producers, busline and highway officials, and congressmen who protect and parcel out the Highway Trust Fund, from which the 90–10 bounty flows.

One fifth of all steel produced is sold for automobiles and highway construction. It is steel's biggest market. Two thirds of all rubber produced ends up on America's highways, and nine tenths of all gasoline, the petroleum industry's major product, is burned up there, too. In fact, as the Ethyl Corporation tells it, 130,000 gallons of gasoline are consumed every minute by motor vehicles, most of which are automobiles. Americans use twenty-three times more gasoline for individual transportation than any other national group. As for auto manufacturers, they watch their sales fluctuate as a mother watches a feverish child's temperature. They sold 8.8 million private automobiles with a dollar value of $19.2 billion in 1968 when private car registration exceeded 84 million.

The construction and related industries have a stake in the program, too. In 1961, it was estimated that every million dollars of highway construction bought 16,800 barrels of cement, 694 tons of bituminous material, 485 tons of concrete and clay pipe, 76,000 tons of sand, gravel, slag, stone, and other mineral materials, 24,000 pounds of explosives, 121,000 gallons of petroleum products, 99,000 feet of lumber, and 600 tons of steel. Multiply those amounts by 15 thousand to equal the $15 billion spent on highway construction in 1967.

The taxpayer plays his role, too, by footing the bill. The only difference is that he has no control over where the money will be spent or where the roads will be built. Moreover, today, the fact that a motorist can drive on our highway system is less the result of an attempt to provide transportation than it is a side benefit of highway construction undertaken for construction's sake and insured automobile sales.

Highway boosters have attempted to make highways answer all of our transportation needs. In 1954, two years before passage of the 1956 Highway Act and establishment of the Highway Trust Fund, there were 9.4 million trucks on all United States public roads hauling 213 billion ton miles of products. (A ton mile is one ton of cargo transported one mile.) By 1966, there were 14.7 million trucks hauling more than 400 billion ton miles between urban areas. The industry has almost doubled in size and service.

The truckers boast that they are moving goods across the nation in tones that suggest that railroads do not exist and are not doing the same job. Automobile ads tell us that car dealers are matchmakers. Highway officials argue that they are for a "balanced transportation system," which means that they will support mass transit construction as long as they can build all the highways they wish. If the congressional guardians of the Highway Trust Fund truly believed in providing transportation, they would be willing to allow trust fund money to finance whichever mode of transportation a community chose. Instead, they shout that highway taxes are collected to build highways only and that the motoring public is paying for more of them, not subway systems or any other form of transportation. Worst of all, the promoters of more roads claim that the system works, when in fact it does so in cities only in the wee small hours of the morning when practically no one is driving. The rush hour is the very time the system is supposed to work and also the very time when it most often breaks down. The highway promoters' answer to this criticism is that the traffic congestion only proves the need for still *more* highways.

For years, highway officials have touted the economic desirability of automobile travel and safety. Today they are more cautious about claiming that driving saves money, but they still cry "safety" when someone criticizes a new freeway. They do not mention that automobile accidents are costing billions in damages and killing more than 50,000 Americans each year. The National Safety Council estimates that more Americans have been killed by automobiles than in all of the wars this country has fought. Yet hungry highway promoters dismiss these statistics as inevitable consequences of our "culture."

Apparently our culture promotes the idea that it is healthy, safe, wise, and economical to fill our large cities every morning with serpentine streams of automobiles whose drivers again each evening wend their weary way out. Apparently our culture, aware that the average automobile carries 1.6 persons per trip and that thus less than 5000 people can travel a single lane of freeway in one hour, while a double-track rail system can move 50,000 in the same time, still prefers the smell of exhaust fumes and the interminable wait in traffic jams.

As former Secretary of Transportation Alan Boyd so aptly stated, during his brief tenure in office, "If someone were to tell you he had seen strings of noxious gases drifting among the buildings of a city, black smoke blotting out the sun, great holes in the major streets, filled with men in hard hats, planes circling overhead, unable to land, and thousands of people choking the streets, pushing and shoving in a desperate effort to get out of the city . . . you would be hard pressed to know whether he was talking about a city at war or a city at rush hour."

Since by 1975 the population may be 215 million and forecasters predict that there will be 98.5 million automobiles on the road, possibly every other man, woman, and child will be operating an automobile by then. The question is where? If the major growth in population occurs in our urban areas and the automobile remains the predominant method of transportation, all of our large city centers will be huge concrete slabs with office buildings interspersed among parking lots and freeways, washed daily by the exhaust fumes of masses of internal combustion engines. Even if the much touted cleaner operating electric car becomes practical for inner-city travel, it will still not solve our traffic and parking difficulties. For while air pollution is an undesirable by-product of our expressway systems, ultimately it is the space which the system occupies that becomes crucial in any economic appraisal.

This space includes not only the very ground, river, or gorge upon or through which the road is constructed, but also the space needed for parking and interchanges and ramps to get on and off the freeway. It doesn't end there. The space next to the freeway is also affected. Sometimes it is isolated by the freeway, such as an expressway running along a riverfront which cuts off access to the water, which might have been used as a means of transportation itself (to say nothing of what it does to the view). A highway can cause repercussions if it takes other facilities such as schools, churches, homes, stores, or parks. A loss of one or all of these facilities can mean a squeezing together or doubling up of remaining like facilities. One less house or school can overcrowd another house or school which attempts to absorb the people displaced by the highway. And there is no guarantee that the highway will actually facilitate transportation.

During off-peak hours some urban freeways can work relatively well, providing motor vehicles with a comfortable and quick system for moving around, another plus for highways. But come 5 P.M. on any weekday, millions of perfectly normal, happy, intelligent Americans become snarling, aggressive, frustrated, or defeated human beings as they vie for road space with their fellow drivers. Not particularly because they choose to do so, but because they have been provided roads to drive everywhere and few suitable alternatives. What happens when commuters, wedded to the idea of driving their automobiles to work daily, are offered a quality alternative?

Special efforts must be made to draw these commuters away from their cars, but the task is not an impossible one. A Housing and Urban Development sponsored demonstration project in Peoria, Illinois, during 1965, which provided a "premium" bus service for factory employees, enticed regular auto drivers onto a special door-to-work bus service. Significantly, free auto parking spaces were available for all employees at each factory location.

Yet 542 commuters chose the bus service. They reported that they felt relaxed and comfortable riding the bus, that it was cheaper than driving a car to work, and that it was prompt and reliable. Equally important, the service proved to be profitable for the bus company.

Some passengers even sold their second car when they learned that the experimental bus service was to become a permanent operation of the local bus company, a relatively positive consumer endorsement for an alternative to automobile transportation.

A significant number of people were lured away from their automobiles even when the service operated in territory served by regular buses, which they could have been but were not using to make the trip to work. The difference was that the premium bus service took passengers from their individual front doors to work in the morning and back in the evening. Twenty-eight percent of the premium bus service passengers were former regular bus riders who switched, but the remaining 72 percent represented a new market of former automobile users. Thus, for every regular passenger the bus company lost to premium service, it gained three new customers.

Michael Blurton, director of the bus project for the University of Illinois, said such a premium bus service could be adapted to larger cities, and he suggests they can be incorporated into a rapid-rail or subway system to pick up commuters at their door and deposit them at the rail or subway line.

Theoretically, if many auto drivers would use this bus service, there would be fewer cars using Peoria's streets and highways during peak traffic hours, the traffic situation would ease, and it would be possible for the highways to operate efficiently. Fewer cars on the streets would make it easier for trucks to make deliveries and buses to pick up and discharge passengers. There would be no pressing need for additional highways.

Although highway systems in our large cities ceased long ago to provide efficient transportation, the American taxpayer keeps on paying good money to have his cities torn up and paved over. The National Planning Association estimates that by 1975, 164 million people will be living in the nation's 224 metropolitan areas. The association further predicts that 60 percent or almost 100 million of these urban dwellers will live in the 25 largest urban areas. Thus it is expected that each of these 25 cities will have an average population of 4 million by 1975. Clearly, all available space in these 25 areas will be fully taxed to provide services the burgeoning populations will demand. But what services? Facilities for automobile travel?

In 1968, there were 100 million motor vehicles operating on public roads. Of that number, 84 million were private automobiles. By 1975, it is estimated that there will be 118 million motor vehicles, 98.5 million of which will be automobiles. The estimate surely will prove correct by 1975 if highway promoters provide the freeways and parking spaces for these automobiles and if our lungs can survive ever increasing air pollution.

To avoid this onslaught of more automobiles, we must stop building freeways and obliging automobile traffic in areas of dense population. We must stop listening to engineers and highway planners, men who explain the effects of displacing people and services in very vague terms. Even more vague, in the mind of the highway planner, at least, is the direct social or economic effect of taking a park or wildlife refuge for highway use. Since highway designers and planners equate cost-benefit in terms of dollar value, it becomes a sticky problem to measure the utility of, say, a public golf course or a bird sanctuary. But they have been convinced in the past that they could prove such public land is less valuable than a highway which destroys it.

Else why would the state and federal highway officials approve a plan to construct a freeway like the North Expressway through the historic city of the Alamo, San Antonio? The center of this city enjoys a park and natural landscape complex virtually downtown which consists of open spaces, college campuses, a river, zoo, golf course, and a flood basin. Now let's see what the highway planners designed for this Texas city.

As proposed, the expressway is to curve and wind its way across an Audubon bird sanctuary and Olmos Creek, a tributary in its natural state which would be converted into a concrete ditch, on along a picnic ground and recreation area, wiping out a Girl Scout Day Camp and nature trail, rise across the Olmos basin to the height of the Olmos Dam, where it would cross, sever a college campus, force an elementary school to close, pass through the zoo, block off the public gymnasium, follow the edge of the sunken gardens, past the outdoor theatre where it squeezed between this and the municipal school stadium, blocking a major entrance, entered residential San Antonio, taking homes, swiping off part of a municipal golf course, and limp home through a wooded portion of the San Antonio River's natural watercourse, one of the few remaining wilderness areas left in the city.

This is a classic example of highway planning. In other cities with expressway controversies, the fight has centered on demolition of a park or disruption of a neighborhood or the severing of a campus or the bisecting of a zoo or of a golf course or the loss of a school or treasured trees. Here, San Antonio has the dubious distinction of falling victim to all of the typical hazards of highway planning. Clearly, the planners of San Antonio's North Expressway did not know where NOT to build. It was only after years of pressure from numerous citizen groups that the Bureau and state highway officials agreed in 1969 to consider tunneling portions of the expressway. At this writing no commitment has been made to tunnel, however.

In late 1966, the same year the North Expressway was proposed

for San Antonio, the Bureau of Public Roads back in Washington
issued a report for fiscal 1966 called "Highways and Human Values."
An introduction to the report stated:

> While the social responsibilities inherent in highway construction have
> always been recognized by the Bureau of Public Roads and the State
> Highway Departments, no 12 month period has produced more ac-
> complishments toward making our highways serve many public needs
> other than transportation. Nor has any comparable period yielded
> greater results in the important fields of highway safety and esthetics.
>   The year was characterized by new emphasis on the total impact
> of highways on people—on their environment, housing, recreation,
> cultural interests, and all the other elements of life in the complex
> latter half of the 20th century.
>   Some new social ideas emerge in connection with the highway
> program, but 1966 was probably more notable for the coming of age
> of concepts dating back several years or even decades.
>   . . . the need for greater attention to those aspects involving more
> than getting the motorist and trucker from here to there became in-
> creasingly apparent and the Federal-State highway partnership began
> devoting a much greater share of its time and talent to the human
> values involved in the Interstate and other Federal-aid highway
> programs.

Apparently the author hadn't heard of San Antonio's North Expressway. Few freeway proposals will do more damage to environment, housing, recreation, and cultural interests than the expressway
as originally scheduled for that delightful Texas city in 1966. Where
is the federal-state highway partnership which the report assured
us was even then devoting a much greater share of its time and talent
to the human values involved in the highway program?

Almost three years after those pious words appeared in the 1966
report, Edward "Ted" Holmes, for many years the brains behind
the planning of Bureau of Public Roads at the federal level, stated
that the north leg of Washington's proposed inner loop should be
placed "along R or S Street off Connecticut Avenue. That area

east of Connecticut could use some redevelopment. It's a pretty grubby area."

That "grubby area" is my neighborhood. It contains deteriorating houses. It also contains renovated houses, and the neighborhood boasts an integrated population of sophisticated city dwellers. Numerous national associations and embassies occupy stately mansions among our tree-lined streets, and the area contains excellent Spanish, French, Japanese, Mexican, and American restaurants and numerous small businesses and shops as well as spiffy boutiques along Connecticut Avenue. The proposed freeway would isolate or obliterate many brownstones and mansions such as the former home of the Willard family, founders of the Willard Hotel, the house where Daniel Chester French lived and designed the Lincoln Memorial, numerous pre-Civil War houses, and a tiny farmhouse that was, in its day, on the outskirts of the nation's capital. It would also slice through an elementary school district which parents and community people recently fought hard to acquire as a community-controlled school.

In other words, the north leg would wipe out the core of this neighborhood of people of mixed ethnic, racial, and economic backgrounds. It would not, however, provide any funds to redevelop the blight that exists in the area. Yet, time and time again, such freeway construction is peddled as redevelopment and progress. It was the specter of just such redevelopment in the form of the north leg freeway cutting through our living room which sparked my interest in expressways back in 1965. I soon found that there were others in the District of Columbia who were fighting proposed freeway systems.

Repeated sorties into the D.C. Highway Department's logic for building freeways in the nation's capital produced ever mounting evidence that such a system would not address itself to the city's transportation crisis. In addition, poll after poll of residents of the District revealed overwhelming opposition to any more road building, and by 1966 suburbanites were expressing a greater interest in beginning a fledgling rapid transit as an alternative to roads. Undaunted, highway planners pressed on bulldozing churches, schools, houses, and parkland.

This book is about the men and institutions who promote highways and how they destroy our churches, schools, homes, and parks.

2. A Commitment to the Motor Age

"The public be damned!"
—Commodore Vanderbilt

The first Portland cement concrete to be used as pavement for a public road in this country was spread in the spring of 1909 along one mile of Woodward Avenue, which led from Detroit to Wayne County's State Fair Grounds in Michigan. It was a meager but prophetic gesture to accommodate automobile travel, then but a novelty.

Fifty years ago there were few such decent stretches of road. There were roads, but most were simply dirt, especially those that extended beyond city limits. Their quality was so poor that travel on them was an unpredictable adventure. The farmer and the city slicker both cursed the mud and mess of our road system well into the twentieth century. Not only were roads of poor quality but they were also limited in length. In nice weather they were usable but bumpy and dusty. In rainy weather most of them became mud canals.

The origins of the U.S. road system sprang from Indian trails and trading pathways which, over the years, were refined as better road-building techniques were developed. For instance, in 1751, the Pennsylvania Road, which extended from Philadelphia west to Pittsburgh, had been transformed from a fur-trading path and Indian trail to a vital lifeline between the colonies and pioneers beyond the Alleghenies. Today it is U.S. Route 30.

In early settlement days, there was a series of such roads—Braddock Road from Pittsburgh to Alexandria, Virginia; the Wilderness Road that wound through the Cumberland Gap; Zane's Trace in Ohio and West Virginia; and even a 700-mile route that paralleled the Pacific Coast beginning at San Diego, touching twenty-one mission settlements as far north as Sonoma, beyond San Francisco.

By 1785, stagecoaches had come into general use, requiring good all-weather roads. The states agreed upon the need for such roads but had no money to build them. Instead, they chartered private turnpike companies to develop and operate good roads. Some were little more than wagon trails, while others were made of wooden planks, a technique which became popular around 1840. Meanwhile, the West was opening up via such routes as the Oregon Trail and the Butterfield Overland Mail.

By the middle of the nineteenth century, the railroads began absorbing most long-distance freight and passenger transportation, and those roads that existed, particularly in rural areas, deteriorated rapidly. While a few urban areas had at least one brick or clay and sand "paved" street, the rural dirt roads grew worse, and a new sport was beginning to catch on with the public that sparked interest in good roads—bicycling.

Enthusiasts were eager to ride their vehicles, but where? City streets were crowded, dusty and narrow, while country roads were bumpy and impossible after rainstorms. By 1880, numerous bicycle clubs joined to form the League of American Wheelmen for the express purpose of promoting good roads and bicycle side paths. Two years later some city streets were well paved but most still remained dusty and dirty. Country roads were usually impassable.

The Wheelmen's call for good roads bore fruit as some states began enacting laws to provide state funds to build highways. Most such early roads were of gravel or macadam, a series of layers of stone. Relatively few were built, however.

The movement for good roads received its most important thrust, in 1893, from the Duryea brothers who introduced the first American-made gasoline engine automobile on the streets of Springfield, Massachusetts. That same year the federal government established the Office of Road Inquiry. Its purpose was to "enable the Secretary of Agriculture to make inquiries in regard to the systems of road management throughout the United States, to make investigations in regard to the best methods of road making and to enable him to assist the Agricultural College and experiment stations in disseminating information on this subject."

The Office of Road Inquiry prepared a Good Roads National Map showing all macadamized and graveled roads in the country. A testing station was established and by 1905 the Office of Road Inquiry and the station were merged into the Office of Public Roads. From there it evolved into the Office of Public Roads and Rural Engineering. The accent was put on getting the farmer out of the mud.

In 1916, the first bill to establish a federally aided highway program was passed by the Congress and approved by President Wilson. Three years later the Office of Public Roads and Rural Engineering became the Bureau of Public Roads. With approximately 3,617,917 motor vehicles raring to go in the country, the 1916 legislation was designed to provide the roads they needed.

This first federal-aid legislation stipulated that each participating state must have a highway department capable of carrying out a sound road-building program. As the progenitor of present federal-aid highway laws, it established a basis for a partnership between the state highway departments and the federal government which remains essentially the same today. States are invited (mainly by the lure of federal matching money) to participate in federally financed highway programs. The states determine what roads to build, the character of their plans and specifications, acquired right-of-way, and award contracts for the work. The Act also established a 50 percent federal matching fund ratio whereby the states and federal government divided the cost of any federal road construction. All federal funds for this program came from general revenue. The Congress periodically authorized a certain lump sum for road building.

Some states did the same, while a few collected revenues specifically for roads by taxing motor vehicles, licenses, and gasoline.

While the states initiated road proposals and awarded contracts, their prerogatives were subject to federal review by the Bureau. In addition, the states assumed responsibility for maintaining all roads. The states were responsible for immediate supervision of all construction work, while the federal government reviewed and approved. The states and the federal government agreed that no toll roads would be built with federal funds. The idea was to provide good, free roads throughout the country.

The main thrust of this program was rural. Most cities by the early 1900s had brick or stone, concrete or asphalt paving, but there were only five hundred miles of paved rural roads in the entire United States. This early road-building program was supposed to connect the city streets with the rural countryside. So work began. Unfortunately, there was apparently a lack of co-ordination between federal, state, county, and other local officials. Many roads were built that seemed to start nowhere and lead nowhere. Some ended abruptly at county or state lines.

The Bureau attempted to correct this situation by issuing a memorandum requesting that each state highway department designate and file with the Bureau a limited, predetermined system to which it would restrict federal aid. The memorandum was generally ignored. And in 1921, when more than 9 million automobiles were registered in the United States, new legislation was passed by the Congress. It corrected the ineffectiveness of the memorandum by passing into law the requirement that all federal-aid money be confined to a designated or predetermined system of main connecting roads, both between states and between counties. In effect, this established what is today known as our federal-aid primary system.

The 1916 and 1921 legislative activity and interest in roads did not go unnoticed among auto interests. Support for the legislation establishing a primary federal highway system came from a then-existing Automobile Association of America, Pierce Arrow Motor Company, Automobile Club of St. Joseph, and the Hudson Motor Car Company.

By 1924, there were 16 million automobiles on the streets and roads of the United States, and state highway departments enlarged as the road-building business mushroomed. During the Depression, for a brief period, the 50–50 federal matching funds ratio was altered, in some instances to 100 percent federal funds, to provide work projects to relieve unemployment. Also, for the first time federal funds were allocated to improve the primary system in urban areas, using the Works Project Administration of the 1930s. In the main, the emphasis remained on construction of the state highway or primary system in rural areas. The accent was still on farm-to-market roads and connecting county seats. Interconnecting highways were gradually linking the states from coast to coast and border to border. Motels, hotels, restaurants, ice cream stands, and souvenir shops crowded both sides of the primary system as millions of Americans not only journeyed to work by car, but ventured far from home for long-distance trips.

The Bureau of Public Roads was shifted from the Department of Agriculture to the New Deal Federal Works Agency in 1939 and renamed the Public Roads Administration. By then, the number of registered automobiles in the United States had climbed to 27 million. By 1941, the number was well over 29.5 million automobiles, which had 156,645 miles of through U.S. numbered state primary highways to drive on.

Under the pressure of World War II, the Congress enacted the Defense Highway Act of 1941 which designated certain highways for troop, war material, and supply movement and placed emphasis on constructing good access roads to military installations. The funding ratio for these defense roads was increased to 75 percent federal and 25 percent state funds instead of 50–50. The rationale for increasing the federal share to 75 percent was national defense. But at the same time, with gasoline rationed, auto production and most regular road-building programs were halted. The automobile took a temporary back seat while public transportation moved masses of people and took over the job of getting them to work. During the war years of 1941 through 1945, auto registration dipped from a high of 30 million to approximately 25 million.

As World War II drew to a close, in 1944, an important piece of highway legislation was enacted. In addition to expanding federal aid to the existing primary (and only) system of federal highways, this legislation established what is still known today as the ABC system. It authorized federal funds on a regular basis for a system of secondary, or B, highways, plus arterials in urban areas, the C portion of the system, as well as the regular, or A, primary system. Significantly, it also called for designation of a new National System of Interstate Highways, not to exceed 40,000 miles, which was to be the backbone of interstate travel. However, that portion of the program never got off the ground, as no money was authorized for it. The federal funds it did authorize were divided as follows: 45 percent went to the ever expanding U.S. numbered primary system; 30 percent for the secondary system; and the remaining 25 percent for streets in urban areas, to be determined according to population, area, and post road mileage. This was the first time the Congress provided federal funds on a regular basis for roads in urban areas. All of these monies were to be matched on the 50 percent formula with the individual states.

Once the war was over, the ABC program began. The 1945 automobile registration figure of 25 million had skyrocketed to 40 million by 1950 as auto production and road building resumed. The auto market grew larger each year as more people brought home bigger pay checks. Everyone wanted a new car and everyone old enough to get credit went out and bought one. Indeed, George T. McCoy, president of the American Association of State Highway Officials, told a Senate roads subcommittee in 1955, "Highways and motor vehicles are truly the keystone of the American way of life."

Meanwhile, the Public Roads Administration in Washington was transferred to the General Services Administration where it remained briefly. In August of 1949, it was renamed the Bureau of Public Roads and was placed in the Department of Commerce, where it remained until April 1967, when it became an arm of the newly created Department of Transportation.

It was during this period under the aegis of Commerce that the massive road program we now recognize as the federal-aid system of expressways and the Interstate System of freeways was launched.

State highway officials and the then Bureau chief Thomas H. MacDonald, who served in that capacity from 1919 until 1953, had been promoting the 40,000-mile Interstate System of highways even before it was mentioned in the 1944 legislation. Although no money had been authorized for the system, they worked diligently to sell the Congress the idea that the country should invest in such a highway system. When MacDonald retired in 1953, he was replaced by Francis V. duPont, former member and chairman of the Delaware State Highway Commission for twenty-three years. Up to that time the major problem in the way of launching an interstate system of the proportions suggested by highway officials and contractors was how to pay for it. The trucking industry said trucks were already overtaxed. The AAA complained that America's automobile owners, too, were taxed to capacity. Automobile manufacturers echoed these cries. The petroleum interests were constantly fighting increased gasoline taxes. The auto manufacturers, petroleum, concrete, stone, asphalt, and rubber producers knew they needed more highways if they were to ensure that people would buy their products. Highway officials and contractors wanted to build more roads, too. All were stymied by the difficulty of selling the program to state governors and the Congress, who in turn would have to sell the idea to the people who would foot the bill—the public.

There had been widespread support for the 1941 legislation that increased federal participation in highway construction to 75 percent for defense purposes. Then the rationale had been defense. So it would be again. But would the defense rationale convince the governors to embark on an expensive construction program that could squeeze state treasuries dry? Wouldn't they simply say that defense was the federal government's concern? Or would they go along, if the federal subsidy was so great that the states had to contribute very little money?

President Eisenhower helped answer some of these questions when, in July of 1954, he waved the promise of a federal $50-billion-road-building project under the noses of the state governors assembled at Bolton Landing, Lake George, in New York State, site of that year's Governors Conference. Eisenhower suggested a grand plan, a highway network that would solve the problems of speed, safe transcontinental travel, intercity communication, and provide access highways, farm-to-market movement, and offer relief to metropolitan congestion, bottlenecks, and crowded parking.

He suggested that the program could be self-liquidating, with tolls wherever possible, or an assured gasoline tax increase and federal help wherever national interests so demanded. He urged that $5 billion per year be spent on the project over the next ten years to boost the economy, and he predicted that such a highway system would pay for itself and reap economic benefits to the country.

It was at about the same time that the President had suggested building a transcontinental highway which would connect East and West, from New York to Portland, Oregon, avoiding but serving the major cities and industrial centers, incorporating existing highways wherever possible. He also proposed a mid-continental highway from the upper Mississippi to the Gulf. Nothing came of these proposals but, when coupled with the $50 billion offer to the governors, Senator Francis S. Case of South Dakota was prompted to predict that the Eisenhower administration might go down in history as the administration of "Ike, the builder."

Vague though the proposals were, they were not too ambiguous to escape the notice of highway interests, who along with Bureau chief MacDonald had been promoting more concrete for years now and had worked hard to get the current appropriation of $875 million, which was the biggest to date.

They were certain to respond to this new proposal from the President; their reaction is well described in the August 1954 issue of *Roads and Streets,* a trade publication representing highway and auto interests, which stated:

> When the initial shock had passed, the Washington Corps of highway experts stationed here to represent the dozens of highway interests reacted swiftly.

That put it mildly. Capitol Hill was flooded with lobbyists representing contractors, oil, auto, real estate, trucking, and concrete interests, all bent on establishing the biggest pork barrel legislation in the history of the United States.

The same issue of the magazine reassured its readers that the business community would back the program:

A fresh approach in Chamber of Commerce thinking on highway construction is expected from a newly formed Chamber committee. Headed by Martin Watson, a highway contractor and former president of the Association of General Contractors of America, the 40-man body will make recommendations on promoting highway construction. Others on the committee with highway interests are Carl Franks, president of the Portland Cement Association, George Kass, Iowa road builder, Pyke Johnson, past president of the Automotive Safety Foundation, and Frank McCaslin, president of the Oregon Portland Cement Company.

Road contractors were performing cart wheels. American Road Builders Association president Robert M. Reindollar, former chairman of the Maryland State Roads Commission, crowed that the President's program represented some of the main recommendations which ARBA had repeatedly made to the Congress, official bodies, and the public. He cited urban congestion and poor rural roads as examples of an obsolete system. He berated Bureau and state officials because, while they were spending money on improving these roads, traffic grew worse. He praised the President's new proposal for a superhighway system, carefully skirting the probability that building a bigger, more expensive version of the existing system would generate its own traffic, clog up and bog down. How such a system would be an improvement over the existing system of urban streets and arterials which were already clogged, or the rural routes, which were used primarily for farm-to-market travel, was a question studiously avoided by the road builders.

President Eisenhower explored the matter further. He appointed General Lucius D. Clay, who had shed his uniform to become

chairman of the board of the Continental Can Company, to head
up a committee to study specific highway needs. The Clay Committee
consisted of the General, Stephen D. Bechtel, president of the
Bechtel Construction Corporation, David Beck, president of the
International Brotherhood of Teamsters, S. Sloan Colt, president
of Bankers Trust Company, and William A. Roberts, president
of Allis-Chalmers Manufacturing Company.

On October 7 and 8, 1954, the Clay Committee held hearings
on the new highway proposal. Those who appeared before the
committee included representatives of the Automobile Manufacturers
Association, the United States Chamber of Commerce, the American
Trucking Association, the American Road Builders Association, the
National Parking Association, the Automotive Safety Foundation,
the National Association of Motor Bus Operators, Sinclair Oil, the
American Petroleum Institute, the American Association of State
Highway Officials, the Truck-Trailer Manufacturers Association, the
Associated General Contractors of America, the National Associa-
tion of County Officials, the American Automobile Association, the
Private Truck Council of America, and the American Municipal
Association, represented by Detroit's Mayor Albert Cobo, as well
as Robert Moses, then the city construction co-ordinator of New
York City. In effect, the highway lobby was given the opportunity to
plead for more highways.

Clay opened the hearings by announcing that the Bureau of
Public Roads had a new estimate for highway needs. The Bureau
had asked the various state highway officials to make their own
recommendations of state highway construction needs. The estimate
was $101 billion when all the state projects were tallied.

In his opening statement, Clay said:

> We accept as a starting premise the fact that the penalties of an
> obsolete road system are large, and that the price in inefficiency is
> paid not only in dollars, but in lives lost through lack of safety, and
> also in national insecurity.

The first witness at the hearings was William J. Cronin, managing
director of the Automobile Manufacturers Association. Clay asked

him if there was a point where availability of adequate highways affects the increase in the use of the automobile.

Cronin answered,

> I think very definitely it does, Mr. Chairman. I think that is particularly true in the large cities where you have the extreme congestion that you find in New York, for example. I think it definitely discourages the ownership and use of both passenger cars and motor trucks.

The next witness was Robert Moses of New York City who, in 1953, had won a $25,000 General Motors Award for an essay on adequate highways. He declared that parkways, expressways, turnpikes, and thruways must go through cities, not around them as generally planned, because most traffic originates and ends in urban centers. Furthermore, he said, ". . . practical solutions of the traffic problems in cities should be co-ordinated with slum clearance, street widening, parks and playgrounds, utility modernization, and other improvements which go with up-to-date city mapping and planning. These incidental features of traffic projects are often neglected by narrow-minded administrators at all levels who can only see one problem at a time. . . . The strategic, military, and evacuation aspects of arterial construction are vital in cities. . . . The needs of cities must not be minimized because they require relatively little mileage. This is strategic mileage of vital importance to both interstate and urban systems. It is the hardest to locate, the most difficult to clear, the most expensive to acquire and build, and the most controversial from the point of view of selfish and short-sighted opposition. Without attempting to override local opinion and dictate from distant capitals, the federal and state governments can help immeasurably to overcome local pressures by establishing engineering and other standards which can only be departed from at the risk of loss of federal and state aid of all kinds."

The last witness of the first day of the hearings was a spokesman from the Automotive Safety Foundation. This organization is made up of groups in the automobile, steel, petroleum, rubber, cement, and auto parts and accessories industries, National Automobile

Dealers Association, leading banks, and auto finance companies. Foundation engineers, the spokesman told the Clay Committee, had concluded studies which showed agreement on the need for a $101-billion expenditure over the next ten years.

AAA's executive vice president, Russell E. Singer, began the second day of hearings.

> We regard the National System of Interstate Highways as the most important element in our entire highway system, from the standpoint of the national economy, meeting the most essential motor transport needs of the nation, and our national defense. . . . Our association has long emphasized the need for adequate urban highway facilities. It is in these areas where the greatest economic loss is occurring due to strangulation of traffic and inadequate terminal facilities,

he told the committee.

Clay questioned Singer: "When you talk of these urban facilities, are you talking of those providing egress and exit, or are you talking about within the city itself?" he asked.

Singer replied, "Both, General. It seems to us that when we talk about an expanded highway program, we have to consider that some 70 percent of all of the traffic that is on the main highways has for its object egress, ingress into the urban areas."

Clay, taken aback, asked, "Would you have the federal government undertake to improve Elm Street?" Singer had no answer for that question, nor could anyone else in subsequent hearings comfortably handle the question of federal funds being used for paving city streets, the approach that highway officials considered to be the key to the whole project. They knew even then that the local traffic would provide the revenue to pay for an interstate system designed for long-haul and rural traffic. The hurdle was how to get the heavy traffic onto the system when heavy traffic was urban and mostly short trips.

The problem kept popping up. A spokesman for the National Association of Township Officials recommended building a toll system for defense purposes, which would have little effect on towns.

He also declared that if instead, the highways were to barrel their way through cities, eating up the greater portion of the money, his group would be against such a plan because they favored rural road improvement.

One of the first to question the rather patent discrepancy between Ike's $50-billion program and the new $101-billion figure was Joseph P. Walsh, general counsel for Sinclair Oil Corporation, who was representing the American Petroleum Institute at the committee hearings.

> We all admit that good roads and sound highway policies are in the broad public interest, but they are also in the direct and immediate interest of our industry, which markets the bulk of its products for consumption by the side of the road,

he began. Yet he went on to express grave concern about the new $101-billion estimate. He reminded the committee that in January 1950, a Joint Committee on the Economic Report submitted an estimate of $41 billion to the Congress for highway improvements. The Bureau of Public Roads estimated the cost at somewhere between $42 and $47 billion in 1951. Robert Moses, in an inspiring $25,000 essay on adequate highways in 1953, had estimated that $50 billion would do the job, Walsh related. And he continued, in 1954, Deputy Under Secretary of Commerce Dr. Charles L. Dearing had estimated the job at $41 billion, while in June of that year, the Bureau had upped its estimate somewhat to between $45 and $55 billion. Yet by September of that same year, the Bureau's estimate had soared to $101 billion. Walsh asked Clay why the figures had doubled between June and September of 1954 from $50 to $101 billion. Clay explained that the new figure was devised from studies submitted to the Bureau by state highway departments. He neglected to remind Walsh that between June and September, President Eisenhower had also suggested sprinkling $50 billion federal dollars over the states.

Alfred E. Johnson, president of the American Association of

State Highway Officials, defended the $101-billion figure. He told
the committee:

> We have no personal interest in this. We have nothing to gain. But
> we have attempted to apprise the people of this problem, which, of
> course, was made more acute by a lack of maintenance and con-
> struction during the World War II period when highways were con-
> sidered expendable. . . . The fact that the United States Chamber of
> Commerce had the meeting on highway finance last December, the
> recent General Motors essay contest on providing for a safe and
> adequate highway system has shown that public opinion has taken
> note of the problem.

Johnson said he favored a program financed 100 percent by the
federal government. He also stressed the importance of obtaining
right-of-way in advance of constructing to be sure highway officials
could get the land to build highways.

The spokesman for the Association of American Railroads brought
some enlightening statistics to the committee. Speaking of the defense
aspects of an interstate system of highways, he pointed out that
during World War II, 90 percent of all military freight and 97
percent of organized military passenger traffic had been moved by
rail. In 1940, rail handled 62 percent of all ton-miles of intercity
freight traffic. This figure jumped to a peak of 72 percent in 1943.
By 1953, it had fallen to 53 percent. He also pointed out that
although references had recently been made to national defense
highway requirements, military authorities for years had pointed
out that a highway system adequate for civilian purposes would
suffice for military requirements with sufficient access roads to military and defense installations.

A. B. Gorman of the Private Truck Council of America expressed
many reservations about building a massive highway program. He
bluntly told the committee that since Bureau estimates had in the
past ranged from $42 to $55 billion, he did not believe the new
estimates were designed to improve long-haul interstate highways
but, rather, city streets. He pointed out that actual highway needs

outside of cities had been well studied by various agencies. He charged that the additional $50 billion tacked on the old estimate between June and September was really designed for multilane highways for egress and ingress to large cities. He pointed to the Los Angeles area where freeways already built or under construction amounted to what he called gold boulevards. "If the citizens of a large city and its suburbs believe that their situation would be improved by building one or several multilane expressways to expedite movement into and out of the city, let them decide by popular vote whether they want it or not and wrapped up in the same vote will be how much they are willing to tax themselves to pay for it," he advised the committee.

Clay explained that the $101-billion estimate included for the first time all city streets and all secondary roads.

Finally, the mayor of the mecca of the automobile industry, Albert Cobo, appeared before the committee. He described Detroit's John Lodge and Edsel Ford expressways and more of the same that were being proposed for the auto capital of the world. He did not discuss the effects or problems these expressways were causing the city. He did state that "more than half of the federal tax on gasoline is earned on city streets," which is also where most highway congestion occurs. He presented the committee a circular depicting a completed expressway system for Kansas City, Missouri. The circular, and Mayor Cobo, boasted that the system would solve that city's congestion at a cost of $50 million of local, state, and federal funds. For that bargain price, Kansas City commuters were to get twenty miles of fast travel motorways. At that time, 1954, federal aid was supporting very few such urban expressways.

But it was certainly true that between 1942 and 1953 the federal government had collected $18 billion in taxes on motor vehicles and related products, while it had spent only $3.7 billion of that amount for federal aid to highway construction. Clearly, highway interests wanted that situation changed.

After sifting through facts, figures, and testimony, the Clay Committee issued a report. It recommended a safe and efficient highway system because it was vital to America's military and civilian defense and to the economy. The report referred to mass evacuation of cities as the civil and national defense function of the system. It recommended establishing a Federal Highway Corporation to oversee the program and recommended that it be financed by bond issue. The report predicted that such a new highway system would reduce current motor vehicle operating costs one cent per mile. It also dealt with urban expressways by suggesting a limit of $4 billion to be allocated specifically to urban arterials of the Interstate System, to provide only for the most important connecting roads— and not for all urban arterials. This was suggested at a time when highway officials were planning more multilane expressways in Detroit, New York, Los Angeles, Kansas City, and practically all major urban areas. Presumably, they would be funded with the regular 50 percent federal matching funds as links in the primary system. Clearly, the highway officials of many states wanted to concrete substantial portions of cities in 1954, but they would not include interstate segments.

In conclusion, the report stated:

> Our cities have spread into suburbs, dependent on the automobile for their existence. The automobile has restored a way of life in which the individual may live in a friendly neighborhood, it has brought city and country closer together, it has made us one country and a united people. But, America continues to grow. Our highway plant must similarly grow if we are to maintain and increase our standard of living. There can be no serious question as to the need for a more adequate highway system. Only the cost and how it is to be met poses a problem.

The governors got together, too, to explore how best to spend $50 billion federal dollars. So did congressmen. Francis duPont resigned as Bureau chief to become special assistant to Commerce Secretary Sinclair Weeks. From this less conspicuous post he lobbied for the new highway program.

All of this activity produced several bills in the Congress. In 1955,

Senator Albert Gore of Tennessee, then chairman of the Senate
roads subcommittee, held extensive hearings on various proposals.
A steady stream of witnesses testified before the subcommittee.
They included representatives from the Commerce Department, state
highway departments, the Bureau of Public Roads, Associated General Contractors of America, American Road Builders Association,
American Toll Ways Authority, Truck-Trailer Manufacturers Association, National Crushed Stone Association, Private Truck Council of America, National Safety Council, Automotive Safety Foundation, and many senators, mayors, and governors. Each in his own
way stressed to the subcommittee the importance of undertaking
this world's largest public works project. Some predicted that the
bigger, newer system would reduce auto accidents and deaths, others
emphasized the importance of relieving city congestion. Still others
claimed they were concerned about improving employment and the
economy, while some dwelt on the importance of the highway
system to national defense. The highway structure would help solve
all of these problems, they said. Final justification for launching
the project was slipped in among all these accolades in the form
of a study conducted by state highway officials. It purported to
show that interstate highways would actually save the motoring
public money—so much per mile—that the system would more than
pay for itself.

The legislative proposals generally called for upping the federal
ante for Interstate System highways beyond the traditional 50 percent
ratio and beefing up the ABC system, too, by increasing the amount
of money annually appropriated, so that these roads would not be
neglected while the new massive program got underway.

Lead-off witness Francis duPont, still special assistant to Commerce Secretary Weeks, unwittingly presented to the committee a
statement that was an accurate portent of the future.

There is widespread agreement that positive steps must be taken to
insure that the Nation's highway deficiencies will not become a
straitjacket to the continued growth of the important aspects of our
economy,

he said. By way of example, he offered the committee a variation
on Parkinson's Law that expenditures rise to meet income. He
demonstrated that congestion rises to meet highway capacity.

> . . . on United States Highway Number 1 between Trenton and
> New York, it became so plugged with traffic that the flow became
> stagnant. Business along the highway deteriorated materially. The
> State of New Jersey . . . commenced . . . construction of route
> 101, which parallels United States Highway Number 1. . . . Today
> this is the New Jersey Turnpike . . . within 2½ years the New Jersey
> Turnpike was carrying as much traffic as United States Highway
> Number 1, and United States Highway Number 1 had five percent
> more traffic than it did originally. In other words, you had removed
> much interstate traffic and put it on a toll road; this made it possible
> for business to return to normal and in fact increase along United
> States Highway Number 1. . . . I think that illustrates the importance
> of the Interstate System.

DuPont did not explain how business, which he claimed had
deteriorated when traffic on Highway Number 1 increased to the
degree that it became stagnant, was able to improve as traffic on
Number 1 increased 5 percent. He also failed to offer proof that
traffic on the New Jersey Turnpike was confined to interstate trips.
C. D. Curtiss, then Commissioner of Public Roads, also in the
Commerce Department, discussed how the Interstate System could
be paid for by the motoring public. He argued that traffic would
increase at a rate sufficient to generate revenue from gasoline taxes
because autos would be enticed onto the Interstate System. Curtiss
based his conclusions on a study conducted by the Bureau of
Public Roads that was based on figures supplied by state highway
departments which proved that increased highway facilities increase
auto traffic.
"Congestion on many city streets has resulted in smaller annual
increases in urban traffic than would be the case if adequate urban
highway facilities were available," he concluded. State and federal
highway officials knew in 1955 that a large increase in automobile

traffic follows the opening of a new highway, adhering to Parkinson's theory.

Rex Whitton, at that time chief engineer of the Missouri State Highway Department, spoke in favor of the proposed Interstate System. Referring to a map of the United States showing all major cities and proposed interstate routes, he said:

> Notice how the interstate routes bind them all together in a single network. Although the system comprises only 1.2 percent of the total roads and street mileage in the country, it serves all the metropolitan districts, 90 percent of all the communities over 50,000 population, and carries more than one seventh of all the vehicular traffic. When completed, in all probability it will carry considerably more of the total traffic. The completion of the system, in other words, will induce traffic.

On the subject of financing the program, most witnesses agreed that government revenues should be used and that none of the new highways should be toll roads. Andrew Sordoni, then president of the American Automobile Association, was quoted as saying, "Toll roads foist the entire cost of such interstate systems on highway users, which is patently inequitable." It was apparent to all that the system would never be built if it was to be paid for by charging a toll for using any portion of the highway system. It made more sense to build a "free" system that would fill up with automobiles burning up gasoline.

One supporter of toll roads appeared before the subcommittee, however. He was S. E. Wiseman, executive director, American Toll Ways Authority, who advocated a system of connecting toll roads such as the then existing Pennsylvania Turnpike, New York Thruway, and Ohio Turnpike. These toll roads were carrying the interstate and long-haul traffic and discouraging local traffic by charging a fee for their use. They also *bypassed* cities rather than entering them. He stressed the importance of keeping excessive traffic away from large urban centers. When Mr. Wiseman finished his testimony, he was dismissed without questioning, a rather flagrant departure from the committee's usual practice of extensive questioning to elicit positive endorsement for the program from highway interests.

Sinclair Weeks, of course, testified in support of a free interstate system so more cars could use the highways and generate revenue to pay for even more roads.

James J. Nance, president of Studebaker-Packard Corporation and president of the Automobile Manufacturers Association, repeatedly referred in his testimony to the "braking effect" of inadequate highways on the country's economy. This point was more clearly spelled out by Senator Case who said that if the 52 million automobiles in the United States in 1955 were on existing highways at the same time, there would be only 700 feet of road available per car. *Business Week* of January 22, 1955, described Americans as "the most mobile people since the era of Genghis Khan." If so, why not make them more so by building more roads?

The New York *Times* editorially supported building the Interstate System, as did most local newspapers across the country. The American people were sold on the idea of driving automobiles, they said, and it was up to the Congress to provide the necessary roads for them. There was no mention of bolstering an already sagging public transportation system with federal dollars.

Several witnesses before the Senate subcommittee stressed how the taxpaying public owed it to various highway interests to invest in the enlarged highway system so they could continue to make a living and prevent unemployment. The program would affect gas station operators, tire dealers, car salesmen, laborers who construct roads, truck drivers, auto insurance salesmen, and all the "little" people who try to make a decent living by working hard. The program could only be beneficial to everyone, each witness seemed to promise. There could be no bad effects.

At that time, the highway program under discussion was patterned after a program which was to distribute 37,700 miles of interstate roads throughout the states and reserve 2319 for "desirable circumferential and distributing routes in urban areas."

Bureau of Public Roads Commissioner Curtiss told the subcommittee that the Bureau could not approve any portion of the Interstate System which was specifically designed to alleviate municipal traffic, and he emphasized that the cities were to take in only long-haul traffic from the system. Yet he also explained to the subcommittee that "The larger the city, the greater the proportion of the traffic which becomes local and transversely the smaller the city, the greater the proportion of the traffic is through traffic." But no one on the subcommittee asked Curtiss how highway officials could justify constructing a system supposedly designed for long-haul traffic that the majority of the population, located in urban areas, who would generate the bulk of the revenue, would demand to use.

The question of building portions of the system in cities, where each mile would be very expensive, was raised.

Rex Whitton came up with a justification for building expensive urban mileage.

> Some sections of our urban expressways cost several million dollars per mile, of which a substantial portion is land cost. But these roads generate vehicular use and therefore highway revenue. . . . In some instances these high capacity roadways generate sufficient highway revenues to make enough to pay for themselves and help pay also for other highways in the state. . . .

Senator Edward Martin of Pennsylvania chimed in with the comment that "Unless the federal government has some control over it, it is awfully hard for us folks locally to resist the great demand to get on those good roads." His caveat was deliberately ignored.

Francis duPont stated that there was no doubt that the trucks would receive the greatest benefit from the proposed Interstate System of superhighways across the country. Only an economist from the American Railroad Association raised the question of the effects on the railroads of boosting the trucking industry. He was ignored.

Perhaps by now, Senator Gore feared that the conflict between long-haul and urban-trip use of the Interstate System was all too apparent, because he recalled Curtiss of BPR to discuss Boston's recently constructed outer belt. It had just been completed as a four-lane highway surrounding that metropolitan area, linking the suburban communities. It had been constructed on the federal primary system for local traffic and was already heavily used.

Gore asked Curtiss how traffic would go to or leave from the city of Boston. Curtiss replied that the city was then engaged in building some elevated arterials. "I do not think there is any plan for an interbelt route, not that I know of." By 1967, an interbelt for Boston was on the drawing boards.

But Gore pressed on about authority to build access roads from the Interstate System to the cities.

"If under this broad interpretation, the Bureau of Roads should be so inclined—and I am happy to say I have never detected any such inclination—political favors could be shown certain cities and certain areas, with the result that 90 percent of the cost of the construction of streets within metropolitan areas could be bestowed. I should hope that the Bureau of Roads would never be so inclined, but the possibility would exist, would it not, Mr. Curtiss?" he asked.

Curtiss replied, "I think the possibility always exists when any executive has responsibility for expenditure of large sums of money to misuse that authority. To my knowledge the Bureau of Public Roads has never done that, and I do not think they ever will."

Gore apparently felt that Curtiss would supply the answer that would resolve the conflict between building a multibillion-dollar highway system for interstate traffic when the traffic and revenue to pay for the system were known to generate from local users in metropolitan areas. Curtiss continued by explaining that the system should be placed in the vicinity of cities and business centers to permit and encourage a desirable co-ordination of highway transportation with rail, water, and air.

Gore, taken aback slightly, commented, "As you read that one, it seems to me, Mr. Curtiss, that you are soon to be in the business of building principal streets within cities." But Curtiss replied firmly, "No, it may sound like that, but it is not intended to," because, he explained, the Interstate System will provide for only a small portion of the movement of traffic of most cities and the routes will be so located as to integrate with the entire urban transportation plan of any city. It would handle long-distance travel only, which would be light. "You see, Senator, it does not take too many of these roads that are described in the previous statement to serve this traffic if it is integrated with the remaining street system," he confidently predicted. Within three years, city governments across the country were busy mapping interstate extensions through their jurisdictions.

Senator Prescott Bush of Connecticut insisted on exploring the contention over financing the system which had arisen. Previous to President Eisenhower's announcement of the $50-billion program, the governors had been in favor of forcing the federal government out of the road-building business and had been pushing for repeal of the federal gasoline tax. The governors intended to reinstitute and collect the tax themselves and build their own roads. Now they were extolling the virtues of a sound federal-state partnership. Why, Senator Bush asked.

Senator Harry Flood Byrd clearly and succinctly supplied the answer.

"First," he began, "I will answer the question about the position of the governors. I was a governor. I imagine the reason the governors favor this now is because they are getting something for nothing. . . . This is the first time to my knowledge that any large sum of road money has been given to the states without matching. . . . This is a giveaway. The federal government has taken over the enormous cost of the Interstate System, and assumes the whole cost. It is not going to be limited to 40,000 miles. In time it may be 50,000 miles, 60,000, 70,000, and 80,000 miles."

He then reminded the subcommittee that the system as originally proposed within the Administration was a closed toll road which the governors wouldn't buy.

He further stated, "This is not an interstate system, as they call it. I will venture the assertion that on most of these roads from 50 to 75 percent of the traffic will be local traffic." There was no exploration of Byrd's remarks. The promise of billions of federal dollars stifled any debate on the obvious conflict between long-distance and urban-commuter use of the system. All other opposition was quickly squelched.

For instance, A. B. Gorman, representing the Private Truck Council of America, pointed out to the legislators that of the estimated $27 billion then proposed for the Interstate System on a 90–10 ratio, $15 billion was earmarked for urban areas while only $12 billion would be needed to construct the rural portions. This lopsided proportion for a relatively small amount of urban mileage was due to high costs of right-of-way in urban areas. Gorman pointed out that 85 percent of truck tonnage was rural while only 15 percent was urban, the portion he represented. He charged that only a small percent of the trucking industry would be burdened with the staggering cost of the urban portion of the system. He recommended that the federal government get out of the highway business. His testimony was received with less than enthusiasm and elicited no questions from subcommittee members.

A less vocal opponent of the program was R. J. Harrod of Oak Park, Illinois, who submitted a statement to the subcommittee for the record. He questioned the wisdom of pouring billions of dollars into a new system of hauling goods and people long distances when the railroads already were doing so. In it he urged that "an impartial study should be made of the hidden potential of the railroad industry before hundreds of dollars of each taxpayer's money are pledged to an expensive highway program." There was no discussion of Harrod's views.

When the hearings moved over to the House Public Works Committee, there was also little debate about whether a massive new highway system was really needed. Most of the discussion was limited to methods of financing the program and hawking the benefits. Secretary Weeks set the tenor of these hearings with the reassurance that "No one questions our need for an expanded highway program. . . . You have 57 million cars on the road today, and you will have 81 million in ten years from now. You have to provide roads to put them on."

But the House committee, too, was plagued with the problem of financing the program. It was considering increased gasoline taxes to either pay-as-you-go or to float bonds to pay for the system. The Congress was in no mood to spend money. During the period 1955–56 when the Highway Act was debated in the House, there was also an ongoing debate over federal aid to education in the form of aid to school construction. Two Montana congressmen, Senator James E. Murray and Representative Lee Metcalf, introduced a bill providing between $10 and $12 billion for adequate classrooms for the ten million children who would be in overcapacity classrooms or obsolete buildings by 1960. Their bill was defeated in the House 224–194.

During DuPont's appearance before the House Public Works Committee, Representative Brady Gentry of Texas asked him, "But is it not true that the highway system needs of the United States of America are almost without limit, and will they not be almost without limit on and on?"

DuPont replied ingenuously, "I hope so."

Gentry then proposed financing education and schools with the kind of bond program being promoted for the highways, to which DuPont replied, "I do not think you can measure the proficiency of those who would be educated. . . . We have no immediate revenue from the schools that we build."

Mr. DuPont's interest in promoting the highway program was further revealed in 1964 when the Supreme Court ordered divestment of the DuPont family's 63 million shares in General Motors. The court ruled that the family's ownership of 23 percent of the auto company's stock lessened competition or tended to create a monopoly by making General Motors a captive customer for DuPont fabrics and finishes. By the early '60s, the DuPonts also owned a sizable interest in U.S. Rubber Company.

General Lucius Clay testified too. He stressed the importance of relieving the traffic jams which had accumulated across the country, jams which were affecting the economy and civil and national defense of the United States. He emphasized his belief that the proposed Interstate System would be a vital link in economic growth of the country, improve our civil and defense posture, and reduce motor vehicle accident rates, rapidly approaching 39,000 fatalities

a year by 1955. Although Clay offered few specific examples of
how the economy would benefit from building superhighways, it was
not difficult for congressmen to imagine that the federal dollars
would provide jobs to labor, profits to contractors, an indirect
subsidy to the auto industry by providing roads to put their cars
on, and more roads to encourage the trucking industry to expand.
Meanwhile, the auto insurance and parking businesses would expand,
as well as driving schools, tire companies, and the petroleum industry
too. None of the congressmen were willing to tackle the problem
of how this massive highway construction program would affect the
railroads, which were, after all, already in the business of long-
hauling goods and people, nor how it would affect public commuter
transportation, which had served admirably in World War II when
no motor vehicles were built for private use and gasoline was
rationed.

Representative Robert Jones, Jr., of Alabama made a feeble
effort to justify the program by asking Clay, "Now, was the conclusion based upon the assumption that it was a federal responsibility to relieve that traffic jam, or was it a sense of responsibility
that arrived out of collection of the 2-cent gasoline tax?"

Clay responded that the conclusion emerged independently from
the calculation that the gasoline taxes would finance a gigantic
highway system. He then reiterated the arguments that such a
program would stimulate the economy and improve driving safety.
He rambled on about the defense aspect of the Interstate System.
It would move troops, weapons, goods, and people, even in case
of an atomic attack, he said. A visitor from another planet might
have assumed from Clay's testimony that we had up to then
devised no means of moving goods and people. The argument that
the system would evacuate cities in emergencies was a popular one
with the congressmen. Yet even Clay cautioned that he could not
say that it would be possible to protect citizens by mass evacuation.

It was left to Representative Charles A. Buckley of New York
to clarify the role national defense played in the legislative program
for the superhighway system. He did so while defending, before
his colleagues on the committee, the construction and financing of

the New York Thruway, which had been labeled a bad idea by anti-toll interests.

His reply to criticism of the thruway was:

No, I say it was a good job and we were quite right. You bring in the Secretary of Defense, Mr. Wilson, and have him testify before this committee. He will say it is a good job because we are all cluttered up in New York City and do not have a highway to drive a car on. There are hundreds of thousands of cars there. You ask him whether General Motors is not stymied in selling cars. If we have good thruways and good highways, people will buy more cars. He would be with us on this bill.

Another witness before the House committee was, again, A. B. Gorman of the Private Truck Council of America. He criticized the high cost of urban expressways with statistics from Los Angeles. The city had a number of multilane highways for the purpose of providing auto traffic in ingress and egress between suburban and urban Los Angeles. Gorman singled out the Harbor Freeway which then was seven and one-fifth miles in length. He pointed out that construction costs of the freeway were $18 million while acquiring right-of-way in this urban area amounted to $40 million, or 70 percent of the actual cost of the freeway, and stated that the urban extensions were the expensive portions of the Interstate System. He also stated that Los Angeles already had evidence that these freeways *induce* traffic and generate the revenue. His testimony was ignored except for an illuminating outburst by Representative Harry McGregor of Ohio who knew that Gorman also worked for oil interests.

"I cannot understand some of the petroleum interests objecting to a needed highway program, whether it is this program or one in the state of Ohio. I cannot understand it, because they have been successful. It seems to me they are not looking any further than the end of their nose. If you do not have good highways you will not continue to build more automobiles, and if you do not have automobiles you will not use gasoline," McGregor said.

On the subject of urban expressways, another witness, Robert
Moses, offered several pointers to the committee members. Speaking
of the various financing methods being considered, he said he
favored borrowing the money and getting on with construction. He
seemed to be confused about the difference between private and
public money, however.

I cannot see the difference between General Motors or Ford borrowing for the expansion of a plant and the government in its various
echelons borrowing in order to provide a road system on which cars
will run. . . . I still have not found anybody who can tell me how
you are going to keep on turning out all of these cars without
decent, first-class, modern highways for them to run on, in particular
on the routes that connect the big cities and their suburbs, and
run through the cities, because that is what we have to do today.
The origin and destination of most of the vehicles, or a large part of
all the vehicles, is in cities.

He was saying this while BPR chief Curtiss was reassuring Senator
Gore that the Interstate System would not serve local traffic as city
streets. Moses elaborated on the effects, well known then, of displacing people, moving houses in the path of a freeway, and he
warned that urban areas with their tacky land acquisition problems
would be the biggest headache, and he suggested securing right-of-
way years in advance to assure that plenty of roads could be
constructed free from the legal tanglements of removing property
owners. He made clear the fact that local road officials had every
intent to ram freeways through urban areas. Yet none of the
committee members questioned this real conflict in the proposed
interstate program.

Rex Whitton elaborated on these urban land problems further.
"You cannot realize, unless you tried to get right-of-way in some
city and move somebody out of his home, the difficulties that we
come up against in getting that right-of-way. People do not like to
leave their homes, and you cannot blame them, but they are in the
way of progress, and so on." Whitton also reassured the committee
that there would be no need to hold public hearings on the urban

portions of "bypass routes" of the system, as he called them, because "The states know the problem best and you can rest assured that the thinking and welfare of the public will receive full consideration."

Whitton left the Missouri State Highway Department to become Federal Highway Administrator in 1961.

Howard Zahniser, representing the Wilderness Society, pleaded with committee members that provisions be made in any bill for an interstate system which would prevent concreting over of wildlife refuges, national park monuments, roadless areas within primitive forests or wildernesses. He was asked no questions and received no assurances from the committee.

It was clear to the committee that highway construction in this country was a never ending process and would never solve our transportation problems because highways induced their own traffic, leading ultimately to new congestion. Representative Jim Wright of Texas, commenting on that very point during the hearings, queried, "In other words, there will be needs that will not be filled under the system?"

State Senator Randolph Collier of California replied, "That is right. And I do not think we will ever meet the challenge finally of highway transportation in its entirety." Wright continued their exchange, "No, the needs are going to grow." Not one of the members of the committee directly questioned the wisdom of investing billions of dollars in a system which they all agreed could never satisfy auto traffic.

But George W. Anderson, executive vice president of the American Transit Association, did try to shed some light on the merits of what the committee members were promoting, even if only for the record.

"We are encouraged to find that planners, city officials, retailers, real estate people, and many other groups are becoming increasingly aware that our problem in the congested areas is trying to move people and not vehicles," he warned.

No searching criticism of the proposed legislation was encouraged. The promised federal money was too persuasive. The congressmen were swept up in their own rhetoric about the benefits of the system—goods would whisk across the country faster, automobiles would have room to "breathe" and smooth roads for long-distance travel, roads would be safer, fewer people would be killed in auto accidents, our civil defense posture would be enhanced. A highway bill embracing the Interstate System was introduced in the House in 1955 and was narrowly defeated because it did not provide a method for financing the program that was suitable to enough congressmen. Some wanted to pay for highways from the general fund, others wished to finance them by issuing bonds. But in 1956, George Fallon proposed establishing the Highway Trust Fund and reintroduced the bill with the new formula. This time it passed.

It was presented as a long-haul through traffic system, a defense necessity, and an improvement in driving safety. Specifications for urban extensions of the system were deliberately glossed over because the system was supposed to be a rural-oriented link-up across the vast United States. By the time the bill came to the floor of the Congress for final passage, the Senate and House investigating committees had heard enough testimony, and certainly the Bureau knew, that the urban extensions of the system were going to foot the bill for the program with their short-distance commuter drivers, and that the city freeways would cause headaches in heavily populated areas. Beyond these facts, highway officials were on record acknowledging that the system would never satisfy traffic demands because it induced its own traffic.

Yet Representative John C. Kluczynski of Illinois defended the House committee's wisdom in promoting the Interstate System with the following comment: "When the pressure was at its heaviest, one of the committee members made this remark, 'We have heard from everyone except the public.' No one can speak adequately for the public except their representatives in Congress. The public has no organized lobby or pressure groups and I am confident that we will give the public proper representation in the consideration of . . . [the proposed highway bill]."

Representative Frank Smith of Mississippi had argued that the gasoline tax increase should fall on highway users rather than the general public, 86 percent of which, he said, would not be using the Interstate System. That was about the closest anyone came to representing the public's interest.

The 1956 legislation itself contained the following provisions:

1. Annual federal authorizations totaling $25 billion through fiscal 1969 to complete the Interstate System. This was the first time Congress provided authorization for a complete highway system.
2. The federal share of the cost was boosted to 90 percent for Interstate projects. The high percentage of federal funds was justified on the grounds that in 1941 the Congress strayed from the traditional 50–50 basis to 75 percent federal and 25 percent state funds for defense purposes as we entered World War II. Members of the Congress and highway promoters repeatedly argued the necessity for this grandiose highway system on the grounds that it was vital to the national defense.
3. There were to be periodic estimates of the cost of the program to be used as the basis for apportioning Interstate funds. Within two years the estimated cost had jumped from $27 to $41 billion.
4. The Interstate System was to be built to standards adequate for anticipated traffic in 1975.
5. It boosted the total amount of funds available for the ABC road systems so that all road building would continue, not just the superhighway system.
6. A special revenue bill established the Highway Trust Fund. This law provided that the fund expire in 1972. All federal taxes on motor vehicles, gasoline, and ancillary equipment began channeling into a special account. Such funds were to be collected until completion of the Interstate System in 1972. These charges include taxes on diesel and special motor fuel, rubber tires and inner tubes, trucks, buses, and lubricating oil. The taxes collected on these items were to be spent "to meet those obligations of the United States . . . incurred under the Federal-Aid Road Act . . . attributable to federal-aid highways. . . ."
7. It required that each highway department hold public hearings on any proposed federally aided highway that bypassed or went through any city, town, or village and consider, too, the economic effects of such a location. After such hearings were held, each highway department was to submit a copy of the transcript of the

hearings to the Secretary of Commerce, under whom the Bureau was then operating.

Another provision of the Act stipulated that the federal government take a long look at highway safety and do something about the increasing number of automobile accidents and deaths occurring annually.

But it was more than concern for safety, economy, civil and national defense that had prompted the Congress to vote for the program. Secretary Weeks himself revealed the source of congressional enthusiasm for the legislation when he reminded the House Ways and Means Committee, responsible for devising a plan to finance the program, that the Interstate System "touches or crosses 406 of the 435 congressional districts."

3. Neither the Quick Nor the Dead Are Safe

"You can draw any kind of picture you like on a clean slate and indulge your every whim in the wilderness in laying out a New Delhi, Canberra or Brasilia, but when you operate in an overbuilt metropolis you have to hack your way with a meat ax."

—Robert Moses, addressing the National
Highway Users Conference, May 1964

What follows is a kaleidoscopic picture of how people in many parts of the country have fought the wanton and often purposeless destruction of their communities by the mania for more highways. The struggle began in earnest in 1956 when cash began pouring into the Highway Trust Fund, stepping up the pace of road construction across the country.

Before 1956, some states, such as Pennsylvania and New York, had built turnpikes and charged tolls. These proved to be excellent revenue generators for the states. The toll roads swept *around* the cities, while arterials carried traffic to and from the toll roads, primarily in heavily populated eastern states. Since the federal road program was relatively minor in the pre-Trust Fund days (in 1952 the federal government appropriated only $500 million for all roads), many other states had been eying toll roads as an answer to the problem of providing the long-distance motoring public with good highways. In Florida, for instance, in the summer of 1952, the

New York engineering firm of Parsons, Brinkerhoff, Hall and Mac-
Donald, not surprisingly, confirmed the feasibility of building a 350-
mile turnpike from Jacksonville to Miami with a westward branch
of 128 miles to Clearwater at an estimated cost of $275 million.
Once the engineers were able to determine that it was "feasible" to
build the superhighway, another study was ordered to establish
whether the road would pay for itself. It was decided that it would.
The route would begin at Jacksonville with a connection from a
$50-million expressway system under construction there.

The 1956 Highway Act discouraged the movement to build such
toll roads. It also stimulated road construction at a time when critics
were beginning to point out that the viability of cities and their
futures were in serious doubt. Yet public officials were to continue
and even accelerate the pace at which they were lambasting metropolitan areas with "urban development" in the form of freeways,
parking lots, sports, and other centers accessible by automobile.

                                                            BOSTON

Opposition to the freeways began slowly and was scattered. It
developed gradually across the country. By the early 1960s, resistance to urban freeway construction had become a commonplace
headache for highway and other public officials. For instance, by
1961, newly elected Governor John A. Volpe, former Commissioner
of Public Works in the state of Massachusetts, former Federal Highway Administrator in Washington, owner of one of the largest construction companies in the country, and former president of the Associated General Contractors of America, announced that he would
fight to get the Massachusetts Turnpike extended from suburban
Weston through the town of Newton straight into the heart of Boston,
a distance of twelve miles.

At the time, turnpike traffic hooked into Boston's outer belt, U.S.
128, then onto arterials which brought cars into Boston. The new
stretch of turnpike was to cut a swath through the heart of the
historic city despite protests of citizens, businesses, and organizations.
Three separate lawsuits were filed by property owners and tenants

of the Back Bay area, all of which were aimed at blocking construction of the highway. They charged harassment by appraisers and public officials. The objectors could foresee what would happen to the downtown neighborhoods when the concrete was poured. Numerous expressways had already intruded on the city.

The Massachusetts Supreme Judiciary Court handed down a ruling in January of 1962 that permitted construction of a proposed center for the Prudential Insurance Company of America in the Back Bay district. The turnpike extension was designed to run through the center via a tunnel. The prospectus for the extension included a contract to the Perini Construction Company of Framingham, a suburban community outside Boston proper. Only the month before, Louis R. Perini, who moved the Boston Braves to Milwaukee in search of a bigger gate return, told Boston's Mayor John F. Collins he was ready to invest millions "in Boston's redevelopment." He said this shortly after the State Supreme Court also ruled that the Scollay Square area of Boston was a blighted area which qualified for urban renewal and thereby was eligible for tax concessions. Back Bay residents lost their suit and the bulldozers and concrete mixers came in. By 1965, the twelve-mile extension was completed. It crashes by and ruins the elegance of old Copley Square and sweeps through to South Station and the site of the Boston Tea Party, after cutting through Haymarket Square.

By 1967, Boston was scheduled for a proposed inner belt. According to then current plans, the proposed $200-million, eight-lane freeway would displace 1300 households, 300 of which were private homes, as it cut a 250- to 300-foot-wide swath. More than 160 of the households had incomes of less than $3000 in 1959, and 250 had incomes between $3000 and $5000. The road would run through the South End, Roxbury, the Fenway, Brookline, Cambridge, Somerville, and Charlestown.

A fight developed over whether to route the road along the Brookline-Elm Street corridor or the Portland and Albany Street path. More than five hundred Harvard and MIT faculty members asked the federal government to halt construction of the Inner Belt until the area's transportation needs could be re-evaluated. In a petition to then Transportation Secretary Alan Boyd, 528 faculty members asked whether the road "needs to be built at all, in view of major new developments which have occurred since the Inner Belt plan was conceived twenty years ago." They further argued that if the Brookline-Elm Street route was chosen, 1200 living units would be demolished, 2300 jobs lost, low-income and elderly family groups would suffer financial and emotional upheaval, and Cambridge would be split in two.

Opponents urged that an integrated master transportation plan be developed that would take into account changing land use arrangements, transportation technologies, and community aspirations.

Executive director of the Metropolitan Area Planning Council, Robert G. Davidson, answered, "A construction hiatus and new planning studies will mean years of delay in affording traffic congestion relief and necessary progress." He labeled the professors' approach as "graphic evidence that a communications gap exists between them and the responsible elected and appointed state and local officials who are charged with conducting the public business."

A Boston *Globe* editorial commented: "For almost two decades responsible public officials and technicians have wrestled with the problem of how best to move ever-increasing volumes of traffic in the Boston metropolitan area. Their master highway plan, including the Inner Belt complex, may have faults. There is no such thing as a perfect solution, but the Inner Belt idea does represent an honest effort. And it will be a reasonably workable one. . . . Where were the academicians eight years ago, when conscientious men were striving for the best solution? Or five years ago? Or even two?

"A decision cannot be put off indefinitely. The threat of traffic strangulation and the depressing effect on the economy because of the long uncertainty are real. With due respect for the nonpolitical position of the professors, and for their concern about the disruption which the expressway would cause Cambridge, we must conclude that following their belated suggestion would lead to the Inner

Belt being 'studied to death.' There comes a time for dynamic action, and that time is now."

By mid-May 1967, Governor Volpe and Public Works Department Commissioner Edward J. Ribbs approved the Brookline-Elm Street route. This triggered action by opponents, some of whom included the 1500 families who would be displaced by the route chosen. They decided to take their fight to Washington to push for the alternate route, arguing that 90 percent of the cost of the project would be coming from Washington. Frank X. Christian, president of the Greater Boston Chamber of Commerce, applauded Volpe's decision.

Statistics from the Public Works Department showed that the road, as chosen, would displace 1669 families in Cambridge and Somerville, 159 businesses, and abolish 2715 jobs. The Portland-Albany route, which was turned down, would have displaced 656 families, 136 businesses, and 7131 jobs.

Cambridge City Councilman Walter Sullivan described the meeting with Governor Volpe to decide the route. "We gave him an argument and he wouldn't bite. He had no consideration for the people in the neighborhood."

State Representative John J. Toomey of Cambridge said, "This is a sorry day for Cambridge. That's all I've got to say," as he stormed out of Volpe's State House office.

Senator Denis McKenna from Somerville was asked if he was optimistic about success in appealing the decision to Massachusetts' congressional delegation in Washington. He replied tersely, "No."

On May 24, nearly one hundred protesting Cambridge and Somerville residents boarded two buses for a ten-and-a-half-hour bus ride to Washington. There they saw Senators Edward Brooke and Edward Kennedy and Congressman Thomas O'Neill, Jr., of Cambridge. As the marchers, carrying their protest posters, CAMBRIDGE IS A CITY NOT A HIGHWAY, trudged along unfamiliar Washington streets, carrying children, asking directions, and pausing for traffic lights, government workers in office buildings clustered at windows and waved.

The marchers were joined by O'Neill as they arrived at the

Bureau of Public Roads. He questioned the need for a road at all. "It's been nineteen years since a basic study has been made on the need for this road. Both would be a China Wall dislocating 7000 people just to save someone in New Hampshire twenty minutes on his way to the South Shore," the congressman told Lowell K. Bridwell, then Federal Highway Administrator. O'Neill opposed both routes.

Msgr. John J. McDevitt, of Blessed Sacrament Church, whose parishioners were in the path of the chosen route, discussed the problem with the senators and congressman. In an obvious reference to Governor Volpe, who had been mentioned as a vice-presidential candidate on the Republican ticket in 1968, McDevitt said, "If I were to seek a position of national importance I would want to have an image founded not on roads but rather on compassion for human beings. That does not appear to be the case." He was then joined by Rev. Paul J. McManus and MIT architect Robert Goodman, who charged that the state highway officials did not study both routes because when opponents asked for the studies of the two routes, Commissioner Ribbs refused to make the reports available.

Senator Kennedy told the group, "This is not just a problem that affects you. You represent something far beyond this—the relationship of a program to people. I am going to do everything to carry your message to every quarter. . . . You have made an extremely strong and impassioned case."

Bridwell promised to check conflicting figures on displacement and job loss provided by the state and the citizens. As a result, two separate studies were undertaken, a "task A study" to determine the need for the highway and a "task B study" embracing possibilities for the route, number of persons and businesses displaced, and relocation problems. Both studies were still in process in 1969.

NEW YORK CITY

In Manhattan, a stormy public hearing was held early in December of 1961 on a proposed Lower Manhattan Expressway, which was to link the Holland Tunnel and West Side Highway with the Williamsburg and Manhattan bridges by a route roughly along Broome and Canal streets. It would consist of ten elevated lanes and displace 1972 families and 804 businesses. Charles J. Murphy of the Automobile Club of New York called the project "essential." A few days later, the Board of Estimate unanimously rejected a proposal to acquire right-of-way for it.

Robert Moses, then federal-state liaison for New York State's road program, continued to press for construction of the expressway, which had been discussed at various levels since 1946. In April 1962, Mayor Wagner and the Board of Estimate called for final hearings on the then $100-million proposal.

There were numerous protesters. Some were not against the expressway; they simply wanted an alternate route over Walker Street instead of Canal, which they claimed would eliminate the need for any tenant relocation and would cost 50 percent less than the approved plan. Wagner said no to this plan.

Early in April of 1963, Robert Moses again urged the city to build the expressway as part of the federal Interstate System with 90–10 financing. Moses stressed that hundreds of millions of federal dollars were available for the project and that none of it should be spurned. He still urged that the expressway run east to west along Broome and Canal streets to the Holland Tunnel.

Meanwhile, a little-noticed project was concluded at the upper end of Manhattan over the trans-Manhattan Expressway east of the George Washington Bridge—four 32-storied apartment buildings containing 960 apartments were built to straddle that expressway. Original ads for the apartments, probably the first to utilize air rights over a freeway project, claimed "New York's Most Fabulous Big-Family Opportunity." A study of tenants in the project several years later revealed the following:

One fifth-floor tenant described life above a twelve-lane highway, "If I were to open the window you would soon find yourself shouting." "We just moved from the fourteenth floor to the twenty-eighth floor, to get away from the fumes," complained another. "We have to rent air conditioners from the management so we

can keep our windows closed to keep from being asphyxiated,"
said another. No one denied that the turnover rate among the
apartments was substantial.

By May 1964, Robert Moses was suggesting a 50 percent increase
in the gas tax to increase federal aid to highway construction.
Addressing the Highway Users Conference members who, the day
before, had been luncheon guests of General Motors, Moses explained how he planned highways.

> You can draw any kind of pictures you like on a clean slate and
> indulge your every whim in the wilderness in laying out a New
> Delhi, Canberra or Brasilia, but when you operate in an overbuilt
> metropolis you have to hack your way with a meat ax.

Two years earlier, Moses had pledged "every consideration to the
human and financial problem" of those who would be removed
by the Lower Manhattan Expressway.

Another public hearing on the expressway was held in 1964.
Seventy-five organizations representing businesses and residents
opposed the road and demanded that Mayor Wagner remove it
from the planning map. Supporters argued that the highway would
provide employment for 2000 construction men out of work after
completion of New York's World Fair. Opponents pointed out that
10,000 workers would lose their jobs in the immediate neighborhood
if it were built.

The president of the East Side Chamber of Commerce said the
expressway would do nothing but connect bottlenecks. Peter J.
Reidy, executive director of the Triborough Bridge and Tunnel
Authority, defended the project. Mayor Wagner still did not give
his approval.

As 1964 drew to a close, plans for the Lower Manhattan
Expressway were revived at still another public hearing which
lasted fifteen hours. The city Board of Estimate heard seventy-four
witnesses oppose it and forty-two defend the plan. Among those
appearing in favor of the project were Robert Moses and several city
officials.

By May 1965, Mayor Wagner announced that the city definitely needed the Lower Manhattan Expressway. As he explained it, "Expert opinion is virtually unanimous. The only way to alleviate the problem is the construction of the Lower Manhattan Expressway." The plan called for the construction of a 460-unit low-rent $10-million apartment building to take care of the 1972 families who would be displaced. For those who could not have one of these units, top priority would be given to the remainder in three hundred housing projects south of Fourteenth Street. The plan also called for setting aside $3 million for those businesses which would have to relocate. Wagner explained that the six-year construction schedule for the project would provide a $35-million overall payroll in the construction trades, hard hit by unemployment. Space under the elevated highway would be used for an attractive retail center. Robert Moses hailed the decision as "most gratifying" and emphasized that the bulk of the cost would be footed by the federal government—$91.8 million federal money, $10.3 million state funds, and $6.8 million from the Port of New York Authority with only $220,000 from the city.

The mayor added that double-decking the George Washington Bridge, construction of the Throgs Neck and Verrazano bridges and new Cross Bronx Expressway had failed to offer a suitable alternative for the downtown expressway as had been predicted.

Later in 1965, Robert Moses was subpoenaed to testify before the New York State Joint Legislative Committee on Metropolitan and Regional Area Studies. The committee held hearings to determine the procedural method by which such highway programs as the Lower Manhattan Expressway and the proposed rebuilding of the West Side Highway were adopted. Moses had suggested both projects in his capacity as New York's representative in federal-state-city arterial project planning. Manhattan State Senator Paul Bookson, chairman of the committee, said the actions to promote the projects indicated that "the Triborough sells ideas without consulting anyone" and was a "superinsulated government." The Lower Manhattan Expressway as planned was in Bookson's district.

At that time, Moses was head of the Triborough Bridge and Tunnel Authority, having served in that capacity for thirty-one years. His current term expires in 1970. General counsel for the TBB&TA told Senator Bookson that the Authority had the legal right to spend its money on projects that would improve the flow of traffic between the bridges and tunnels it operates. Authority lawyers argued that it could also use some of its funds to relocate people living where the expressway would be built.

In his mayoral campaign of 1965, John Lindsay endorsed the communities' opposition to the expressway, a position he abandoned upon taking office. He did attempt to placate opponents by opposing the superhighway as an elevated expressway, opting for a cut-and-cover project, which in effect did nothing to lessen the impact of the proposed expressway on the Lower East Side neighborhood.

By 1967, Percy Sutton, Manhattan Borough president, suggested that the proposed Lower Manhattan Expressway be wiped off the planning maps rather than wipe out the ever increasing number of families and businesses in the path of the route. Shortly thereafter, Lindsay was advised that the highway might be tunneled. A public hearing on the expressway was again held in April 1968, at which time the Lindsay administration defended the need for the expressway. Information from the hearing was submitted to the Bureau of Public Roads, which finally approved the right-of-way on July 24, 1968. The Lindsay-backed proposal consisted of a series of tunnels and open cuts and was labeled as "probably the most dramatic breakthrough the nation has yet seen in the planning of highways through congested urban areas . . . an excellent example of planning. . . ."

As the project was planned, it would take a year of further study, two years to construct, and a new price tag of $150 million for its 1.5 mile length from the Holland Tunnel on the west side of Lower Manhattan to the Williamsburg Bridge on the east side along Broome Street. It would consist of ten lanes, a center mall, and emergency parking facilities. The open cut would extend from the Williamsburg Bridge to the Avenue of the

Americas. The remainder would be tunneled. Assemblyman Louis DeSalvio replied, "The underground idea is better than the elevated highway proposal, but we don't want to see any highway at all." Interestingly enough, the Lindsay administration neglected to apprise the Bureau of certain information concerning the expressway which was gathered by traffic and land use planners for the Lower East Side Civic Improvement Association. The data included the fact that development of new office space in Lower Manhattan failed to bring on the predicted increase in vehicular traffic in the area. Furthermore, there has been a decline of nearly 100,000 jobs in the goods-handling (truck-using) industries in Lower Manhattan since 1960. Also, the cut-and-cover plan still advocated by Lindsay would result in the loss of an additional fifteen blocks on either side of the right-of-way containing businesses employing some 10,000 additional unskilled and semiskilled workers of the inner city. Worse still, Lindsay and Moses had based their claim for the need for the highway on two studies undertaken by the engineering firm of Madigan-Hyland. Those 1963 pleas by Moses to build the expressway on the Interstate System had rankled opponents, who charged that they should not have to sacrifice their neighborhood communities for interstate "through" traffic. In 1964 and again in 1966, the engineering firm submitted identical reports to Moses and the TBTA with traffic figures that showed that 80 percent of the expressway traffic would be local in nature, not interstate. The studies were based on 1958 traffic counts, meaningless by 1968 when the project won BPR approval, and even more so by 1978 when the expressway would open for traffic.

By November of 1968, the Department of Air Resources of New York's Environmental Protection Administration released a study of vehicular air pollution potential from the proposed LME. The New York Scientists' Committee for Public Information labeled the study's predicted levels of pollution as capable of "seriously [impairing] the health of people living and working in the neighborhood of the Expressway." The concentration of CO in the trench, the committee warned, can cause "headache, dizziness, [and] lassitude." State and local environmental health officials agreed on the need for further study of the effects of air pollution resulting from the highway. Instead, Mayor Lindsay requested $750,000 from the federal government to study the corridor through which the route of the proposed expressway would pass. Interestingly enough, the consultants on the study would not examine the need for the expressway, alternate routes, the extent to which surface improvements could meet the claimed traffic problems, nor air pollution.

Congressman Edward I. Koch (D., New York), who has fought the construction of the expressway since he was councilman for the borough of Manhattan, discussed the project with then Bureau chief Francis Turner in January 1969. At that time Turner reassured him that it was still possible for the whole project to be scrapped.

Congressman Koch maintains that since 1941 the city of New York, the state, and the federal government have conspired to destroy a neighborhood by means of the expressway, because the state and city have promised contracts (and here he likes to quote Murray Kempton's remark that union members would pave over their grandmothers if it paid $3.50 an hour).

Finally, in August 1969, the City Planning Commission recommended against building the expressway. The Board of Estimate met and voted to demap it, thus killing the project. Mayor Lindsay, facing a tough election in November, once again reversed his position and, as a member of the Board, voted against the expressway. Thus, it took twenty-eight years of wrestling with bureaucrats and politicians for residents and businessmen of the area to obtain a victory that merely maintained the status quo of their neighborhood.

NEW YORK STATE

Residents of Manhattan's Lower East Side were not the only New Yorkers embroiled in a freeway battle, either. In May 1965, Governor Nelson Rockefeller announced plans for a new Hudson River Expressway which was to generate anger, gossip, political fights, and exasperation in a struggle between officials and residents of the Hudson River bank. The governor's plan was to build the expressway along the east shore of the Hudson River between the Bronx and the town of Beacon, forty-seven miles north. Although it was to be an Interstate project, financed with 90 percent federal funds, there had been no public hearings, as required by law, before the announcement. The residents, businessmen, and town mayors were against the plan. One Dobbs Ferry resident charged that the governor intended to pave the river with concrete. The route would consist of an expressway and an alteration to existing Route 117 in Pocantico Hills, site of the Rockefeller estates. A bill establishing the projects was introduced in one house of the state legislature on a Monday and in the other on the next day, late in May. The bill was signed by the governor the following Saturday.

Late in June, Representative Richard Ottinger, whose district embraces Westchester and Putnam counties where the expressway would be located, announced that Secretary Udall had requested that federal funds be withheld from the project until passage of a congressional resolution then in the works that would establish a Hudson Highlands National Scenic Riverway. Udall feared that the road would impair the area's scenic beauty.

A spokesman for the Department of Public Works in Albany countered that the state would proceed to acquire land for the expressway despite lack of federal funds because the frozen funds would be used only in the last stages of construction, anyway.

Rockefeller established a Hudson River Commission to conduct a study of the river valley and made recommendations to him that would protect and enhance the area's scenic and historical and cultural resources. Brother Laurance Rockefeller was named chairman of the commission.

In early July 1965, J. Burch McMorran, head of New York State's Public Works Department, announced that the tentative proposal for the Hudson River Expressway would be the basis for discussions with the newly formed commission and officials of the communities affected. Ossining's mayor charged that a newly proposed 3.5 mile spur from Route 9 on the west side of the county to the Taconic State Parkway and Route 9-A farther east was being planned as part of the expressway project to take traffic away from the Rockefeller estate in Pocantico Hills. As he explained it, traffic on two-lane 117 through the governor's estate would be diverted to the new road and leave 117 virtually a private road for the Rockefeller family.

An editorial in the New York *Times* warned of the prospect of trucks and buses roaring along the banks of the Hudson and asked why the governor had not included the project in a scenic road and parkway study then being undertaken by a federal task force with the co-operation of local governments.

Late in July 1965, the state Public Works Department invited the mayors of the towns affected to attend a closed meeting to discuss the expressway. Every municipality objected to the project. The mayors labeled it a "gasoline alley" for trucks and buses. The day after the meeting, the department officials announced that the state planned to proceed with the expressway. Governor Rockefeller said the expressway would not be a gasoline alley but would instead enhance the valley's scenic beauty.

Secretary Udall reiterated his stand that the expressway must not be constructed, as did then Under Secretary of Transportation in the Commerce Department Alan Boyd, who also stated that no federal funds would be used for construction of such a highway.

By August, Mr. McMorran felt called upon to explain the need for the Hudson River Expressway. He said, "Surely no one can question the need for affording traffic congestion relief in the Hudson River corridor. We have no intention other than to give a useful utility that will be a credit to the communities concerned, will do much to enhance scenic and cultural values, and will open to the state, nation, and world the majesty and grandeur of the valley."

Within three weeks, the state had scrapped plans for constructing the portion of the expressway between the Tappan Zee Bridge to the Major Deegan Expressway in the north Bronx, but continued to plan construction from Tarrytown north to Beacon.

Governor Rockefeller was accused of trying to rewrite Washington Irving's "Legend of Sleepy Hollow" with his plans for the River

Expressway. Opponents charged that the highway, already labeled a destroyer of the scenic beauty of the valley by residents of the area, would also quadruple the value of 3000 undeveloped acres on the Rockefeller estate. "The Headless Horseman of Sleepy Hollow's literary fame today thunders through the countryside astride a bulldozer rather than a 'stallion,'" Assemblyman Lawrence Cabot charged.

Rockefeller answered these accusations by saying that Mr. McMorran had explained to him the necessity for construction of the 9 and 9-A spurs to the expressway and he pointed out that it was the governor's duty to support long-range plans of the department aimed at meeting future needs essential to the people in all parts of the state. Rockefeller explained away charges that he intended to develop the 3000 acres by saying, "We have no intention of developing, the beauty . . . would be spoiled by this multilane commercial superhighway."

While the governor was asking participants at a conference on natural beauty for "bold thinking and imaginative solutions" to New York's planning of pollution and conservation problems, pickets paraded outside the meeting protesting construction of the Hudson River Expressway and the 9-A spurs around the governor's estate. The opposition charged the expressway would be a 60-mile-an-hour whizz-way with belching trucks and auto exhausts.

Rockefeller explained that as governor he had no choice except to support the recommendations of the State Public Works Department.

Next, neighbors of the Rockefellers who lived in Sleepy Hollow Valley went to court to block bulldozers from blazing a new path for 117 and spurs 9 and 9-A through or near their homesites. They wanted the road contained in the path of the old road through the middle of the Rockefeller estate in Pocantico Hills. The old road winds close to the homes of Nelson, David, and Laurance Rockefeller. A replacement had been sought for it by the Rockefellers since 1932. The 1965 legislation creating the Hudson River Expressway explicitly called for a route to the expressway through the middle of the Rockefeller family estate.

But McMorran planned to reroute most of the 3.5 mile spur north of the estate property. Plaintiffs told the court that the most suitable plan would be to widen and straighten out old 117. The new route would invade "the very center of Sleepy Hollow Valley, an historic shrine and irreplaceable American heritage."

Late in June 1966, they had their day in court battling both the Hudson River Expressway and rerouting of 117. Joseph A. Romano, Assistant State Attorney General, told the court, "I am shocked that the plaintiffs are not pleased with the new alignment and instead are thinking up little gimmicks, picayune arguments, and ethereal ideas to mislead the court."

A spokesman for the plaintiffs said the legislature had specified a definite alignment for the new road and that Mr. McMorran was ignoring it. Mr. Romano replied that this was Mr. McMorran's privilege and duty if an inferior route was to be avoided.

The citizens lost their case and appealed it to New York State's Court of Appeals, highest court in the state. This court reversed the lower court decision and ruled that the superintendent of Public Works cannot change a legislatively determined route.

Then the Public Works Department announced plans to convert a four-mile stretch along the Hudson riverbank between Ossining and Tarrytown into a riverfront park with sandy beaches, fishing piers, marinas, and bicycle and hiking paths. The project was acknowledged to be an adjunct to the proposed expressway which would parallel the park. The park plan was introduced by the governor's advisory committee, the Hudson River Valley Commission. The Public Works Department also took the opportunity to issue a dire warning about 117—the old road had become unsafe. Built for 1900 vehicles per day, it now was carrying 5000.

Meanwhile, the Citizens Committee for the Hudson Valley discovered that state Public Works Department maps prior to 1961 showed I-87 farther east, also under attack, was originally routed near the Hudson riverbank, through the Rockefeller estates in Pocantico Hills. Subsequent maps showed I-87 rerouted through neighboring estates in Bedford, North Castle, and Purchase, much farther east and away from the river. A document was prepared by the state Public Works Department in 1962 to justify the move. They explained to angry residents of eastern Westchester that the superhighway had to go through their towns rather than the Rockefeller estate because the former route was so close to the Hudson River Valley that it would be in direct competition with the state's thruway which parallels the Hudson's west bank. Yet, the Citizens Committee pointed out, three years later a special bill establishing the Hudson River Expressway that was even closer to the thruway was defended by the Public Works Department as essential. The committee expressed concern for the "broad and almost unassailable delegated rights of eminent domain" the state enjoyed to confiscate whatever private property it wanted for highways.

As Rockefeller campaigned in the fall of 1966, he was met by pickets carrying signs reading THE ROCKY ROAD TO RUIN and WE WANT CONSERVATION, NOT CONCRETE. The state Department of Public Works labeled both I-87 and the Hudson River Expressway as essential.

An editorial in the New York *Times* of November 20 made a telling point. "As neighborhoods are sliced in two and cemeteries are relocated, neither the quick nor the dead are safe. Every major city from Boston to Los Angeles is festooned, draped—or is it strangled—with ribbons of concrete."

Up in Castle, New York, Route 117 crept along. Supervisor John F. Reed, Jr., charged that the segment between Hawthorne and Katonah would destroy homes and mar the colonial appearance of Chappaqua, an unincorporated residential community in New Castle. It would affect 108 such homes, he explained, wiping out some, taking away the front lawns of others, and pass just in back of still others. Already, a little more than one mile was completed between North Tarrytown and Hawthorne, at a cost of $7.2 million, while the remainder was tied up in a court suit. Critics continued to point out that the choice of this route, near North Tarrytown, removed 117 from the rim of the Rockefeller estate. Supervisor Reed said at the time that all the community wanted was a local road and that he understood the state to want only the same. Yet the state was acquiring a 125-foot right-of-way for

a four-lane and center island road. State engineer John Manning
said redevelopment of 117 was essential because of faster and
heavier traffic. He reported that the firm of Edwards and Kelcey
had been retained to draft alternate plans for the stretch between
Hawthorne and Katonah and that when final plans had been endorsed by the state's engineers, a public hearing on the project
would be held. In other words, the residents could fight over
alternatives, but only alternatives.

Meanwhile, farther up the Hudson, the New York State Department of Public Works and the Ulster County sheriff teamed
up to evict eighty-three-year-old Elizabeth Collier from her historic home in Highland, New York, to make way for a new four-
lane interchange to the Poughkeepsie-mid-Hudson Bridge. The
house, built in 1819, was known as the Reuben-Deyo Halfway
House. It had once served as a tavern for stagecoach stops on
the trip from Albany to New York in another era.

The sheriff and public works personnel removed the retired
Hunter College professor and her belongings to a small tenant
house nearby that lacked electricity and plumbing. Mrs. S. Jeffrey
Starin and a group of historians from nearby Newburgh had purchased the house for $205 when it was condemned by the state
more than a year before. The historians intended to move the
house to preserve it, but they could act only when Miss Collier
was removed. Mrs. Starin had arranged for the donation of a
parcel of land to receive the house and the Cross Country House
Movers were alerted to be ready to move immediately. On the
appointed day, as Miss Collier was evicted, Mrs. Starin and her
group asked for an hour to remove the house. Instead, state
employees swept the house clean. Then they ordered demolition
by a bulldozer waiting in the wings. The house was reduced to
rubble in a matter of minutes, as onlookers wept and threw
stones at the machine which ground up the house. Afterward,
Miss Collier's cat was discovered to have been destroyed when it
hid in the house during the confusion that reigned. Searchers
combed the rubble to recover doorknobs, hinges, carvings, and

other artifacts from the old home. Miss Collier died in a fire that destroyed the tenant house shortly thereafter.

Today, Mrs. Starin refers to the state's Public Works Department as The Department That Gives the Public the Works. She theorizes that the state refused to await the house movers because saving the old house would have set a precedent contrary to the philosophy of state officials. Mrs. Starin's group was in the process of having the old tavern declared a national historic monument. In 1966 she hired a consultant, who suggested to the state that the plan to place the interchange route in the path of the house would create a dangerously sharp curve, but to move it some twenty feet beyond the house would be in the interest of public safety as well as avoiding destruction of the landmark. His report was ignored. The Hudson River Valley Commission sat on its hands.

Today, concrete covers the site of the former tavern. Mrs. Starin has personally recorded several accidents which have resulted on the curve highlighted in the consultant's report.

Downstream from the new Poughkeepsie interchange, the first public hearing was finally held on the proposed Hudson River Expressway in June 1967, more than two years after legislation for the project was rammed through the legislature. Opposition at the hearing ran 15 to 1.

Next, Governor Rockefeller telephoned Secretary Udall and asked him to reconsider his position. Udall ordered a full review of the proposed expressway. In June 1968, the Department of Public Works, which had switched labels and was now designated as the Department of Transportation, held still another public hearing, which ended at 1:00 A.M. There were three speakers for the expressway, ninety against.

By noon of the day following this second public hearing, the New York Department of Transportation had filed an application with the Army Corps of Engineers for permission to build the expressway, permission they needed because 3.5 miles of the highway would extend out and over the Hudson River on fill, placing a portion of the highway in the jurisdiction of the engineers. Residents expressed fears that this portion of the con-

struction would destroy the habitat of the river sturgeon and affect
newly planted shellfish beds. It was clear from the plan as presented
that the expressway would open up the Rockefeller property at
route 117, one half of which, Rockwood Hall, had been rezoned
commercial for shopping centers, high-rise apartments, and light
industry. The Rockefellers donated the other portion, that nearest
to the Rockefeller homes, to the state as a park.

By May 1968, a task force, appointed by Secretary Udall at
Rockefeller's urging, reported its review of the expressway. It offered no new information from that on which the Secretary had
earlier based his opposition, but recommended that he change his
position.

Meanwhile, the governor's Hudson River Valley Commission
held hearings on the project, hearings at which there was overwhelming opposition. Nevertheless, in July 1968, the commission
went on record approving the expressway. The approval was written
by executive director Alexander "Sam" Aldrich, a cousin of the
Rockefellers.

At about the same time, Secretary Udall received from still a
second task force a report signed by Harry Rice of Interior's
Bureau of Outdoor Recreation, approving the expressway, although
it added, somewhat ingenuously, that the state Department of
Transportation had not considered any alternatives.

Thereupon, Udall informed the Corps of Engineers that he was
withdrawing his objections to the project, which allowed the engineers to hold hearings and then issue the state a permit to
build the highway. The Corps of Engineers held their hearings on
the proposal January 6, 1969. The opposition was 90 to 4. On
January 22, Governor Rockefeller called Secretary of the Army
Stanley Resor and requested the permit. On that day the permit
was scheduled to be issued the following week. On January 24,
a group of citizens filed suit against Resor, newly appointed Secretary of Transportation Volpe, newly appointed Secretary of the
Interior Walter Hickel, and Burch McMorran on grounds that the
Department of Transportation had not given approval to the project,
nor had the Corps of Engineers or Interior investigated alternatives.

Meanwhile, the state has proceeded to acquire land for the right-of-way of sections of the expressway. Despite federal officials' claims that no federal money will be spent on the highway, a Bureau spokesman in the right-of-way office has since stated that the expressway is being built to conform to federal standards and that it is possible that the state will ask for reimbursement of construction expenses.

Westchester and Putnam county residents in New York State were not sold on highways, either. Many of them had attended in February of 1962 the state Department of Public Works public hearing on plans to route I-87 as a twenty-nine-mile expressway through those two New York State counties located just north of New York City.

A crowd of about 750 persons turned out for the hearing. They spoke, applauded, and booed to express their opinion of alternate routes submitted by the Public Works Department. State engineers at the hearing, which was held at the Westchester County Center, wanted to determine by a "full expression of local opinion" whether I-87, the last "sizable" chartered segment of interstate highway in the state, should go east or west of Byram Lake in the towns of North Castle and Bedford.

At a similar hearing in neighboring Mount Kisco a year before, the easterly, or Chestnut Ridge, line was officially being considered. The opinions of eight hundred persons obtained in a twelve-hour public session were studied by highway engineers, and months later they drafted a westerly alternate route through the Byram Lake area and ordered the hearings in February of 1962.

As planned, I-87 would run north and south through east central Westchester from the intersection of the Cross Westchester Expressway and Hutchinson River Parkway in Harrison to the also planned east-west I-84 near Brewster in Putnam County, following already-built state Route 22. Public Works Department officials estimated that if the easterly alternate were chosen, it would cost $56 million and $4 million more if the westerly route were used to skirt Byram Lake. The entire stretch would be financed with 90 percent federal funds, 10 percent state.

Citizen responses at the 1962 hearing varied. Some preferred
an even more westerly alignment along the Hudson River or
parallel to the Saw Mill River Parkway. But most of the controversy
centered around the east-west routes at Byram Lake near the
Connecticut line. The Westchester Citizens Alliance, land owners
in Purchase, declared that New York State had not demonstrated
a need for a superhighway nor justified the tremendous expense
to taxpayers to build the highway.

Cecil E. Heacox, secretary of the state Conservation Department,
warned officials that the easterly route would traverse two important
and significant wildlife sanctuaries, the Arthur W. Butler Memorial
Sanctuary and Westmoreland Sanctuary. And, he reminded them,
the westerly route would traverse the Leonard Park and March
Memorial Sanctuary.

The Westchester Citizens Alliance raised to the ceiling of the
auditorium huge gas-filled balloons bearing signs which read ROCKY
AND 87 GO WEST, recalling charges that I-87 originally was
drawn up to go through the western portion of Westchester County
but had been shifted eastward to avoid going near the Rockefeller
estates in Pocantico Hills. North Castle's supervisor, John A.
Lombardi, led his constituents into the hearings waving small
American flags. He declared that the old easterly, or Chestnut
Ridge, route would be better from the standpoint of distance, cost,
engineering, and construction difficulties.

State officials left the hearing with much information and many
attitudes to ponder. They also had the help of an editorial in the
Times which in part warned, "It is as dangerous to leave roads
purely to the engineers as it is to leave war to the generals."

Even after the hearing, so much interest and opposition had been
generated by plans to build I-87 that more than one hundred
additional communications were sent by interested citizens and
groups to the regional office of the state Public Works Department.
A spokesman cautioned that a decision would not be made for
several months and that then it would take two years to draw
up plans for the route.

In mid-April of 1963, Connecticut's Governor John Dempsey

was asked to approve construction of a one-and-one-half-mile segment of I-87 which New York State engineers planned to cut through a small corner of Fairfield County in Connecticut. New York State highway engineers said that an alternate route would affect New York City's water reservoir at Rye Lake and the Westchester County Airport. But the North Castle Democratic Committee of Connecticut urged Governor Dempsey to "force New York State to reconsider an ill-conceived plan." The governor in turn awaited the recommendation of Highway Commissioner Howard Ives. To help him make up his mind, citizens had prepared numerous and vociferous protests against the superhighway. He also had to consider the fact that I-87 north of Fairfield where it crossed back into New York State again might be successfully opposed by the Bedford Association, estate owners, the representatives of the Butler and Westmoreland wildlife sanctuaries, and numerous town officials who did not want the freeway.

In May, a suit was filed in New York State's Supreme Court by ten Bedford residents to block construction of I-87 along another controversial segment through the northeastern section of Westchester County. In court, the Bedford residents protested against constructing I-87 on their ridge. They said they preferred the Mount Kisco route which they claimed would cost $20 million less. They also charged that J. Burch McMorran, state public works superintendent, had originally chosen the Mount Kisco route because it would help commerce and cause a minimum of harm to residents. The state's attorney argued that the present route would save the state $4.3 million, produce a road .7 of a mile shorter, and not be destructive to the countryside. He also noted that the present route had Bureau of Public Roads approval.

In June 1963, the State Supreme Court acted on the suit brought by Bedford residents to block I-87. Supreme Court Judge Justice Gerald Nolan dismissed the suit, saying:

> As private citizens, petitioners apparently seek to act as champions of the community in requiring the superintendent to defend his official act. However commendable that purpose may be, it does

not provide petitioners with a cause of action, nor may the constitutional questions which they present be decided in the absence of special injury or damage to their personal or property rights.

Disheartened, but not resigned, Bedford residents were already planning to take their case to the state's higher court of appeals.

At just about the same time, Bedford's Connecticut neighbors at Greenwich learned that despite their protests, Connecticut State Highway Commissioner Howard Ives had approved construction of I-87 one and one-half miles through the town. Ives explained that engineers could find no other path. While Connecticut residents were grappling with that headache, I-87 was disrupting plans for New Castle Township in New York State. State highway engineers asked town officials to halt two housing developments and construction of a $1.25 million golf course planned between Byram Lake and state Route 22 because they were in the projected path of the highway.

Early in December 1964, the Bureau picked and approved the final route for I-87 through Westchester County. It was to be east of Byram Lake and would run between the Butler Memorial Sanctuary and the Westmoreland Sanctuary, despite the fact that the state had favored a westerly route which would have gone through the Marsh Sanctuary. Rex Whitton, then Federal Highway Administrator, announced that the decision was based on many considerations, the primary one being that the eastern route would cost $4.5 million less than the westerly route. Then, too, he said, the approved route would affect eleven acres of wildlife sanctuary, while the alternate route would have taken sixteen. The chosen route also would take twelve less parcels of land and affect fewer existing buildings.

He promised that landscape architects would be brought in by New York State to make the new six-lane route esthetically pleasing to adjacent land users and the motoring public. The new highway would serve truck traffic. No official suggested improving state Route 22 which paralleled the proposed I-87, nor did they suggest not building it at all.

The county Planning Department as well as county officials had constantly opposed the use of Chestnut Ridge, as had the state Department of Public Works until Washington made clear it would reject the western route. Thus residents of the alternate routes were pitted against each other and no one could think of a way to avoid building the road at all. The Bureau made its decision solely in terms of the cost, since neither route would please everybody.

Meanwhile, that section of I-87 routed through Westchester County and a corner of Connecticut near Greenwich was started. It consisted of nine miles and started from the Cross Westchester Expressway in Harrison, onto state Route 22 in Armonk, New York, via estates in Purchase and others, across country club property and Manhattanville College lands, around the west side of the Westchester County Airport, a 1.39-mile sprint through estates in Greenwich, Connecticut, and back into New York State near the Armonk Airport. As it approached Byram Lake and northern reaches, it faced more resistance.

In August 1965, a tug of war developed again between property owners in the path of I-87 as it emerged from the Connecticut state line and aimed for the wildlife sanctuaries along Byram Lake. Although the BPR approved the eastern route, property owners there were unhappy and Mrs. Lyndon B. Johnson asked Mr. Whitton to look into the route and re-examine it. Meanwhile, the state was ordered by Whitton to halt land acquisition along the route.

During the second week of 1966, residents involved in the I-87 dispute heard from Mrs. Johnson. In an Armonk, New York, schoolhouse, more than two hundred residents, mostly homeowners, who were opposed to the westerly route near Mount Kisco, listened intently to a letter from Lady Bird. She expressed the hope that highways and expressways "can enhance the beauty of our landscape." The audience began hooting, stomping feet, and laughing derisively.

"Lady Bird Johnson's letter is what we get from Washington when we object to a superhighway going through our living rooms," shouted one angry resident.

Just a year earlier, residents of the Hunts Woods area of Mount Vernon, New York, had attempted to reach Mrs. Johnson when state and federal officials signaled the go-ahead to fell 150-year-old beech trees along a two-mile wooded section of the Cross County Parkway in Westchester, which they wanted to widen to eight lanes. Residents of the area attempted to reach Mrs. Johnson at the White House by telephone as the bulldozers moved in. Their attempt was futile. She was discussing civic improvement at a Washington conference on Natural Beauty. The parkway was widened and many of the fine old trees were removed.

Early in 1966, the consulting firm of Charles H. Sells, a former state superintendent of public works, submitted a study showing that the westerly route for I-87 away from Chestnut Ridge and Westmoreland Sanctuary would be a better route, since the easterly route, then the choice, would need an additional $17.9 million in related highways in the area.

By mid-April 1966, New York conservationists knew they had lost the long battle to prevent I-87 from being built along Chestnut Ridge in Bedford and North Castle. Secretary of Commerce John T. Connor and Rex Whitton overruled their objections to the route. The federal officials argued that rather than destroying the area's natural beauty, the highway would improve it in spots and open it up "to all the people." The highway was scheduled to skirt and sometimes cut through some private estates and pass between the Westmoreland and Arthur W. Butler wildlife sanctuaries. Whitton explained in a letter, "It is our thought that this highly scenic area should be dedicated to all the people and not restricted to the few who know about its location." Commenting on the engineer study charging there would be an additional cost for ancillary highways to I-87, Whitton said that the cost of these roads would not be a consideration anyway. He reassured everyone that federal engineers had made no such blunder of overlooking costs of collateral roads. Mr. McMorran concurred with the choice of route for the superhighway.

This final decision out of Washington was in defiance of recommendations of Secretary Udall, Governor Rockefeller, who this time apparently did not feel obliged to support his superintendent of public works, the New York State Conservation Department, Westchester County Planning Department, and other public officials.

Rural areas were no less affected. In mid-December 1963, another highway controversy flared anew, this time involving a sparsely populated area of New York State. The Public Works Department had for ten years planned to reconstruct the stretch of Route 17 which wound its way from Binghamton east to the Hudson River. They planned to convert it into a four-lane divided expressway. But opposition began when the state revealed its plans for the highway along the Beaver Kill and Willowemoc creeks in Sullivan County. Trout fishermen were up in arms over the effect construction would have on this world-famous fresh-water fishing paradise. The sportsmen suggested an alternative route to avoid disruption of the streams by construction equipment. It was rejected by Superintendent J. Burch McMorran as "utterly impractical," but he promised that during construction every precaution would be taken "to avoid or minimize even temporary disturbance to the stream."

Harry Darbee, chairman of the Beaver Kill and Willowemoc Rod and Gun Club, observed that in the past, engineers had destroyed stream beds by building bridges "like a kid sitting on the floor building a bridge with blocks."

Mr. Darbee collected 17,000 signatures of protest from trout fishermen from Hawaii to Alaska who had visited the area and sent them to Governor Rockefeller. The governor would not interfere. Nor would Secretary Udall. As planned, the original Route 17, a twisting, winding, two-lane road, would become a service road, and new Route 17, financed with 50 percent federal and 50 percent state funds, would become a four-lane highway, part of the Southern Tier Expressway. It would cross each of the streams and zigzag across old 17 with about thirteen bridges in a twenty-mile stretch. The fishermen and opponents of the new expressway favored building the new highway into the terrain instead of down in the stream beds, but McMorran insisted that such an alternate route would cost $1.9 million more than the plan approved by the state Department of Public Works. The state's plan would take two factories and numerous houses. Mr. Darbee said that the community of Roscoe was divided on the issue, with real estate interests and parties expecting to make money by selling land for the highway pitted against those who wanted to preserve the streams. There were also many who wanted a new highway but not at the expense of the streams.

Mr. McMorran told fishermen who objected to the bridges in the streams that they would be helped because trout were famous for loafing under bridges. But the fishermen countered that bridge piers could raise the level of water, increase the velocity of the flow, which in turn would then dig holes and displace sand and gravel which would form bars. Bottom disturbances could also clog pools in which the trout gather and kill tiny plant life on which fish feed. But the bulldozers came to Beaver Kill and Willowemoc.

In 1964, the Seneca Indians on the Allegany Indian Reservation near Salamanca in southwest New York State had lost a seven-year battle with the federal government over another segment of Route 17. It all began when the Kinzua Dam project in northwest Pennsylvania was undertaken by the Army Corps of Engineers. The dam flooded a third of the reservation. A treaty signed by George Washington in 1794 promised the Indians the right of perpetual occupancy. The courts decided in favor of the government and ruled that the Congress had the intention to break the treaty when it directed construction of the dam. The Indians were later awarded $15 million for their flooded homes.

After the dam was built, the engineers found that it would be necessary to relocate that portion of Route 17, the two-lane highway which stretches across New York's southern tier, that passed through the remainder of the reservation.

It is the policy of the army engineers to replace any highway they disturb with the exact type or "in kind." But New York State's ambitious Department of Public Works had long been anxious to convert Route 17 into a four-lane limited access Southern Tier Expressway. The army entered into an agreement with the state whereby it acquired land for four lanes of road instead of two, and the state paid the difference between the land needed for two and four lanes.

The Indians objected to the fenced superhighway on grounds that it would divide the reservation in two, cut off communication between the halves, and bar access from one portion of the reservation to the other.

In a 2 to 1 decision, signed by then Judge Thurgood Marshall, the Second Circuit United States Court of Appeals ruled that the law establishing authorization for the dam project gave the Secretary of the Army the necessary authorization to replace or relocate highways and to determine necessity for condemning Indian land.

Judge Leonard P. Moore dissented, with a longer argument than the justification offered by the majority. He protested that the Secretary of the Army should not be authorized to condemn private property, much less Indian treaty-protected property. "Under the guise of a road of a higher standard, New York State is, in effect, promoting a public highway project independent of the water resources projects authorized by Congress. . . . Would it not be more consistent with the Indian policy so frequently expressed by Congress and the Supreme Court to let Congress decide whether it wishes to give the State of New York the power to condemn land for a superhighway, rather than impute to Congress an intent to invest the Secretary of the Army with such powers?" he asked.

"At a time," he continued, "when so much attention is being paid to so-called 'civil rights' which are statutorily created because of certain racial problems, some consideration might well be given to the Indian race and those 'just rights' which President Washington assured the Senecas this Government would protect."

In February 1967, Governor Rockefeller announced that he was going to the voters in November to ask their approval of a $2.5-billion bond issue to finance highway and mass transit construction in the state.

Citing the need to provide the state with a balanced transportation system, the governor ticked off the following proposals as "musts":

1. Southern Tier Expressway (old 117 which affected the Seneca Reservation and Beaver Kill and Willowemoc creeks)
2. Genesee Expressway
3. Long Island Expressway
4. Interstate 84
5. Bruckner Expressway
6. St. Lawrence Scenic Highway
7. A newly proposed Nu-Way
8. Arterials in Buffalo, Niagara Falls, Rochester, Syracuse, Binghamton, Utica-Rome, Albany and environs, Yonkers and New York City, Route 7, the LaSalle Expressway, an east-west Poughkeepsie highway, Hudson River Expressway, and Sunrise Highway

Turning to mass transit, he explained that "some of the specific projects which might benefit from comprehensive aid for mass transit include new and improved mass transit systems for the state's major cities, extension and improvement of the New Haven, Long Island, and other essential railroad commuter service, right-of-way, and the development of high-speed rail transportation to our major airports."

State Senator Edward J. Speno of Nassau proposed that a board of highway planning review be formed to pass on the merits of road projects in the state. Others took up the cause and soon it was suggested that such a board study alternate modes of transportation that might better serve a given area, avoid destruction of scenic values, historic sites, and natural resources, and consider the effect on local governmental planning and public need and convenience based on current highway capacities.

Governor Rockefeller stumped New York State to sell his $2.5 billion bond issue that would appear on the November 7, 1967, ballot. He had explained when he introduced the idea in February that the bonds would be amortized from the state's general funds, not by highway users' charges alone. Addressing the New York State Auto Association in that fall of 1967, he said, "We can no longer expect that the subway, railroad, air, or bus riders can be expected to assume all the financial (operating) responsibility for mass transit, or that highway users should, as a class, shoulder all the burdens of an improved highway system."

In Rochester, he told the Chamber of Commerce, "If past experience prevails, the improvements in highways alone under the bond issue would be accompanied in the counties of Monroe, Genesee, Livingston, Ontario, Orleans, and Wyoming by 185 new, relocated, or expanded plants, $111.2 millions in plant investment, 11,700 more jobs, and $77 million added annually to payrolls. . . . Construction of these roads alone would generate an additional 1500 on-site and 3900 related off-site jobs in these counties." He estimated that the state's population would expand by 1.5 million persons and the number of registered automobiles by 1.1 million in seven years. If the additional cars were lined up bumper to bumper, he explained, they would stretch from Bangor, Maine, to San Diego, California. To allay fears that the bulk of the money would go to New York City, he said it would be spent in direct proportion to the population and needs of each area.

Early in October, the New York State AFL-CIO endorsed the bond issue.

By late October, VOTE NO! TRANSIT BONDS—LASALLE EXPRESSWAY bumper stickers were appearing on hundreds of automobiles around the town of Tonawanda, a well-to-do suburb of 110,000 just north of Buffalo, New York. Angry citizen groups from Tonawanda and North Tonawanda voiced opposition to construction of the expressway from Niagara Falls to Buffalo through their residential community. This proposal alone convinced town residents that they must vote against the $2.5 billion bond issue. Other opposition to Rockefeller's bond issue stemmed directly from plans for the Hudson River Expressway and a Rye-Oyster Bay Bridge. The LaSalle Expressway would split school districts and remove homes and small businesses, opponents charged.

"It's nonsense to argue that highways are necessary to bring in light industry. Not through a built-up residential area, they're not," a resident argued.

Representative Otis Pike of Riverhead, Long Island, called the bond issue economically and sociologically disastrous. State Senator Bernard C. Smith debated Pike, calling the issue a necessary crash program to meet impending transportation crisis growing out of an estimated increase of five million persons and four million automobiles by 1990. The bond issue, he argued, was the best way to avoid putting the state's transportation needs in annual competition with vital educational and social programs, as if this were not desirable! Then, too, Governor Rockefeller had assured the state's AAA that amortization of the bonds would come from the state treasury's general funds.

Mayor Lindsay endorsed the bond issue at the end of the month. The lion's share of mass transit funds, $1 billion, would go to New York City's rail system, and most road money to upstate. When Lindsay dropped in on the Catholic Guild of the city's Department of Highways, which was meeting at the Commodore Hotel, he told them, "I hope you will all spread the word. It would mean a lot of jobs."

Not everyone agreed. R. Bradlee Boal of the Council of Better Transportation Planning opposed the issue in a debate with Dr. William Ronan, Rockefeller's chairman of Metropolitan Transportation Authority, on a television station in New York City. Boal pointed out that with federal matching money, the $1.25-billion portion of the bond issue would really amount to $5.3 billion for roads but only $1 billion of the issue would be spent on public transit, where the need is most critical.

At the close of October, Governor Rockefeller received upsetting news. A poll revealed that only 30 percent of the people of New York had heard of his bond issue proposal and he was told the opposition would turn out in numbers at the polls in November. So he encouraged formation of a nonpartisan citizens group to work for the bond issue. It was called Action for Transportation in New York State. It had an announced budget of $750,000 and was supported by business organizations and labor unions. Almost overnight, a vigorous campaign was launched over television and radio as well as in newspapers and on billboards, subways, and trains. Up in Albany, a bill by Senators Edward Speno and Whitney-North-Seymour, Jr., to establish a road review board died in committee.

One of the strongest opponents of the bond issue was the Atlantic Chapter of the Sierra Club, whose members urged New Yorkers to vote against it. They argued that the bulk of the money would go for unnecessary and unplanned roads that would destroy the countryside and lead to further deterioration of public transit. Lindsay, Senators Javits and Robert Kennedy supported the governor's proposal. Rockefeller answered these charges. "It is only when there is hectic, last-minute road building that you don't have a chance to save beauty areas." By the first of November, New York State had a new Transportation Department whose function it was to co-ordinate all transportation. J. Burch McMorran was appointed chairman of the new department.

The New York *Times* carried an editorial just before the November 7 election in support of the bond issue.

As election day drew closer, bond proponents argued that highways, airports, bus lines, tunnels, and other facilities built with the money would expand business, which would expand state revenues, which would help pay for the bonds. They won. The bond issue was approved 3 to 2 by the voters.

By the time Governor Rockefeller had entered the 1968 presidential race in June 1968, he was pouring an estimated $5.5 million into campaign advertising. One of his television spots demonstrated the governor's concern about air pollution. It showed a man with a dozen cigarettes in his mouth and a fistful in each hand. The message came via a voice which said, in part, "Just breathe for twenty-four hours and you get what you'd get from two packs of cigarettes every day." This was followed by a description of Rockefeller's record on air pollution. "Four more years for the governor, and New York could break the air pollution habit . . . four years of somebody else [man coughs] . . . and who knows?"

This is the same Rockefeller who, along with members of his family, owns vast holdings in the Standard Oil Company, whose brother David is director of B. F. Goodrich Company, and himself successfully sold a bond issue largely devoted to constructing more highways in New York State. He was aided by Dr. William Ronan. Ronan, described as one of the palace guard during Rockefeller's inept bid for the presidential nomination, receives $70,000 in salary as chairman of the Metropolitan Transportation Authority. As a public official, he receives a salary second only to the salary paid to the President of the United States.

Opposition and criticism of highway construction continued across New York State as more and more money was collected for such projects. Big and small communities felt the onrush of the bulldozer. In The Branch and neighboring Smithtown on Long Island, residents fought the widening of Route 25 into a four-lane divided highway. They argued that the project would change the atmosphere of the region where Walt Whitman had once lived while teaching at the village of The Branch School. Mayor John W. Jones said the widening would provide no benefits to Smithtown and that the town did not need it.

But a number of businessmen in the area urged that the highway construction be accepted as "progress." Mario Remo, an official of Mays Department Store in Brooklyn, announced that a branch store was being considered for the area. He cautioned, however, that Mays would not invest the five to seven million dollars for the project if the road widening project did not go through. He pointed out that better roads would be an important ingredient in the store's appeal to residents in surrounding areas. Countering this argument, Frederick Froessel, lawyer for the First Presbyterian Church, said, "Smithtown does not need Mays."

An official of the Public Works Department said he could not understand the opposition, since all historic houses in the area would be spared. He was referring to twelve Early American homes with neat picket fences which stretched about one mile along the north side of the highway. The village had designated the houses as historic to preserve the town's colonial atmosphere. Speakers pointed out that those houses had never been restored or rebuilt and had been in continuous use as dwellings, some since the 1700s. Although the road widening, they argued, would not disturb the houses, it would necessitate removing huge elms, oaks, and locust trees that lined the south side of the street to make a mall and new traffic lanes. One of the homes, the Hull Conklin House, was pre-Revolutionary, angry residents pointed out. Ultimately, they were able to work out a compromise with highway officials whereby Route 25 remained untouched while an adjacent route was improved without affecting the character of the area. Other communities across the nation were not to fare as well when they tangled with the bulldozers.

PENNSYLVANIA AND POINTS SOUTH AND WEST

New York was not the only battleground.

Residents of Philadelphia objected to plans for the Southwark Expressway. As approved by the state Highway Department, 131 certified historic houses on Front Street would be razed, and the Gloria Dei "Old Swedes" Church, the oldest in Pennsylvania, would be isolated on an island between railroad tracks and the elevated barrier of the expressway. Dedicated in 1700 and declared a national historic site by Congress in 1942, Gloria Dei Church was for decades the center of a Swedish settlement above the banks of the Delaware. Opponents of the thirty-two-mile project requested that the route swerve a short distance to the east and be depressed for a quarter of a mile. Across town, the Franklin Institute received a $149,500 contract from the Highway Research Board to study the effects of highway landscaping and determine whether or not it affected nearby property.

In Virginia, a quiet campaign was organized to save a Frank Lloyd Wright house from being razed for a four-lane superhighway, I-66, through Falls Church, a small town eight miles from the White House.

The house had been condemned by the Virginia State Highway Department and was about to be demolished. It was built by the famous architect as an example of good design at low cost. The Highway Department offered its owner, Mrs. Robert Leighey,

$25,605 for the 1940 four-room house plus its one-and-one-half-acre wood and stream setting.

Douglas B. Fugate, Virginia State Highway Engineer, said that the state's plans had gone too far to change or reroute I-66. Acting as quickly as they could, Secretary Udall and members of National Trust for Historic Preservation arranged to have the house moved out of the path of the highway and to a suitable setting at Wood-lawn, near Mount Vernon, Virginia. Mrs. Leighey was finally paid $31,000 for the house, which she donated toward the moving expenses. Despite hints from the Bureau of Public Roads that it, plus the state, might be able to pay the cost of moving with 90–10 money, Mrs. Leighey's donation plus anonymous gifts footed the $50,000 moving bill.

New freeway plans for Cleveland put the affluent Shaker Heights community in an uproar. An 8.7-mile, eight-lane freeway was proposed as a secondary access route to downtown Cleveland from Interstate routes that proceeded on to Buffalo, Pittsburgh, and New York.

Shaker Heights Mayor Paul K. Jones declared:

> We must decide now whether we regard freeways as masters or servants. I think we must weigh the values involved. Is faster traffic flow more important to any of us than our homes, our neighborhoods, and their schools and churches?
>
> Have we become so callous that we can disregard the value of irreplaceable parks and historical landmarks? Are we willing to tolerate anything simply because 90 percent of its cost would be footed by Washington?

The planned freeway will take 810 homes and 75 commercial properties, of which 75 homes and 5 businesses were in Shaker Heights.

Out in the West, a dispute arose over a north-south freeway through and around Sacramento, California. The state Highway Commission designated a route between Second and Third streets, through "Old Sacramento." Highway planners were urged to consider an alternate route on the west side of the Sacramento River which would bypass the city but connect to its bridges. Backers of this alternate route were making an effort to save thirty-one historic buildings in the old section of the city that were in the path of the proposed highway. A study by the National Park Service found that "there are historical values in Old Sacramento important to the community, the state, and in a degree, to the nation." The Park Service urged that Old Sacramento be preserved and restored as far as would be practicable.

The Sacramento city planners and state Highway Commission stuck to the original choice, selected by state Highway Engineer J. C. Womack, despite Governor Pat Brown's disapproval.

Then a report out of San Francisco warned that traffic jams had become monumental on the Golden Gate Bridge, indicating that the area was in need of a new transportation facility.

Back in 1963, the bridge's fourteen directors hired the consulting firm of Ammann and Whitney to study the possibilities of a mass transit facility over the bridge. The firm's report stated that a second deck on the bridge to carry a rapid-rail system was unfeasible. That decision was a blow to San Francisco's fledgling Bay Area Rapid Transit System, which wanted to extend across the bay into Marin County north of the city.

In 1965, the directors hired the same firm, which reported that a second deck would be practical but for *automobiles*. They claimed that the difference between auto and rail traffic was that trains caused vibrations. This decision chilled proposals to build an underwater tube or hopscotch to Alcatraz and Angel islands, to shore with a new bridge. A high-speed ferry system was also proposed. Each of these proposals would probably be more expensive than a second deck on the bridge. The plan to double-deck the bridge would require costly off-ramps in San Francisco proper and result in dumping more cars into congested downtown San Francisco, which had gone on record against building any more freeway facilities.

In New Orleans, residents of the Vieux Carre section were exasperated with the Bureau of Public Roads in Washington and Louisiana state highway officials and vice versa. For ten years, engineers had been planning an interstate route, originally conceived by Robert Moses back in the forties, to run along the city's waterfront. The latest plan called for routing it across Jackson Square, a national historic landmark in the old French Quarter, in the form of a six-lane elevated expressway. The expressway would cut off the square from the open view of the Mississippi River. By July 1969, federal officials had agreed to remove the expressway from the historic area but were still determined to pour a freeway somewhere in the vicinity as an alternative.

In September 1967, the federal government appropriated $4.8 million to hire architects, sociologists, economists, and city planners to work together as a so-called "design concept team" on a proposed freeway through Baltimore.

The team's objectives were supposed to be to integrate freeway design with overall city planning, avoid large-scale displacement of people and disruption of neighborhoods, and destruction of worthy old buildings. They were encouraged to come up with ideas on how to use freeway construction to create new housing, community centers, and parks along freeway routes and enhance the city in general. The design concept was first proposed as a sweetener by architect Archibald C. Rogers and other colleagues when it was apparent that the freeway program might be halted by bitter controversy. The J. E. Greiner Engineering firm of Baltimore, House Public Works Committee Chairman George Fallon's district, and the architectural firm of Skidmore, Owings and Merrill, of Washington, D.C., represented two of the disciplines involved in the Baltimore design concept team.

The design concept team discovered that the proposed freeway, as planned, would cut through Rosemont, a middle-class Negro neighborhood, one of the most stable and cohesive neighborhoods in the city. More than 70 percent of the families there owned their own homes and only 18 percent of the residents would consider moving unless forced to. Community participation, income and educational levels were considerably above the city average. The incidence of juvenile delinquency, crime, and welfare dependence was not higher than elsewhere. As proposed, the freeway, I-70-N, would bisect the neighborhood and displace 68 businesses, which provided 490 jobs, and 880 families. It would also isolate 500 households from the remainder of the community.

The team estimated that tax losses to the city would amount to $233,000 a year and indicated that some areas faced certain blight if the freeway went through. The team reported it planned to investigate opponents' claims that the freeway was not needed nor justified. It also planned to study an alternate route and alternate means of moving cars and people. State Highway Director Jerome Wolff grudgingly agreed to allow further probing by the team but warned that "this is the first and last change" in the design team's limited mandate. As set up, the team was severely handicapped by the terms of the contract it negotiated, which permitted it to work only within the highway engineers' long-predetermined freeway corridors.

By 1969, Baltimore's freeway plans had been approved by federal, state, and city officials. Only the residents continued to resist. One major expressway was routed through Fells Point, a waterfront neighborhood dating back to 1732, consisting of a small collection of federal-style houses similar to those in Washington's historic Georgetown, which members of Baltimore Heritage, Inc., were interested in restoring. The Heritage group, along with twenty-two residents and businesses in the paths of the freeways, filed suit in Federal Court to stop the highways when it became clear the design concept team was rubber-stamping the whole project.

And so the skirmishes between the road builders and the communities continued, in Morristown, New Jersey, Mount Vernon, New York, Milwaukee, Detroit, Chicago, Wilmington, Delaware, and Seattle.

Nowhere did the strong-arm tactics of the Congress of the United States surface with such clarity as in May 1966, when a long-smoldering freeway fight erupted in the nation's capital. It began as a struggle between federal agency and civilian members of the National Capital Planning Commission, which at that time had to approve public works projects in the capital. The District of Columbia, without home rule since the 1870s, was at the time governed by three presidentially appointed commissioners, one of whom was, as member of the Army Corps of Engineers, responsible for the District's Highway Department.

As a federal official and member of the NCPC also, Brigadier General Charles M. Duke, the engineer commissioner, pressed for a $700-million freeway program at the Planning Commission meetings. Citizen members of the Planning Commission, appointed by the President, successfully blocked Duke's proposals in an effort to reflect the views of the voteless citizens in the city. The result was a deadlock.

President Johnson stepped in and requested that an established Policy Advisory Committee, composed of seven representatives of major District and federal agencies, make a recommendation. The PAC turned to the D.C. Highway Department, which hired the Arthur D. Little Company, a management consultant and research firm, based in Cambridge, Massachusetts, to make a two-month study of Washington's freeway plans.

The resulting "Little Report," as it became known, called for a moratorium on *all* freeway construction in the city. Engineer Commissioner Duke was stunned to learn that the report found: (1) existing plans for freeway extensions were "based on insufficient data, and on questionable assumptions, and forecasting techniques"; (2) transportation planning had "been carried out with inadequate regard for long range economic and social impact," both points made repeatedly by an ever growing number of citizen groups in testimony before NCPC officials, the District commissioners, and before Senate and House subcommittees which approve District budgets and appropriate matching funds for highways as well as every other expenditure by the District government. The PAC, in turn, recommended to President Johnson that the city's freeway program be restudied and each project reviewed.

President Johnson issued a statement that the recommendations were reassuring to him, members of the Congress, and the "citizens" of Washington. He had misjudged citizens of D.C.

Commissioner Duke decided not to accept the PAC statement, although he was a member of the committee and the statement had been adopted unanimously. He contacted the Director of the National Parks Service who, as a member of the NCPC, had voted against the freeways because they would take parkland along the historic Mall and elsewhere. Duke offered to replace in cash or kind the parkland in the city and to tunnel the south leg of the inner loop under the Lincoln Memorial and along the Mall. The Parks director agreed to switch his vote, leaving the citizen members of the NCPC in the minority and negating the PAC statement. Duke subsequently went before the NCPC and received approval without further study for all his freeway projects from the new majority.

One of the members of the NCPC was Walter McCarter, who was in charge of building the congressionally authorized D.C. subway, then only in the planning stages. Representative William Natcher of Kentucky, chairman of the District of Columbia Appropriations Committee in the House, had repeatedly threatened that he would withhold subway funds from McCarter until the freeway system was begun in the District. Thus McCarter voted for freeways.

As freeway proposal after freeway proposal won approval from the new NCPC majority, citizen anger waxed hotter and hotter.

One of the proposals was yet another Potomac River crossing, to be called the Three Sisters Bridge. The first week in November 1966, the Washington *Post* reported the findings of the most recent study conducted by the Metropolitan Area Transit Commission, which revealed that the number of vehicles crossing the river into the city increased sharply during the year, while the total number of people riding in these vehicles dropped.

The bridge proposal was the kickoff point for an inner loop through downtown Washington. The new bridge itself was to connect at parkland on both the Virginia and District sides of the river. The loop was aimed through the inner ghetto areas of the city. Another portion of the proposed freeway system was aimed at other parkland and through businesses and residential areas of both black and white Washingtonians.

When it became clear that neither the District commissioners, the NCPC, nor the congressmen on Senate and House District committees, who ultimately determine the fate of the city, were responsive to citizen opposition to the freeway program, opponents regrouped to take their case to court. More than fifteen citizen organizations, both within the District and in neighboring Maryland and Virginia, as well as individual property owners, joined the suit. They charged that proper public hearings had not been held on four separate projects, that certain federal agency members of the NCPC voted illegally through "alternates" who were sent to represent them at NCPC meetings, while citizen members did not vote in such a manner, that certain NCPC members were guilty of conflicts of interest, among them District Engineer Commissioner Duke, who voted as a member of the NCPC on his own highway department proposals, and that the city Highway Department had failed to comply with the District's own 1893 Highway Act, which set strict requirements that had to be met before any highway could be constructed in the city. The deposition of Commissioner Duke revealed what had been going on between the city fathers and city business interests as well as the Highway Department.

Duke admitted that no public hearings had been held on the latest alignment of the North Central Freeway, which was scheduled to be built through a business and mixed, but predominantly black, neighborhood. He claimed he had been assured that all BPR requirements had been met with regard to all Washington freeway projects.

"The funds would not be given if they had not met the requirements established by the Bureau of Public Roads. . . . I am confident as I am sitting here that not only have the requirements of the BPR been met with respect to all of these projects, but the interest of the citizenry has been met at the same time."

He explained that if officials believed they could further improve the location of the freeway and reduce adverse effects of the freeway, *then* they held public hearings. But if they felt that the changes that had been made and the appearance of the freeway represented the best possible location and that further public hearings would not result in improvement, then no further hearings would be required. "If we don't think that constructive suggestions with respect to the improvement of the facility would be forthcoming from a public hearing, we would not hold one. We would hold one if we thought that the hearing would produce constructive suggestions." That the law required the hearings seemed to elude him.

Duke also admitted that neither he nor the other two District commissioners had read any of the transcripts of the only public hearings, held years before, on the contested freeway proposals. As for voting as a member of the NCPC on projects his highway department submitted for approval, Duke explained that it was perfectly proper for him to vote on his own projects because he was sure the proposals were in the public interest.

At the time of his commissionership, Duke was a trustee of the Federal City Council, an organization whose members are reluctant to describe its function or purpose. A spokesman for the organization explains that they cannot give out printed information on the council's activities or even its purpose, but she describes it as "a non-profit organization for the betterment of D.C." Others describe it as a businessmen's organization whose purpose is to promote legislation that will advance the interests of businesses in the Washington area. Members include car dealers, department store owners or executives, lawyers, managers of the city's major newspapers, D.C. Highway Department officials, and one Louis Prentiss, former executive director of the American Road Builders Association.

Freeways have always been popular with the Federal City Council. Periodically, Duke briefed FCC members on the need to build more highways in the nation's capital. As if that weren't persuasive enough, FCC hired Lloyd Rivard of the Automotive Safety Foundation, an organization supported by petroleum, rubber, and automobile manufacturers, to study freeway needs in the District of Columbia. So impressive was Rivard's report that Duke hired him away for his own highway department. The Federal City Council presented Rivard's study to the House D.C. Appropriations Committee, headed by Congressman William H. Natcher.

Then Lieutenant Colonel Louis W. Prentiss, Jr., son of the road builder, became Assistant Engineer Commissioner for the District. Duke also explained that he, Rivard, and Duke's director of highways, all public officials, met in executive session with members of the Appropriations Committee. In the deposition taken of Duke

pertaining to the citizen lawsuit, he was asked if he consulted with
Congressman Natcher about withholding funds for Washington's subway. ". . . I certainly would not deny that in the course of our
discussions this problem came up," he answered.

Duke left for an army assignment in Saigon at the end of 1966.
Meanwhile, residents of the Washington metropolitan area awaited
the court's decision.

In November 1967 the lawsuit filed by District, Maryland, and
Virginia residents against pending freeways in the District of Columbia was dismissed in the United States District Court by Judge
Alexander Holtzoff. The *Evening Star* crowed in an editorial several days later: "Judge Holtzoff's favorable ruling on the legality of
the District freeway system represents, at this point at least, a clear-
cut victory for the city. . . . The legal challenge was brought by a
citizen group which, during the past several years, has explored every
means at its disposal to harass Washington's freeway program in the
hope of bringing it to a standstill. Its District Court suit has dredged
up a hodgepodge of complaints—most of which Judge Holtzoff de-
cisively rejected last week."

The citizens took their case to the Federal Court of Appeals, while
the proposed Three Sisters Bridge near the Georgetown waterfront
got a red signal from then Secretary of Transportation Alan Boyd,
who decided the project needed more study. Critics of the bridge
proposal kept arguing that it was not needed.

Representative William Cramer, ranking minority member of the
House Public Works Committee, said the District "is the clearest
example where the freeway problem is muddled and has sharply
destroyed the effectiveness of the Interstate System. I, for one, do
not intend to stand by and see this done." He spoke as the House
approved legislation to add two hundred miles to the existing Interstate System and give state highway departments permission to
shift already approved routes with the further approval of the Secretary of Transportation. Cramer explained that changes could be
made in routes but only if the abandoned route is "not essential to
completion of a unified and connected Interstate System." No portion of the system could be removed, leaving a gap. "For example,"

Cramer explained, "this bill would not authorize the elimination of the Three Sisters Bridge or the North Central Freeway as part of the Interstate System here if the sections of highway are essential . . . and in my opinion they are essential."

Cramer said that the states had agreed to finish the full Interstate System as a condition of getting federal funds. If the District is not compelled to finish, other states with similar big city problems would want to get off the hook, too, he claimed. But this was a straw man. The urban-freeway controversies in no way blocked completion of other roads. An investigation into specific controversial freeway projects in New York City, Baltimore, Chicago, Detroit, and San Francisco by the General Accounting Office elicited this response from Bureau officials:

"The unresolved locations in metropolitan areas are vital links in 'metropolitan transportation systems' and will improve metropolitan traffic circulation, relieve local street congestion, and provide service through the central district or between the central district and rural interstate highways. *However, these segments are not vital links of a 'unified national network' and failure to complete these segments will not prevent the completion of an integrated and completely operational interstate system. It is possible to either delete the controversial route segments from the Interstate System entirely or to make substitute interstate connections.*" (Author's italics) The report was released almost four months before Cramer's statement. Furthermore, state highway departments are *encouraged* (by 90–10 funds) to participate in the interstate program, not *obliged*.

Among those controversial freeway segments mentioned in the report and deemed nonessential to the Interstate System were the freeways under study by Baltimore's design concept team, the Lower Manhattan Expressway, and controversial freeways in Chicago, Detroit, and San Francisco.

House roads subcommittee chairman, Congressman John Kluczynski, scheduled hearings the second week in December to air Washington's freeway snag. Testimony was presented by Maryland, District, and Virginia highway officials, two congressmen from

neighboring Maryland districts, two congressmen from neighboring
Virginia districts, and Secretary Boyd.

Boyd, as lead-off witness, explained that he was in favor of dropping three proposals for the capital, including the Three Sisters
Bridge, because it would channel traffic into the north leg of a
proposed inner loop that had not received approval. Construction of
the bridge at this time "simply would transfer a growing traffic jam
from the Virginia side of the Potomac to the interchange at 26th
and K streets," he said.

The Transportation Secretary also opposed plans to tunnel under
the Tidal Basin near the Lincoln Memorial to connect with the
South Leg Freeway, which would dump three lanes of traffic into
the three lanes of traffic already moving on that freeway. He said
that Bureau officials themselves had "characterized this tunnel expressway as a cannon which will literally fire three lanes of traffic at
three lanes already on the expressway." The one-mile-long tunnel,
to cost about $100 million, would be only a marginal improvement
over existing surface streets around the Basin, he argued. As for
the North Central Freeway, he described it as an eight-lane recipient
of traffic combined from one six-lane freeway in neighboring Montgomery County and another six-lane freeway from Prince Georges
County, both in Maryland, to bring traffic into downtown Washington.

"We want that bridge," said Subcommittee Chairman Kluczynski
anyway. Serving notice that he expected Boyd to approve the new
Potomac bridge by the end of the month, the chairman added, "If
he doesn't act, the Congress will. That's a mandate."

Suddenly the National Park Service announced it had planned all
along to close Memorial Bridge across the Potomac to commuter
traffic and limit it only to vehicles visiting Arlington National Cem-
etery. Virginia Highway Commissioner Fugate offered this as still
another reason for building the Three Sisters Bridge. He said that if
Memorial Bridge were closed, the existing bridges would not be
able to handle the traffic. The House Public Works Committee sent
Boyd a letter demanding that he approve the Three Sisters Bridge
or face legislative action directing that the bridge be built. The com-

mittee said it expected Boyd to consult with District city officials on the assumption that their position would be favorable.

The city's officials had changed. President Johnson had abolished the old District government of three commissioners and replaced it with one commissioner, a deputy commissioner, and a city council of nine. The nation's capital, more than 60 percent black, now had a black commissioner, Walter Washington, who was immediately dubbed "Mayor Washington" by hopeful residents. Deputy Commissioner Thomas W. Fletcher, fresh from San Diego, was white, and the council was a balance. All were appointees.

Blacks watched Mayor Washington hopefully. Whites did too, banking on his empathy for the large number of residents who would be uprooted by any freeway plans.

Especially encouraging was a speech Deputy Fletcher delivered in New Orleans in the fall of 1967, shortly after he was appointed. "In my opinion, the day of the urban administrator is gone—even the city manager who considers himself an administrator. . . . We can no longer solve the city's problems with the planner and the highway engineer. They are no longer speaking to the needs of the urban area." What is needed, he told his audience, "is a strongly motivated political decision maker" combined with active citizen participation in the decision-making process. "The people can make decisions and if we don't give them the right to make decisions, we're all in trouble." Referring to Washington as "the most important city of all the cities in the United States, if we cannot provide government that is decent and workable, God help all the cities in the United States," he said. Despite these pious declarations, Fletcher, by May 1969, was secretly negotiating with Kluczynski for freeways for D.C. and seemed not interested in the people's right to make decisions in his city.

As Congress was awaiting Boyd's decision on the Three Sisters Bridge, District residents held their breaths awaiting appellate court action on their lawsuit, and Walter Washington sent his proposed city budget to the new City Council. It included funds for both the South Leg of the proposed inner loop and the North Central Freeway. On the first day of public hearings before the City Council, representatives of fifteen organizations testified against the projects. The freeway program was labeled "institutional racism" and the men who run it, "lily-white bureaucrats . . . who live in Maryland and Virginia," by one white suburbanite who testified. He was referring to the District's highway director and chief highway planner, both of whom lived in suburbia far beyond the District line. Another witness testified that the city already has more than 4000 cars per square mile and more than 30 percent of its land devoted to streets and highways. As the parade of anti-freeway witnesses continued, there was a flurry of activity among organizations favoring freeways. Representatives of these groups quickly signed up to appear before the council. They said they did so after news accounts told of the sharp feelings expressed at the hearings against spending money for highways instead of other city services, and because of relocation problems for displaced families. The pro-freeway people were: Harold E. Wirth, chairman of the District Representatives of Rubber and Tire Manufacturers; Paul L. Pascal, general counsel for the Greater Washington Food Wholesalers Association; and Glenn T. Lashley, public relations director for the District Chapter of the American Automobile Association.

Wirth demanded an end to the delays in freeway construction and said that businesses had moved to the suburbs but "they have moved where the freeways are. You have no freeways here. Build freeways and you'll get them back."

The *Evening Star* editorialized: ". . . the jettisoning of local highway funds at this point would jeopardize the availability of millions of dollars in federal matching funds for highways." No discussion of whether the highways were needed—concern only for all that nice federal money.

Next, the Washington *Post* moaned: "If downtown residents, increasingly in lower income groups, are to work at all, government must enable them to get to and from work. These are the citizens who have the greatest stake in a transportation system built around the necessities of a population that finds it increasingly difficult to get satisfactory work in their immediate neighborhood." There was no mention of the embryo-planned subway system.

The lawyers for the citizens' lawsuit received a temporary injunction from the Appellate Court which prevented the District Highway Department from proceeding with the freeway program. Secretary Boyd did not meet Congressman Kluczynski's ultimatum for approving the Three Sisters Bridge by the first of January 1968.

By mid-January of 1968, Secretary Boyd still had not assured Congressman Kluczynski that he would push construction of the Three Sisters Bridge. And as for the North Central Freeway, Boyd courageously told a television audience that "political clout" and not traffic demands had determined the proposed route for the bitterly opposed freeway. Boyd said that traffic studies had shown a greater need for a route in fashionable Georgetown along Wisconsin Avenue, where businesses and residents do have clout. He charged that the freeway was continually pushed across town, away from the white affluent area west of Rock Creek Park, where Wisconsin Avenue is located.

Mayor Walter Washington claimed he was taking no position on the freeways when he included appropriations for them in his budget, which was submitted to the Congress. He then said his decisions would be keyed to Boyd's moves. Boyd said the decision should be made locally and his decisions would be keyed to Mayor Washington's moves.

In mid-February 1968, the Federal Court of Appeals heard the lawsuit brought by citizens in the District of Columbia against pending freeway proposals and decided in favor of the citizens, overruling the lower court. In their decision, in which all three judges concurred, they wrote, "These projects generally affect more people and larger areas of the District than any other type of street, and therefore are potentially more destructive of esthetic values and fundamental property rights. To allow the District government to build large expressways without regard for (the 1893 highway law), which was initiated for the express purpose of preserving the L'Enfant street plan, would be inconsistent with history, a strong tradition and express statutory language. The public hearing . . . forces the [city's] administrators to spell out the reasons for their decision —a check and balance basic to our entire system of government.

Though the District Commissioners are appointed rather than elected, their primary interest is the District of Columbia, and, therefore, they are likely to be more responsive to a group of District residents . . . That is, it is probable that a group of District of Columbia citizens would have more leverage on the final decision if their opinions were presented to the District Commissioners, a local interest group."

In the wake of the citizens' victory, Congressman Kluczynski promised to introduce a bill *ordering* the District Highway Department to construct the freeways. And Congressman Natcher renewed his threat to withhold funds for the subway system if the freeways were not built. "On this committee, we have believed sincerely for a number of years that there is a place in our Capital City for the freeway system . . . along with a rapid transit system."

On March 18, Congressman Kluczynski introduced a bill, H.R. 16000, to force the District's freeway program *despite* the court order. Groups opposing the freeway system labeled his action dictatorial and undemocratic because the legislation included an ultimatum to the District government, the Department of Transportation, and related agencies to complete the system, which by then was estimated to cost $772 million.

The bill stated that "notwithstanding any other provision of the law or any court decision or administrative action to the contrary, the Secretary of Transportation and the government of the District of Columbia shall, as soon as possible after the enactment of this section, construct all routes on the interstate system in the District of Columbia. . . ."

Defending his decision to introduce the bill, Kluczynski said, "The legislation is necessary to accomplish what the Congress intended when it passed the 1956 Federal Highway Act."

Lobbyist Harold E. Wirth predicted the bill would receive substantial support. "This is the nation's capital, and it belongs to all of the people. Congress is the voice of all the people in the United States speaking," he crowed.

The *Evening Star* editorials burst forth with dire warnings that utter chaos would result if the freeways were not built.

Congressman Kluczynski held hearings on his proposed legislation for the District highway program the first week in April 1968. More than seventy citizens' associations signed up to testify.

The lead-off witness was Charles Cassell, a member of the Black United Front, an organization of moderate and militant blacks. He referred to freeway supporters as the Road Gang who insist on creating more massive concrete canyons containing accelerated treadmills for rapidly dumping pollution-generating vehicles into a downtown area already hopelessly congested during rush hour. He said the issue was black and white in the sense that they were white men's roads through black men's homes. "I wish to remind you gentlemen that in giving aid to the forces militating against the desires and well-being of the majority of the residents of Washington, D.C., you would be confirming the findings of the President's Commission on Civil Disorders; namely, that recent unrest and frustration of poor people stem from long years of exploitation, neglect, and abuse reflected in callous and cavalier attitudes on the part of local governments, in this case aided and abetted by the Congress. . . . This . . . is the stuff that civil disorder is made of, and bayonets and Stoner guns cannot replace sincere response to the desires and needs articulated by the public, and this has been articulated by that suit and by the constant remonstrations on the part of the public, to both the city government and the Congress, regarding the damage done to the city by freeways. . . . Citizens in this city are also completely aware that no solution to this crisis is valid which accepts the premise that the automobile is a fixed factor around which all plans must center." He called for restricting automobiles from entering the city.

Congressman William Cramer responded, "I do not intend to dignify his statement by asking any questions." Questioned later about Cassell's testimony, Cramer ingenuously commented that some people say they wish they could get housing outside the city, but protest when the government wants to pay them for their present homes. He charged that Cassell did not suggest any solution to the traffic problem of the city. Cramer said he was sure Negroes could move into any neighborhood they chose if they wanted to.

Other witnesses representing various District neighborhoods fol-

lowed. All opposed construction of more freeways. Perhaps the
most dramatic witness was Sammie Abdullah Abbot, a white resident
of suburban Maryland, publicity director of the Emergency Committee on the Transportation Crisis, an organization of citizen groups
joined to stop the freeway program and support the proposed subway.

Abbot waded in by reciting a dialogue he had heard between a
newscaster and Congressman Kluczynski. The chairman of the House
roads subcommittee had said, "We've got to get the traffic moving.
For instance, the rain this morning evidently tied up all the roads
and our office staff was more than an hour late coming to work."

Abbot charged that the tardiness of Kluczynski's staff might be
reason enough to fire his employees, "but it is sure not enough reason to engulf the nation's capital in freeways eight and ten lanes
wide. . . . I read quotations attributed to you in the press using
the same reason; namely, that the traffic problems of congressional
employees and staffs justified the freeways. The fact that these employees work for Congress does not in the slightest reduce the de-
structiveness and debilitating effect of freeways upon citizens whose
taxes, I may add here, pay for the salaries of Congressmen and their
staffs. . . .

"Now, another reason we are gathered here today, according to
newspaper accounts, is that Congressman Kluczynski wants to get
Congressmen Broyhill and Gude off your back," Abbot added. Broyhill's district is across the Potomac, where a substantial number of
his constituents live in Broyhill Estates residences, built by the congressman's relatives. Gude's district is adjacent to the District city
line in Maryland.

Abbot also discussed racism: "If an individual white racist, bigot,
destroyed an individual Negro's home by dynamite, he would be
universally condemned by the officials, the press, and the public,
but when a governing body, be it Congress or a city council, pro-
mulgates a policy of urban freeway or urban renewal and unleashes
a set of bulldozers to drive thousands of families from their homes,
demolishing established and integrated communities, then only the
victims object as in the case of Watts, Newark, etc.

"This official action is called institutional white racism which uses the planning process to the detriment of the increasingly all black and poor inner city vis-a-vis the almost all white affluent suburbs. . . . Last year where all fifteen of the top planners in the District of Columbia Highway Department and Planning Commission were white, thirteen of the fifteen lived in Maryland and Virginia suburbs. . . . This institutional white racism exists all the way up through the councils of governments to the very halls of Congress. Otherwise, how could we still in this critical year of 1968 advocate and try to ram through freeways which will, if built, create the conditions to duplicate the Watts explosion in every major city of the land."

At one point in the hearings, Kluczynski was moved to comment: "This is the capital of the free world. People from Illinois come here by the thousands. We have millions of people coming in from all over the country to the great city of Washington, D.C., which will be the greatest city in the entire world in the next few years. I am happy to see people coming in from Chicago, Illinois, here, and I would like to entertain them, take them around, show them, 'These are your buildings; this is what you came to the nation's capital for with your children.'"

That was April 2, 1968. Within three days, Dr. Martin Luther King, Jr., was dead and sections of Washington were burning, sections which few tourists from Illinois or any other state had ever seen.

And so the parade of witnesses continued, each telling the roads subcommittee members that the automobile as a prime mode of transportation in cities is outdated, destructive, and unnecessary. A few challenged the wisdom of continuing the Highway Trust Fund in its present form, suggesting that the money be made available for the mode of transportation a community chooses, rather than financing only auto-oriented transport.

After the congressmen had heard from the freeway opponents, they heard from freeway boosters. These included representatives of taxicab companies, paving contractors, the Washington Board of Trade, rubber and tire manufacturers, American Society of Civil

Engineers, D.C. Bankers Association, Downtown Progress, Airport Transport, Washington Building Congress, labor unions, department stores, local chambers of commerce, concrete firms, automobile dealers, bus companies, realtors, automobile clubs, truckers, and local suburban government units.

Although District of Columbia residents have no congressman to represent them, suburban congressmen appeared before the subcommittee. They pleaded for more freeways. Representative William L. Scott of Virginia plugged the proposed bill. He said it was necessary to build the proposed highways to get his constituents who are employed in Washington to and from work. He predicted the downtown business area would wither away and suggested if the freeways are not built, shopping facilities and government offices might be moved out to the suburbs.

Representative Gilbert Gude of Maryland said dislocated people should be paid a fair market value for their property and that housing should be built by utilizing air rights around and over freeways. He did not offer to house them in neighboring Maryland.

Miles L. Colean testified for the Federal City Council. Its position was that, among other things, the freeways were needed because "jobs are going begging in the suburbs and along the Capital Beltway. The underemployed or unskilled workers in the District need jobs. . . . Traffic and parking on Washington's overburdened streets may soon make many of the city's residential neighborhoods unlivable. Constant traffic congestion poses an increasing danger to pedestrians, especially to children." He did not explain how the freeways would rid neighborhood streets of the clutter of cars parked on both sides of the streets, the effect of autos everywhere. He also asked for a higher federal payment for property of persons dislocated. Members of the Federal City Council are Senator Alan Bible, at that time chairman of the Senate District Committee; Congressman John L. McMillan, Bible's counterpart in the House; representatives of General Motors, Ford Motor, a Chevrolet dealer, Texaco, Inc., Goodyear Rubber and Tire, realtors, Washington's two major newspapers, Standard Oil and U.S. Steel. All had addresses in affluent neighborhoods and half lived in suburbs of the District of Columbia.

After the hearings, the congressmen went into closed session to decide on what bill to present to the Congress. There was no doubt in the minds of freeway opponents that the House roads subcommittee would report out a bill demanding construction of the city's freeways. It did. But rather than bring this bill to the floor of the House where it might be defeated for being too dictatorial, the bill was tacked onto the upcoming 1968 Federal Highway Act, a bill particularly popular during an election year because it promised large federal funding for all areas of the country.

At about the same time the hearings were held on D.C.'s freeway legislation, a group described as District citizens and businessmen organized a drive to aid Senator Bible in his campaign for re-election in the form of a $50 "thank you testimonial." Secretary-treasurer of the affair was Retired Major General Louis W. Prentiss, a special consultant to ARBA, now with the AAA, still a member of the Federal City Council.

Mayor Washington was told what position he should take on freeways in an *Evening Star* editorial which read, in part: "Congress' first obligation is to see that a reasonable freeway program, as part of a balanced system with rail transit, is built. Mayor Washington, for his part, has a strong obligation to assure Congress of his total support in that venture."

In light of the attitude the newspapers have taken on the freeway issue, it is interesting to note that Washington *Star* vice president John W. Thompson, Jr., and Washington *Post* board vice chairman John W. Sweeterman and vice president Gerald W. Siegel are members of the Federal City Council and weekly receive their dose of freeway promotion to crank into their editorials.

In June, when the House Public Works Committee packaged the District freeway legislation into the 1968 Federal Highway Act, both the *Star* and the Washington *Post* praised the strategy. The *Post* editorial commented: "There is a powerful argument for Congress to go as far as it can in making the policy decision even if it cannot at this time resolve all the controversial details." The *Post,* with its national liberal reputation, has been for years a champion of home rule for the colony of the District of Columbia. Its liberalism ends with that lip service.

In the May presidential primary, both the Humphrey and Kennedy ballots in the District of Columbia asked if citizens favored a city referendum on each highway project proposed by the D.C. Highway Department. The pros won, 19 to 1. More than 93,000 voted in favor of letting the residents make these decisions. Less than 5000 who did not opposed the citizens' choice referendum.

At the same time, a *Post* education reporter was writing articles about the shortage of funds for the District's sagging school system which had proposed a summer enrichment program aimed primarily at helping the ghetto disadvantaged. The original request was trimmed from $19 million to $1.3 million by school officials themselves and the House Appropriations Committee which controls the flow of federal cash for all District programs trimmed it further to $675,000, whereupon it was approved by the Senate and the House. Mayor Washington added $186,980 to lift the program to at least a workable level. Although 1967's summer program for the city was almost $3 million, and there was end proof of the effectiveness of some of the programs, in 1968, funding totaled $862,000 and reached 10,000 fewer youngsters. "The children who will lose educational opportunities because of limited funds include many with behavior or academic problems. They often need just an extra push to help them stay in school another year," one *Post* article stated. D.C. residents had repeatedly requested that the money spent out of the city's general fund for highways should have been spent on improving schools, welfare, and recreation facilities.

Congressman Natcher froze the District's subway funds with a promise to release them when freeway construction began. As planned, Washington would undergo the disruption of subway and highway construction simultaneously.

The City Council and the National Capital Planning Commission both agreed on a modified freeway plan for the District in December 1968, that eliminated key links in the system demanded by Congress. When President Nixon took office in January 1969, he appointed a new chairman to the council as well as one new member. When it became clear the council would not budge, he hovered over Washington in a helicopter with his Secretary of Transportation, John Volpe, one rush-hour morning to observe traffic conditions. Ironically, he commented, "I sure am glad I don't have to drive to work."

Meanwhile, subway advocates in the city were alarmed that Congressman Natcher had not released the funds to begin that project. He reiterated his argument that every freeway had to be built if the subway was to be built.

White House pressure prevailed, and on Saturday, August 9, 1969, the City Council met for the announced intention of reversing itself to allow construction of all the freeways demanded by Congress. The council was able to do so only after fourteen of more than two hundred protesters were arrested. The council chambers was emptied following a slug fest between freeway foes chanting, "Sell-out" and police ordered to clear the chambers. Nixon immediately telephoned his council chairman and congratulated members for "their courage in taking this difficult but necessary action."

At this writing, the citizen groups who successfully blocked construction before are again in the courts attempting to prevent Congress from forcing more concrete on the nation's capital.

". . . Senator Jennings Randolph is not only our friend, he is one of us."

—John P. Moss, president, American
Road Builders Association, 1966

The continuing momentum for the highway program is provided by a staggering number of private interests. The average motorist is unaware of some of these organizations because many are closed clubs, although they testify before congressional roads committees whose purpose it is to determine how many highways the public is supposed to need each year. Many public officials whose duty it is to protect the public are themselves members of these closed clubs.

One such group is the American Road Builders Association, which began in 1880 during the era of the bicycle as the American Wheelmen. ARBA has 5300 members representing the entire highway construction industry, including highway contractors, manufacturers, and distributors of highway construction equipment, materials producers and suppliers, faculty members and students of engineering colleges and universities, engineers, investment bankers, state and federal highway officials, and members of Congress. Half the members are contractors. The association is located, appropriately, in a new building side-by-side with the Donohue Building which houses the Federal Highway Administration in Washington's southwest renewal area.

According to association literature, its purpose is to assure "long-range soundly financed well-planned highway and airport programs adequate to serve the growing demands of traffic, our advancing economy and the requirements of national defense." ARBA explains that there is nothing wrong with public officials belonging to ARBA, a trade association, because ARBA speaks for its entire membership and feels that the views of the highway officials who administer the program are important in the process of developing policies which are in the best interest of the highway program as a whole.

Association policies are dictated by a board of directors representing every segment of the highway industry and officials at every level. ARBA recommendations are supposed to be limited to those items which are best for the country and in the best interest of the overall highway program, association spokesmen say. They also boast that "We are accepted as an objective non-self-serving witness when we appear before Congressional committees."[1]

Some of those recommendations which ARBA has decided are best for the country have included positions against the following: equal employment opportunity regulations; use of highway trust funds for beautification of highways, mass transit, or any other purpose except construction of more roads; cutbacks or curtailment of designated urban connections of the Interstate System which would disrupt neighborhoods, destroy businesses and homes, and which citizens opposed; use of highway money to pay the families or businesses displaced by highways or assistance to relocate displaced families in "decent, safe and sanitary" dwellings.

Major spokesman for the association had been until 1968 General Louis J. Prentiss (retired), of the Army Corps of Engineers. A graduate of Engineering School, Camp Humphreys (Fort Belvoir, Virginia), and the Command and General Staff School, Fort Leavenworth, his military assignments included training, supply, administration, construction, and command responsibilities. One of his last assignments was Engineer Commissioner for the District of Columbia.

[1] *American Road Builder*, April 1965, p. 45.

He retired from the Army April 30, 1956, to become executive vice president and secretary of ARBA May 1, 1956, a position he held until retirement in December 1967, after which he remained an active booster of freeways for Washington as a member of that city's Federal City Council. The association boasts an annual budget of over half a million dollars, more than double the funding size when Prentiss took over in 1956.

According to Prentiss, membership in ARBA brings invaluable services from its Washington-based office, such as the assembling and interpretation of information, which is to a large degree a matter of having proper contacts. It takes time to develop these contacts. Prentiss boasts that collectively the ARBA staff claims more than one hundred years of experience in dealing with Congress, federal agencies, and highway-related associations, including executive experience with the Bureau of Public Roads, the Corps of Engineers, the District of Columbia government, and the American Association of State Highway Officials. ARBA staff members have worked for state highway departments and with members on Capitol Hill. "Together, we are personally acquainted with literally hundreds of key people in the federal community," he says.

This is no idle boast. As an example, a picture taken at the 1962 annual fall meeting of the West Virginia Contractor's Association, one of ARBA's offspring, showed Prentiss conferring with Congressman George Fallon, then chairman of the House roads subcommittee, Congressman John M. Slack, West Virginia, and West Virginia State Highway Commissioner Burl A. Sawyers.

Then, too, ARBA's most famous "graduate" is Senate Public Works Committee Chairman Jennings Randolph, of West Virginia, who had been treasurer of ARBA for ten years when he successfully ran for the Senate in 1958. While at ARBA he had also been an assistant to the president and director of public relations for Capitol Airlines. After joining the Senate, he became an honorary member of the association, as did Congressman Fallon.

Traditionally, the Federal Highway Administrator has been a member also. Rex Whitton saw no conflict of interest as a member of ARBA while he was also representing the public as administrator of all federal highway programs. Nor did Lowell Bridwell, his successor, or Francis Turner, as chief of the Bureau of Public Roads.

ARBA has for years been able to sprinkle public officials among its private interest membership. In 1966, the president of ARBA was J. Burch McMorran, then superintendent of Public Works of New York. A vice president that year was J. C. Womack of California, along with J. C. Dodell, Jr., president of the Codell Construction Company of Winchester, Kentucky; W. K. Cox, Caterpillar Tractor Company of Peoria. Robert S. Holmes, general manager of highway construction marketing for U.S. Steel of Pittsburgh, was president in 1967 and 1968.

Some of the directors whose terms expired in 1967 were Mason Butcher, manager of Montgomery County, Maryland, a suburb of Washington, D.C., and Donald O. White, president of the American Asphalt Paving Company of Chicago. Other directors included E. J. Donnelly of the J. E. Greiner Engineering Company of Baltimore; Howard G. Minier of the Washtenaw County Road Commission, Michigan; Tom Airis, director of the District of Columbia Highway Department; Eugene V. Avery, chief engineer, St. Paul; S. N. Pearman, chief highway commissioner, South Carolina Highway Department; F. D. Lyons, Oklahoma Department of Highways; and Walter Johnson, Kansas State Highway Engineer.

Another of ARBA's past presidents is Enoch R. Needles of the engineering firm of Howard, Needles, Tammen and Bergendoff. This firm can boast that it has averaged, for every working day, the design of public works facilities with a value of about $1 million for more than ten years and that in its fifty-year history it has studied, reported on, and certified the financial feasibility of $3 billion in actually constructed public works projects. This is also the firm Rex Whitton joined when he retired as Federal Highway Administrator.

Other past presidents of the association are, beginning in 1957, a former director of the District of Columbia Highway Department; 1958, the president of the Koehring Construction Equipment Manufacturing Company; 1959–60, the president of the Nello L. Teer construction company; 1961–62, the chief highway engineer, Department of Public Works and Buildings of Illinois; 1963–64, senior vice president of Allis-Chalmers Manufacturing Company; 1965–66, president of the Moss-Thornton Construction Company. At this writing, Robert J. Holmes of U.S. Steel has been succeeded by Robert G. Bartlett, formerly head of Pennsylvania's Highway Department, as president of ARBA. Likewise, it is possible for ARBA members to become public officials through appointments, as did Winton Blount, President Nixon's choice for Postmaster General.

ARBA officers and committee members for 1968–69 include former President Holmes; vice presidents Elmer Timby of Howard, Needles, Tammen and Bergendoff, T. F. Hobart, Southern Amiesite Asphalt Company, E. H. Holt, Barber-Greene Construction Manufacturing Company, and L. R. Gillis, assistant state highway engineer, California Division of Highways. J. N. Robertson, a former director of the D.C. Highway Department, is treasurer, the post formerly held by Senator Randolph.

The directors for 1968–71 include public officials of cities and states and highway departments, members of engineering firms, contractors, plus representatives of the Asphalt Institute and the Aluminum Company of America.

The association has a pledge and an official prayer. The Road Builders' Pledge, adopted by the Board of Directors in 1962, states:

> We, the Members of the American Road Builders Association, recognizing that the public investment in highways and airports is vital to the social and economic future of our Nation, and in the conviction that adequate highways and airports are essential to the National Defense, pledge ourselves, on our honor, to conduct our business affairs as a public trust, ever mindful that we bear an obligation to our country which demands the highest standards of performance and of ethical conduct and an active faith in the future of our Nation.

The "Prayer for America's Road Builders" was adapted from a blessing by the Reverend Raymond F. Wrenn at the Virginia Road Builders Association banquet in 1965.

> O Almighty God, who has given us this earth and has appointed men to have domination over it; who has commanded us to make

straight the highways, to lift up the valleys and to make the mountains low, we ask thy blessing upon these men who do just that. Fill them with a sense of accomplishment, not just for the roads built, but for the ways opened for the lengthening of visions, the broader hopes and the greater joys which make these highways a possibility for mankind.

Bless these, our Nation's road builders, and their friends. For the benefits we reap from their labors, we praise thee; may thy glory be revealed in us. Amen.

The organization publishes a monthly magazine, *American Road Builder,* called "The Voice of the Highway Industry." General Prentiss used it well as his vehicle for communicating to members. Early in 1957, for example, Prentiss wrote an article in which he dismissed citizens who opposed plans to build freeways in cities. His article proved to be a good example of the kind of thinking prevalent within highway promoting circles. The article was entitled "Public Relations—the Engineering of Consent."

General Prentiss wrote: "The Highway Act of 1956 authorizing the Interstate System provides that each state will hold public hearings wherever the route bypasses or goes through a community. Naturally, this was done in order that the interests of the local people can be taken into consideration prior to making a final decision on the location. The truth is, however, that the local people are not entirely aware of their best interests. They do not know for sure just what the new highway will mean to them. That is why those who oppose a proposal usually appear in large numbers and talk longer and louder than do those who favor the project. And that is precisely why a softening-up or pre-selling public relations campaign must be waged in those communities before the public hearing is held. The citizenry must know that their gains will offset many-fold the small loss of a few dissenters who for personal reasons resist the proposal. Opportunities to accomplish this pre-selling job should not be overlooked by state highway departments, chambers of commerce or other civic groups interested in area progress." Beside the article was a slogan in large type with the message A FEW MUST SUFFER SO THAT MANY MAY BENEFIT.

But there were many people who did not buy Prentiss' argument that highways were always beneficial.

A group of civic planners, municipal engineers, and transit operators had gathered in Chicago in 1957 to learn of the accomplishments, capabilities, losses, advantages, and social acceptance of mass transit in Chicago, Cleveland, San Francisco, Toronto, Philadelphia, New York, and Boston. The point was made time and again that mass transit is the key to survival of metropolitan areas with their concentrated businesses, shopping, industrial, and cultural core surrounded by suburbia. It was also pointed out that the survival of cities is dependent on rapid transit, whether surface or subway. The many advantages of moving people by rapid transit were convincingly presented. Commenting on these points, Prentiss said he agreed that the possibility of halting or at least slowing down the ever increasing volumes of metropolitan peak-hour traffic through its use does offer a partial solution to urban traffic strangulation worries that cannot be ignored. But, he said, regardless of the type of mass transit offered, whether it is bus, trolley, monorail, subway, or surface rapid transit, the first and foremost problem is not how to finance, build, and operate it, but how to make travel on it "attractive enough, cheap enough, and convenient enough to get you and your friends to ride it so that my friends and I can drive our cars in greater comfort and safety and be assured of a place to park." This describes all too well the average attitude of too many metropolitan dwellers, the general warned. Many such persons look covetously at the Highway Trust Fund to provide money for nonhighway systems, he said. Instead, he suggested, express buses should be put on median strips of urban freeways. "If those who seek to solve the mass transportation problems of the metropolitan areas would recognize that Congress does not intend to permit the Highway Trust Fund to be diverted to purposes or objectives other than those specifically stated [in the 1956 law] and would look to other sources of funds for financing, I am sure that the entire highway industry would gladly co-operate with them in seeking a satisfactory solution and early solution to their problems," he said.

In October 1957, C. W. Enfield, general counsel, BPR, wrote a contradictory article in ARBA's publication: "The highway program offers a golden opportunity for cities and towns to coordinate urban rehabilitation and redevelopment with highway construction in eliminating blight and slums and *in halting the flight to the suburbs.* Good roads, particularly freeways, allow the suburbanite to travel from his residence to his downtown place of business, or where he would like to shop, in less time than the city dweller can travel a much shorter but more congested route. *This not only promotes the subdivision and development of new areas* outside of metropolitan centers and results in better and fuller utilization of land, but preserves businesses and property values by making the metropolitan central business district more accessible. *Freeways frequently open up new areas,* and by minimizing the travel time between such areas and the metropolitan centers, transform otherwise low value land into desirable residential, commercial, and industrial sites. Obviously, *such extension of metropolitan limits* results in greater land utilization and increased property value which is particularly true with respect to land that is adjacent to or in the vicinity of freeways. The modern highways that are already in operation and are a part of the new Interstate System are providing fast, safer, and cheaper travel and shopping services and greater job opportunities. Everywhere they have been synonymous with industrial and residential growth." (Author's italics)

At ARBA, words were not enough. General Prentiss scooted off to Hollywood to hire professional actors to make a movie, entitled *We'll Take the High Road.* It was described by the association as follows: The movie opened with a scene of a traffic jam. The camera moved from one jam to another as a narrator explained that the traffic mess was intolerable. Then he set the scene for appearances by President Eisenhower and then Federal Highway Administrator Bertram D. Tallamy, hot off the New York Thruway. They explained how the new federal highway program would benefit the country.

Then the scene shifted to the town of Hilldale and a luncheon gathering at which the mayor introduced a speaker, a Bureau engineer who explained how important the national system of highways would be for America's future. Emma Glock, president of the Hilldale Historical and Beautification Committee, thought the idea was lovely. The head banker of the town thought it would be good for the economy of the whole country. (The banker's home was a lovely old mansion belonging to the family for generations.)

Suddenly the town received the news that a freeway was to serve Hilldale. The town became panicky. The local restaurant owner, gas station owner, farmers, and Emma Glock proclaimed they didn't want it. Emma thought it would destroy beauty: These people are afraid of the unknown and unseen effects of the freeway, the narrator added.

Next, a public hearing was held at which the state engineer explained what the freeway had to offer the town. Arguments broke out. Everyone had a pet project to defend. The projected route and the alternate routes were debated. Questions were asked and accusations hurled. The state engineer answered them honestly and intelligently. As he did so, the camera took the audience on a magic-carpet tour. The movie-goer saw practical applications of aerial surveys, electronic computers, heavy construction equipment, materials, and supplies. Numerous other details of efficient highway construction were shown. Then, while a moving human interest story unfolded, the freeway came to Hilldale. ARBA readers were told that the banker in the movie was the citizen hardest hit by construction of the new freeway, but he was a rational man and resolved his many conflicts in the interest of the community. Other residents argued that Route A should not be picked, that Route B would be better. Still others favored Route C. The villain was a Mr. Snavely who didn't like the idea of freeways. "Why should outsiders come in and tell us where the freeway will go?" he asked.

A review of the movie in *Roads and Streets* rated it "terrific." "It will surely soften up many of your human road blocks because the viewer will inevitably identify himself with one or another of the characters."

To further bolster highway acceptance, Prentiss outlined a ten-point public relations plan for state and other highway officials on how to deal with the press and assure favorable publicity, in which he stressed the importance of a good image.

Among the techniques, he suggested: "Call on the editor of the local newspaper and present in a clear and concise manner the state of the plan, and the engineering, traffic, and economic reasons behind the plan. The known objections should be set forth and the fact emphasized that meeting these objections would create other objections equally or more serious. Point out that the benefits to the many will unavoidably cause inconvenience to a few. The editor's support should be sought editorially together with objective news coverage prior to any public hearing. Furnish him appropriate material.

"Call on leading bankers. They are silent partners in every step of your construction program, and, in addition, their banks stand to benefit from the economic boost which is invariably experienced in areas served by modern highways. Feed them facts and figures. Their opinions are respected and their lead followed by many community leaders. Arrange to have the ARBA motion picture *We'll Take the High Road* shown in every luncheon club, chamber of commerce, PTA, and church meeting in town. Have it shown on TV as a public service. Give the area saturation treatment prior to the public hearings.

"Organize militant support for your plan. Don't let the record of the hearing reflect only the opposition. See to it that a convincing presentation of the sound justification of your plan is made by a highly respected local man whose interest in the project cannot by inference be said to be self-serving," Prentiss advised.

Prentiss' plan continued, "Be sure that the official conducting the hearing gives careful and courteous attention to all objectors. Let no one leave the hearing with a feeling that he was not given a fair chance to raise and support his objection. The attitude of the opposition is very important, for frequently following a hearing they are the ones with whom you must negotiate for purchase of right-of-way. If you place all witnesses under oath, you will eliminate a lot of extraneous and exaggerated material. Whenever it is decided to acquire right-of-way, send a personal letter signed by you to each landowner. . . . Carry the battle to the opposition. Go to the major trouble spots yourself. Inform the public of your personal interest. Let them see in the press and by personal appearances that you are getting first-hand information. . . .

"Don't let the opposition build up a position from which it will have trouble retreating without loss of face. The longer you delay launching your offensive the longer the petition lists will grow and, although many who sign petition lists do so only to accommodate a friend, a bulky petition may subject you to undesirable pressure. Make your final decision as promptly as possible after a careful review of the transcript of the hearing. Accept good recommendations presented at the hearing. It will increase the public's confidence in you."

He concluded that the job of public relations for the accelerated highway program is too big to be handled by one man or by single units. The Bureau of Public Roads and organizations such as AASHO (American Association of State Highway Officials) and ARBA must help. "Competition today is too keen for the TAX dollar. The public decides where the tax dollar is spent. Everyone interested in a sound highway construction program wants to keep the program rolling; good public relations backed by sound engineering and economic planning will insure the essential public support to accomplish this end," Prentiss declared.

Late in 1957, the County Division of ARBA held its national highway conference. Among those attending were regulars in Tennessee highway circles: Judge Beverly Briley and Robert Everett, executive secretary of the Tennessee County Services Association, composed of judges, highway officials, and others interested in activities at the county level in Tennessee.

Shortly thereafter, Everett, or "Fats" (he weighed 363 pounds), as his friends called him, a member of ARBA's County and Local Roads Division, was elected to the United States Congress. He asked for and received an assignment on the House roads subcommittee. Judge Briley went on to become Mayor of Nashville, which by the mid-1960s was to be embroiled in a fight over a freeway first planned through white neighborhoods and businesses and later shifted into black neighborhoods.

At about the same time, in 1957, C. D. Curtiss, Bureau of Public Roads commissioner, retired from public office and promptly became a special assistant to General Prentiss.

The organization displayed its patriotic posture in a Fourth of July editorial in 1958 which read as follows:

"Be first to place hat over heart when the Flag should be saluted.

"Be first to applaud Old Glory anywhere and anytime that we can, in good taste, pay this respect.

"Be first to stand, and do it proudly when 'The Star Spangled Banner' is played.

"Give the youngsters a spark of patriotism that will light their pride in America.

"And remember always that the 4th of July Celebration is in honor of the beginning of a way of life . . . only the *beginning.* We must maintain it."

One of the clearest portents of the future of suburban development, as seen by ARBA, was offered by Nebraska State Highway Engineer L. N. Rees in an article in ARBA's magazine in 1958: "The proposed highway improvement program offers a golden opportunity for cities to co-ordinate urban rehabilitation and redevelopment with highway construction in eliminating blight and slums. Good roads, particularly freeways, bring the suburbanite's residence within shorter driving time of his downtown place of business and where he would like to shop. This promotes subdivision and development of new areas outside metropolitan centers and results in better and fuller utilization of land; it preserves businesses and property values in the metropolitan central business district by making it more accessible. . . . Freeways frequently open up new areas, and by minimizing the travel time between such areas and the metropolitan center, transform otherwise low value land into desirable residential, commercial, and industrial sites. Obviously, such extension of metropolitan limits results in greater land utilization and increased property values, which is particularly true with respect to land served by the improved highway system." This article simply paraphrases the article presented by BPR general counsel Enfield in the October 1957 pages of the ARBA publication.

This philosophy was to be the wave of the future, not because it had overwhelming support from planners and city officials, but because the 90–10 money was available. Criticism of freeways was seldom entered in the printed pages of *American Road Builder*. In fact, between 1957 and 1968, only the voice of John J. Matthews, executive director, Allegheny County (Pennsylvania) Planning Commission in 1961, questioned the wisdom of the engineers. "Must we design our highway systems and parking garages so that everyone can drive downtown instead of relieving part of the traffic load at a lower public cost by improving mass transit systems? Will we continue to delude ourselves that low-cost housing can be provided on large lots, knowing that the costs of street paving, sewers, and water lines are directly proportional to lot frontage? Are we married to the notion that residential areas and schools must be so remote from each other that we must spend up to 10 percent of the school budget in bus transportation at the expense of the teaching program?

"Let us consider several facts: More new homes lack public sewer connections today than a generation ago; slums are being created faster than we can eradicate them; before the coming of the white man, an Indian could walk across Manhattan Island faster than the trip is made today in a $5000 350-horsepower automobile. . . . Perhaps we can uncover some explanations for the mistakes which we have made in the past and which we continue to make. For one thing, I believe that we should free ourselves of the notion that public bodies actually play much more than a passive role in the process of community growth. The really important decisions affecting the form and functions of urban and suburban areas are made by the multitude of private landowners, realtors, merchants, bankers, industries, home builders, home buyers, and others, each of whom can be expected to act only in the light of his own financial position and personal judgment." Mr.

Matthews did not appear in the pages of the Voice of the Highway Industry again. Nor did any other criticism of freeways.

But freeway boosters did, and one of the most avid was former ARBA treasurer Jennings Randolph, elected to the Senate in November 1958. Once there, he sought and received membership on the Senate roads subcommittee. Shortly thereafter, his name, and soon his articles, made a predictable appearance in ARBA's magazine. The organization's executive committee reported to its membership readers that newly elected Senator Randolph of West Virginia would have a prominent voice in highway legislation before the Senate and reassured the highway industry that key congressmen still held their positions on Ways and Means and the Senate Finance Committee.

Randolph had been a representative in the Congress from 1933 to 1947, when he was defeated. During that time he was a ranking member and eventually chairman of the House subcommittee on roads. At that slot, he conducted hearings on laying the groundwork for the vast interstate system then being promoted. He sponsored the first federal aid-to-airports legislation. He was chairman of the Airport Panel, United States Department of Commerce, which studied the advisability of federal aid to airports. He served as president of ARBA's Municipal and Airport Division and vice president of the National Aeronautics Association of America.

Shortly after the elections of 1958, the New England Road Builders Association held a dinner at ARBA's annual meeting in Dallas. Joseph R. Perini, past president, was among the contractors and public officials representing New England. The speakers included Senator Dennis Chavez of New Mexico, chairman of the Senate Public Works Committee, moderator DeWitt Greer of the Texas Highway Department, Representatives William Cramer and George Fallon. The group sitting at the dais was referred to by ARBA as "this powerhouse of Congressional highway legislators who launched the convention, keynoted future legislation, and answered questions posed by an intensely interested audience." The major address was delivered by newly elected Senator Randolph. In his speech he remarked, among other things, that "As much as we need vast highway developments, we must do our utmost in careful planning to avoid strangling ourselves with our own improvements."

To prevent just such "strangling" from occurring in the nation's capital, the Congress in 1960 passed legislation which, in effect, called for construction of a rapid transit system in the District of Columbia. The legislation also contained a proviso halting all freeway construction in the northwest quadrant of the city for five years or until such time as the rail system is completed and given a fair trial. ARBA chief Prentiss reacted quickly: "The law sets an extremely dangerous precedent, for it is based on the theory that it is sound practice to ignore the findings of the planning engineers and to nourish the groundless hope that a rail transit system will solve the transportation problem alone and thereby make urban freeway construction unnecessary. . . . It is an open invitation for every city to put its highway plans on the shelf and concentrate its energies on the construction of rail transit lines. . . . It is noteworthy that most mass transit promoters nowadays are casting covetous eyes on highway trust funds as a potential source of revenue for their transit schemes." He was plainly concerned that new mass transit might demonstrate the senselessness of more and more city busting roads. So, to assure his readers that congressmen were not going "soft" on the nation's road program, Prentiss burst into print with an article entitled "Advise and Convince," in which he bluntly told his readers how pressure was being applied to keep the road program rolling. "In order to get the needed Congressional support for the public works program, Congress must be *advised* and *convinced*. . . . Generally speaking, the public's attitude is: 'I want better and safer highways—period.'"

In November of 1961, Prentiss felt called upon to defend the Highway Trust Fund partially because there had developed a great deal more interest in public transportation as a solution to ever increasing traffic problems in large urban areas. In an article entitled "The Threat to the Highway Trust Fund," he explained that there is a direct relationship between traffic volume and highway user tax revenues. Any diversion of these user tax revenues to

purposes other than the federal highway program would be an attack
on the basic concept of the trust fund, he warned darkly. Because
expenditures are so closely linked to revenues, ARBA was appre-
hensive of proposals which might add new costs without improving
the highway system. President Kennedy, he continued, had recommended that state highway departments be required to give assurances to the Secretary of Commerce, as a condition for federal
participation in highway projects, that decent, safe, and sanitary
housing would be made available to tenants displaced by such
construction, in suitable locations and at prices they could afford.
The President had also recommended that the definition of "construction costs" reimbursable to the state by the federal government
be modified to include "the administrative costs incident to furnish-
ing such housing," Prentiss warned.

Low-cost urban housing is not abundant and low-income families
must have places in which to live; this is one of the many national
problems, Prentiss allowed. But it is not certain, he wrote, that state
highway departments are the best equipped agencies to handle
housing problems. Also, no sound estimate of the cost to the
states or to the Highway Trust Fund of such a displaced persons
program has been stated, he complained. There was reason to be
concerned that this proposal would divert highway funds to housing
construction, or, at least, the administration of an urban housing
program, Prentiss warned.

The mass transportation problem posed another major potential
threat to the "integrity" of the trust fund, the ARBA chief said.
Then he traced the history of transportation studies in the nation's
capital, studies which had resulted in engineers' proposal that both
an urban freeway system and rapid transit facilities be provided in
the major commuter corridors of the city.

"Rail transit facilities in the Washington area are needed. In
spite of the fact that existing commuter rail lines are almost invariably operated at a loss, the wishful thinkers believe that new
rapid transit lines will make a tremendous hit with the public, attract great numbers of riders, and prove without a doubt that the
estimates of urban highway needs have been overstated," Prentiss

explained, bemoaning the fact that the Congress had directed construction of expressways in the northwest quadrant of the city be postponed until the proposed subway line was completed.

"There is a corollary to this line of thought," Prentiss wrote. "If the unproven proposition that urban highway construction plans can be cut back by building transit facilities is accepted, it follows that the cancellation of the highway construction plans will result in a surplus of highway funds, as compared with a great shortage of ready money available for construction of subways. Therefore, it is argued, the highway users should be made to pay for the rail transit facilities which are being built for their benefit." This seemed like heresy to Prentiss.

Then he pointed out that the Interstate Commerce Commission reversed its historical position and recommended to Congress that railroad passenger service be subsidized, specifically, commuter service. He quoted from the ICC report: "A nation that is serious about propelling a man to the moon should be able to solve the mundane problem of moving its citizens dependably and comfortably some 50 miles or less from home to work without multiplying ribbons of concrete and asphalt that would strangle the central cities they are supposed to serve."

Here again, Prentiss warned, was the unspoken suggestion lurking in the shadows that by cutting back the highway program funds could be freed for improving rail commuter service. Prentiss avoided commenting on the other implication of the statement he quoted, i.e., that highways are undesirable and *not* the most efficient manner of transportation. He continued, "It appears probable that at the next session of Congress, legislation will be enacted establishing a Department of Urban Affairs and Housing to unify federal jurisdiction over programs directed at the solution of urban problems. It is certain that this new federal agency will attack the urban transportation problem. It will not be surprising if a diversion from the Highway Trust Fund is proposed eventually." Prentiss was clearly alarmed at such a prospect.

In April 1962, Representative George Fallon addressed ARBA's annual convention. "Of course, I keep in touch with many of your problems through contact with your national headquarters staff here in Washington. . . . However, I am never completely educated on any subject, and on this extremely vital subject of highways, I seize every opportunity to learn what I can from conversations with road builders.

"When we were in Atlantic City a year ago I participated in a panel discussion with other members of Congress on the subject of highway problems. The problem in the forefront of our thinking then was that of finding means to finance the interstate and ABC programs. . . . Our major project just now is the ABC program." He then proceeded to explain to the contractors where their next bundle would be coming from in his new bill. Then he launched an attack on a proposal to provide housing for persons dislocated by highways. "Another proposal made by the Administration last year concerned the relocation of families displaced by federal-aid highway construction. President Kennedy expressed the belief that highway officials should assume the responsibility of seeing to it that such displaced families are suitably relocated. I am very sympathetic to the principle expressed by the President. I believe that the government must make adequate provision for relocating displaced families. Last year the Subcommittee on Roads tabled the Administration's proposal, not for lack of sympathy but because the proposal was presented in such a vague fashion that none of us could tell what the impact on the Highway Trust Fund might be, or what administrative complexities would be put on the shoulders of highway officials. Again, I must point out that there is no money in the Highway Trust Fund for purposes not contemplated in the Highway Act of 1956."

Early in 1962, President Kennedy proposed an amendment to the Federal Highway Act to provide that by July 1965 all highway projects in urban areas, submitted for approval to the Secretary of Commerce and the Bureau, be consistent with comprehensive development plans for the metropolitan area in which they would be constructed. This meant that urban centers had to have a master plan for all types of transportation, and was aimed at preventing the then current practice of constructing freeways whether or not the individual community wanted or needed them. ARBA had comments on this proposal. "No reasonable person can object to the intent of the proposal. Surely, new urban highways should be considered as segments of the total transportation system of the metropolitan area, and surely, when 'soundly based' judgments indicate the necessity of rail transit to bring the system into 'balance,' highways should be planned accordingly. And, certainly, each metropolitan area should have its comprehensive development plans, necessarily including plans for highway development."

But after this lip service, Prentiss, speaking for ARBA, then repeated the history of the nation's capital, where money was spent on planning and freeways were to be frozen in the north quadrant until the subway was built.

"In Washington, at least, it would have been helpful if someone had the authority to step into the petty arguments, knock heads together and insist that the comprehensive plan developed through so much trouble and expense be carried out," Prentiss proclaimed.

Then the director of the District of Columbia Highway Department, Harold Aitken, came up with a solution to the tug-of-war over public transportation and highways. "Americans have shown their preference for highway travel, let's give them what they want—mass transit on our highways! We have known for some time that one lane on the freeway serving buses can move approximately 20,000 to 25,000 persons per lane per hour and still have the capacity left for other traffic." He pointed out that a properly designed lane could easily accommodate 700 buses per hour. Thus, with 55 persons per bus, 38,000 persons could be moved per lane.

He continued, "Some of our friends who are primarily interested in recreation sometimes take us to task in our highway planning and construction. It is appropriate to remind them that auto riding for sightseeing and relaxation constitutes the biggest single type of diversion or relaxation or recreation, according to the recent report to the President and the Congress by the Outdoor Recreational Resources Review Commission. The report shows that such driving is the greatest single recreational activity now, and estimates that it will be substantially in excess of all other activities, except swimming, in the year 2000," he added. He did not point out that while driving is one of the most popular recreational activities, most driving today is *not* for recreational purposes. Nor did he explain that most scenic parkways, built originally for just such recreational driving, had become expressways, most definitely not suited for pleasure driving.

The final version of the Highway Act passed by the Congress in 1962 provided that the Secretary of Commerce would approve only those highway projects in urban areas of 50,000 population that proved to be based upon a continuing comprehensive transportation plan worked up between states and local communities. The same Highway Act included what Prentiss labeled a controversial item which "proved to be that which appears in modified form, as section 5 of the Act, entitled 'Assistance for Displaced Families and Businesses.' As originally proposed by the Administration," he explained, "the section would have required state highway departments, as a condition precedent to federal concurrence in projects for right-of-way acquisition or actual construction, to satisfy the Secretary of Commerce that provisions had been made to relocate displaced families in 'decent, safe and sanitary' dwellings, equal to or better than their original dwellings and in addition be equally convenient to public facilities and places of employment. ARBA's testimony on the bill contended that the provision was unworkable and would result in costly delays in urban construction. This touched off lengthy discussions among members of the House and Senate Public Works committees.

"As a result of these discussions, numerous alternative provisions were proposed and, as finally adopted, the requirement is only that the state highway department guarantee 'relocation advisory assistance' to displaced families," Prentiss was able to boast. He added that there would be a $200 ceiling imposed on payments to families and $3000 on businesses. He said that ARBA objected to these provisions also, since there was no provision for replacing these munificent sums out of the trust fund.

ARBA's interpretation of the comprehensive planning provisions of the 1962 Highway Act were revealed in testimony delivered by Prentiss before the House roads subcommittee a year later when Washington's National Capital Transportation Agency recommended a moratorium on freeway planning on grounds that the District of Columbia's proposed rail line would obviate the need for several expressway projects.

"Highway construction in urban areas is the most urgently needed part of our national highway program, and the most difficult. It is the most urgently needed because it will provide the highways which carry the greatest volume of traffic. Hence, they are the facilities which will serve the greatest number of people. It is the most difficult to plan because urban highways must be built in the places where real estate is already being used most productively. This means that any urban highway location will be opposed by those whose property, interests, comforts, or conveniences are threatened.

"The law does not require a transportation plan. It requires a transportation process, or in other words, the working arrangements from which highway plans and plans for other affected forms of transportation will be soundly developed, carefully co-ordinated, and continuously evaluated." In other words, transportation plans be damned, let's build the freeways.

As 1965 approached, ARBA began a campaign for an ever bigger highway program to follow the 1972 deadline for completion of the Interstate System and demise of the trust fund. Prentiss was able to get the ball rolling by raising the question of future highway needs before the House roads subcommittee. Chairman Fallon acted quickly by introducing a Highway Needs Study bill in the House which requested the Bureau and state highway departments to draw up plans for post-'72 needs. The House passed the bill but no action was taken in the Senate. Meanwhile, Fallon moved up to become chairman of the parent Public Works Committee, and John Kluczynski became chairman of the roads subcommittee.

ARBA continued to push for passage of the Needs bill although Rex Whitton had already undertaken a similar study for the Bureau of Public Roads. Presumably, the BPR study might conclude that there is no pressing need for more roads. However, ARBA thought it wise to obtain legislation regardless of the preparation of a study which might conclude that there is no need for the legislation.

Prentiss explained his reason for continuing to lobby for Fallon's bill despite the Bureau study: "It would establish a target date and give the study a degree of prestige and authority it does not now have. Moreover, it would spell out what might be called the specifications for the study—what topics must be covered, on what points recommendations must be submitted, and to what date the projections of highway needs should be made. In the absence of specifications we run the risk that the study may be abridged, delayed, or even distorted through political accident or caprice. I say this without throwing aspersions at any political party but simply as a reflection of the practicalities of politics."

While the Needs Study bill was being kept warm by the House roads subcommittee and highway interests, President Johnson introduced Lady Bird's beautification bill.

Prentiss testified on the beautification bill before Kluczynski's committee that Congress must not use Trust Fund money, but must instead provide another source for the money to pay the advertisers to remove their signs and foot the bill for cleaning up highways. When he testified before Senator Randolph's Senate roads subcommittee, Prentiss suggested that the auto excise tax, then about to be phased out from the general fund, be transferred to the Trust Fund to pay for the beautification program. As finally enacted, the beautification bill provided that the general fund would provide the necessary money, $160 million for 1966 and 1967 each.

Senator Randolph, chairman of both the Senate's Public Works Committee and its roads subcommittee, received ARBA's annual award in 1966. ARBA president John P. Moss, of the Moss-Thornton Construction Company, said of Randolph during the award ceremony, "Quite often, if not always, the winner of the ARBA award for outstanding contributions to the highway program is a man who has also contributed to the success of our association. Such is the case this year. Senator Randolph is a former president of ARBA's Municipal and Airport Division, served on the association's board of directors, and was for ten years treasurer of ARBA. In short, Senator Jennings Randolph is not only our friend, he is one of us."

Public Works is Senator Randolph's major assignment. His other assignments include only membership on the Senate Labor and Public Welfare Committee, which handles legislation pertaining to coal mining, for which West Virginia is well noted, but he does not chair any of Labor and Public Welfare's subcommittees. West Virginia's other senator, Robert Byrd, doesn't even belong to the Labor and Public Welfare Committee, so it cannot be argued that the state's other senator is vigorously representing West Virginia's coal interests. Randolph sought assignment to, and subsequently worked his way up through membership and then chairmanship of, the roads subcommittee and finally to chairman of the parent Public Works Committee, although his West Virginia constituency does not represent highway interests nor has West Virginia ever been designated as the hub of the highway construction industry.

Articles by Senator Randolph appeared in four of the twelve issues of ARBA's publication for 1967. The first was entitled "The Cutback in Federal Aid Highway Funds"; the second, "Deferment of Highway Construction? No!"; the third, "Financing the Remainder of the Interstate System"; and the fourth, "Highway Construction Funds Endangered."

Unwavering in their loyalty to America's highway industry, Senator Randolph and Congressman Fallon were among the officials who broke ground for ARBA's new headquarters building in March 1964. Representative Fallon received ARBA's annual award in 1965, a year before Randolph. Previously it had been awarded to Bertram Tallamy, Julien R. Steelman, Nello J. Teer, Jr., past presidents, and John Mackie, Michigan Highway Commissioner, later elected to Congress.

The highway construction interests are attuned to the needs of other related interests, too. For example, ARBA's magazine reproduced portions of a speech made by John E. Swearingen, chairman of the board, Standard Oil Company of Indiana, before the

American Petroleum Institute's division of marketing in 1966. "Unless we work vigorously for the development of an adequate system of rural highways and urban roads and streets, the American motorist will be throttled by traffic, and many governmental restrictions as well.

"Look at our cities. As congestion increases, we hear a rising chorus of attacks on the automobiles which use our urban streets. Serious proposals are already being advanced to ban private cars from the central city. Some are suggesting all electric cars for in-city driving. The proponents of mass urban transportation are mounting vigorous attacks against construction of the urban expressways that increasing traffic volumes—and our customers—will require."

When he was ARBA president, Burch McMorran contributed to the pages of ARBA's publication, too. In 1967 he commented, "During this past year there was quite a bit of talking about developing an electric automobile as a means of reducing the pollution of the air caused by gasoline fumes. This may be of tremendous significance to future transportation historians, perhaps not. Speaking as a highway official, I'm sure that I will see the significance of the electric car when the gasoline tax ceases to be a convenient method for making sure that every motorist makes a reasonable contribution to the cost of building and maintaining highways, in proportion to his use of the highway system."

The highlight of ARBA's May 1967 sixty-fifth annual convention was the "Industry Talks to Congress" panel discussion, featuring Congressmen Fallon, Kluczynski, and Cramer. Senator Randolph was scheduled to appear but at the last moment had to cancel and fly back to Washington before the panel discussion. Others included Dr. H. N. Huntzicker, president, Portland Cement Association; Gerald T. McCarthy of Tippetts-Abbott-McCarthy-Stratton, consulting engineers; Paul F. Phelan, technical director, road materials, Koppers Company Incorporated; Richard R. Stander, president, Mansfield Asphalt Paving Company; and John W. Thompson, Sr., president, Thompson-Arthur Paving Company.

Cramer stated that the drive for highway construction funds had not been commensurate with the drive for other less essential funds and that the country should not launch into new areas until highway construction needs were met. The panel also discussed a recent presidentially ordered cutback in highway trust funds, and it was decided that joint House and Senate subcommittee hearings should be held on the "crisis."

On the very day the hearings were held, the Administration loosed some $175 million in deferred funds and Bureau of the Budget director Charles Schultz testified that 1968 funds would be even greater than 1967's, with $4.4 billion available. The congressmen promptly issued a joint statement that "Too often, necessary actions are misinterpreted because of a failure of communication," after which they recessed the hearings.

Accumulated criticism of urban freeways prompted Senator Randolph to hold hearings on the subject late in 1967. The express purpose of the hearings was to find out why the public was fighting freeways and what could be done to eliminate the objections raised at public hearings. By this time freeway construction had been halted in numerous cities.

And in the House, George Fallon asked for "help" from the highway industry in formulating 1968 highway legislation for future needs after the expiration of the 1972 interstate act. "We need the expert knowledge of the highway industry, its forward-looking attitude and co-operative approach. Together, we can work for legislation which can solve some of these pressing problems facing road construction in the United States."

ARBA obliged him by testifying before the House roads subcommittee on new legislation. Then president Robert Holmes urged that more money be appropriated for the ABC program in the future as well as more money for rural and urban highways. Then the executive director of the Ohio Contractors Association, Karl L. Rothermund, told committee members that cutbacks in the highway program were very unpopular with contractors. He launched into the matter of the relationship between employer and employee on highway construction jobs. "By presidential directive, the authority of the state highway director to award highway contracts has been seriously eroded. Now, the Office of Federal Contract Compliance is to consult with the low bidder after bids are taken. From these consultations, the OFCC will determine if the bidder has 'a positive posture (on equal opportunity) employment' and then recommend (or not recommend) the award of the contract. We feel that this action will completely disrupt the competitive bidding system under which our great highway network has been and is being built."

ARBA's executive vice president Burton F. Miller testified later on the subject of equal opportunity employment. "At its sixty-sixth annual convention in Las Vegas last month, ARBA expressed by resolution its support of the principles of equal opportunity to employment for members of all races, and noted that America's highway builders are taking positive action to ensure equal opportunity for all. At the same time, the association stated its unequivocal opposition to those regulations and practices which interfere with the contractual relationship between the contracting agency and the contractor, or which impose financial burdens on the contractor without provision for indemnification and reimbursement. . . . We call your attention to the fact that, as of today, there is no national application of these procedures. The plan was first put into effect in California as a pilot project. It was subsequently moved to Ohio and Pennsylvania. Today these are the only three states that have had any experience whatsoever under these new procedures. It is our opinion that the procedures which have been in use in these three pilot projects are absolutely impossible of compliance, either by the industry or the state highway departments." Miller told the subcommittee that compliance would destroy the competitive bid system.

ARBA, which is so proud of its Road Builders' Pledge, and which bursts forth with patriotic prose on national holidays and has published "A Prayer for America's Road Builders," adopted in 1968 the following resolution: "The Association considers it to be a matter of settled policy [national] that discrimination in employment practices is inequitable, unjust, and economically unsound; that the association is already working toward and will continue to work toward the development of an affirmative program to ensure equal employment opportunity in the construction industry." Nevertheless, the resolution went on to explain that the association deplores those equal employment opportunity regulations and practices including pre-award procedures which interfere with the contractual relationship between the contracting agency and the contractor, and those which impose on the contractor unreasonable requirements with respect to locating and hiring workers who have specific scarce job skills and are members of a specific minority group.

These heavily qualified equal-opportunity goals were formulated during a meeting of ARBA's executive committee held at Sea Island, Georgia, early in 1968. The members of the executive committee of ARBA's Contractors Division were invited to join in the deliberations. They included a member of the Tennessee Highway Research Program, University of Tennessee, Portland Cement Association, Southern Amiesite Asphalt Company, Heffner Construction Company, Thompson-Arthur Paving Company, Koehring Company, Tippetts-Abbett-McCarthy-Stratton, Barber-Greene Company, ARBA president Holmes, Timby, and other ARBA officials, none of whom could be described as totally attuned with the widest interpretation of the public interest.

Congressman Fallon asked for ARBA's help in mid-1968, too, when he faced stiff competition in Maryland's primary. He got it when General Prentiss arranged a testimonial for Fallon which netted $15,000 for the Baltimore representative's campaign kitty. Prentiss was aided by the Washington Board of Trade, the D.C. Road Builders, and the Federal City Council. In fact, Prentiss was treasurer of a "National Committee to Re-elect George Fallon" which consisted of road building interests such as contractors, engineers, products manufacturers, suppliers and lobbyists. Friend and neighbor Edward J. Donnelly, of the J. E. Greiner Engineering firm, went to work to raise funds, too, because "Fallon has been good for the state and the industry." A new parallel Chesapeake Bay Bridge in Maryland, authorized under Fallon's chairmanship, will yield the Greiner firm approximately $5 million in engineering fees. The firm does most of the engineering work for the state of

Maryland and in the past five years has done $18 million worth of business with Maryland's State Roads Commission alone.

Another highway booster group, the Associated General Contractors of America, AGC, is much more diversified, although its membership boasts even more highway contractors than ARBA —3423, to be exact. AGC has a total membership of 8416. Many highway contractors belong to both AGC and ARBA. The AGC is concerned with all contracting work, and mainly new building. It excludes public officials. Yet it does have a joint committee set up with highway officials to keep in touch with public administrators of our highway program.

The association testifies regularly before congressional committees also, but does not claim to have any former members in the Congress. John Volpe was AGC president when he resigned his office to run for and win the governorship of Massachusetts, however. It does offer its member contractors an organization which nationally and locally "enables him to speak with an authoritative and persuasive voice before the Congress, and state legislators, federal, state, and county and municipal construction contract-awarding agencies to support needed construction appropriations."

AGC has joint committees with the American Concrete Paving Association, American Institute of Architects, American Public Works Association, American Society of Civil Engineers, National Asphalt Pavement Association, National Ready Mixed Concrete Association, among others. In addition, AGC and AASHO regional associations meet regularly across the fifty states.

The AGC serves highway contractors specifically by promoting the "orderly development of adequate highways and airports for the purpose of keeping highway and airport construction programs on a sustained rather than haphazard basis, along with congressional testimony to ensure a large volume of highway and airport construction at the least cost to the taxpayer."

AGC's transportation policies claim to stress the need for overall, integrated transportation systems, encompassing "all proven modes of transportation" but are geared to the idea that highways will continue to be the dominant force and a major transportation mode for years to come. "The need for more and better highways grows. The planning of any transportation system should reflect this need," the association's policy paper states.

It goes on: "The need for rapid, efficient transportation from the suburbs to the center city becomes more acute each day. We believe that the most practical and economical way of filling this need is by the use of exclusive bus lanes on the highways. While there may be specific locations where other modes—rail, subway, etc.—might be more practical, we are convinced that the exclusive bus lane offers a flexibility that other modes do not have. . . . Monies dedicated to the Highway Trust Fund should be used only for the construction of highways and for the administrative functions of the Bureau of Public Roads. The funding of other forms of transportation should come from those who use and benefit from those forms. We recommend the development of limited access forms of transportation as an integral part of the airport facility, serving only airport traffic, to international airports. We support the joint development concept, which is designed to make the maximum use of both space and funds in locating and building urban freeways. This, we believe, makes the most efficient use of both money and space. It also makes possible a rebirth of the downtown area, with its consequent benefit to the city tax rolls."

AGC vice president L. P. Gilvin, president of the Gilvin-Terrill Highway Construction firm, which does $8 million of highway construction each year in Texas, testified before the House roads subcommittee in May of 1968 on 1968 legislative needs.

He stated that money for both TOPICS (Traffic Operations Program to Increase Capacity and Safety), a program to step up capacity and safety of our present highways as an alternative to building new expressways, and beautification should not come out of the Highway Trust Fund, but that money for advance purchase of right-of-way, which would enable states to get land years ahead of construction, should come from the fund. As for the recently suggested fringe parking facilities, he said, "The AGC recognizes the need for the development of adequate parking facilities on the outskirts of metropolitan areas, as well as in the center city. We in no way object to the development of fringe parking areas and agree that they should complement the exclusive bus lanes. Again, however, the cost of their development should not be paid by the Highway Trust Fund without additional money going into the trust fund for this purpose." Billions for highways, but not one cent for parking.

"Again, in accordance with our policy statement, if parking facilities are developed for use of other modes of transportation, such as mass transit, rail or subway lines, we believe that the users of those modes of transportation should pay their share of the cost of the parking facilities."

AGC did not support a proposal to increase federal payments for homes and businesses taken for highways even after federal officials admitted that displaced persons were not receiving a just amount. As one AGC highway division spokesman said, "It seems a shame to pay for a new house with air conditioning and plumbing when they lived in shacks full of rats before."

Another organization very much interested in road construction in the United States is the National Highway Users Conference, consisting of more than 3000 member groups active in state divisions of the association. According to NHUC literature, it is a conference of associations and companies concerned with the advancement of highway transportation in the public interest. It is supposed to serve as a forum for the discussion and exchange of ideas affecting highway transportation's progress. It acts as a clearing house of information on research and engineering activities, legislative reporting, highway safety, and other pertinent developments of interest to the users of America's highways.

Membership includes bakers, bottlers, dairymen, livestock growers, rural letter carriers, fruit and vegetable producers, and retail merchants; civic groups, farm organizations, safety organizations, passenger car, bus, and truck groups, hotel and motel associations, utilities, shippers, and manufacturers; purveyors, such as the producers and dealers in the motor vehicle, petroleum, rubber, and automotive parts industries, and labor unions.

NHUC began in 1932 when Alfred P. Sloan, then president of General Motors, called into conference the diverse groups interested in highways. Sloan was NHUC's first chairman in 1932 and continued in that post until 1948.

The big event of NHUC is its biannual conference at which hundreds of delegates from the state HUCs assemble to discuss state and national problems confronting highway transportation. They thrash out problems that would hinder the growth of automobile transportation. "Through research, analysis, and digests, through press releases and bulletins, and through thousands of personal contacts each year, NHUC is a trusted source of news and data for its constituent groups and for the public press," according to NHUC.

Current chairman is J. N. Bauman, president of White Motor Corporation of Cleveland, who succeeded H. E. Humphreys, Jr., former president of the United States Rubber Company (now Uniroyal, Inc.). Other chairmen were Albert Bradley, who was executive vice president and chairman of General Motors, and William S. Richardson, president of B. F. Goodrich Company.

Unlike most highway interest groups, NHUC does not lobby before congressional committees. This is because member groups may not agree on policy. The American Automobile Association supports higher taxes on trucks to pay for roads while, not surprisingly, the American Trucking Associations are against such legislation. But members do testify as individuals. Members of the Board of Directors of NHUC include AAA, American Bakers Association, American Bottlers of Carbonated Beverages, American National Cattlemen's Association, American Petroleum Institute, American Trucking Associations, Automobile Manufacturers Association, International Association of Ice Cream Manufacturers, McGraw-Hill Publishing Co., Inc., Michigan Bell Telephone Company (telephone companies own some of the largest fleets of small trucks), National Association of Motor Bus Owners, National Automobile Dealers Association, National Grange, National Milk Producers Federation, National Rural Letter Carriers' Association, Private Truck Council of America, the Rubber Manufacturers

Association, Truck-Trailer Manufacturers Association, United Fresh Fruit and Vegetable Association.

NHUC claims that its goal "has been and will continue to be that of serving those who seek to assure an ever brighter future for highway transportation consistent with the interests of the individual citizen, the national economy, and the national security." The rubber, petroleum, and automobile industries pick up the tab for NHUC.

Their most recent biannual congress, the twelfth, was held in Washington in April 1968. An armed forces color guard marched into the Washington Hilton Ballroom to commence the opening of the program. One of the speakers was State Senator Randolph Collier, chairman of the California Senate Transportation Committee. Speaking on proposed rail transit plans for urban areas, he said, "Should feasible plans be developed, I believe it is essential that they be financed locally, by the communities affected, and then only after the financing plan and the revenue measures to support it have been submitted to popular vote in those areas. . . . Several proposals have been made in our legislature, designed to finance rapid transit systems by drawing on highway user funds. Fortunately, however, highway funds in California are protected, as they should be, by our constitution."

He went on to discuss some of the criticism leveled against highways and noted that despite continuing attacks on freeways, an April 1 Highway Research Board study indicated that 80 percent of people believe the automobile is the ideal mode of transportation and only 12 percent indicated a preference for public transportation. He did not mention that nearly 50 percent of these same people said they still used automobiles despite the problems the vehicle causes because there was no alternative method available.

Dr. Robert Brenner, deputy director of the National Highway Safety Bureau, newly created under the Department of Transportation, told the NHUC audience that upwards of one hundred research grants to industries, foundations, universities, and government agencies had been awarded recently, and four hundred applications for funding of safety projects from the states were received and being considered. He was followed by Thomas Mann, president of the Automobile Manufacturers Association, who described the advantages of bus rapid transit over fixed-rail systems. "If, for example, the business center should move, fixed rail cannot readily move with it. Or if the suburbs, which trains and subways serve, should later decline or change in character, fixed rails would have an even more difficult time accommodating to change." He did not mention the movement of businesses to the suburbs as a result of the change the automobile had caused in urban areas. He continued by pointing out that bus rapid transit has an "unmatched capacity" to adjust quickly and at relatively low cost to an infinite variety of change as well as provide service to people who want to travel across town from one suburb to another or who work in the central city and wish to visit widely dispersed areas in the suburbs.

"To be sure," he conceded, "bus travel will have to be speeded up." Addressing himself to the charges that automobiles and their use destroy the beauty of the city, he said, "Important as the esthetic is, and the quality of urban environment *is* important, cities must also provide for the less romantic but nevertheless essential needs of their people, including adequate transportation. The challenge today is to harmonize our transportation with our need for pleasant, healthful urban environments—to harmonize the desire of people to live in uncongested areas with their need for convenient, flexible transportation." This is the man who represents the industry which bitterly fought exhaust control devices for automobiles.

Other participants in the program of the conference were from the Private Truck Council of America, American Trucking Associations, General Tire and Rubber Company, and governors, highway officials, both federal and state, state senators, and engineers.

Some of the biggest problems plaguing NHUC and all highway related interests were summed up as questions in their February 1968 quarterly publication, *Highway User*. They included the following: Why may the Highway Trust Fund be in greater danger now than ever before? What are some new gimmicks being advanced for dipping into state highway funds? Will future highway plans emphasize a federal-aid urban system? What super-new plans show buses as the most practical answer to mass transit? How much joint planning among all kinds of planners makes for progress? Will the "people's platform"—public highway hearings—become quicksand in which highway plans are dropped and sunk, year after year? What new burdens on highway development are being planned for "social uplift" programs?

Yule Fisher, publisher of *Highway User,* explained that new gimmicks refer to the growing movement in California, in particular, to divert state highway tax revenues to other modes of transportation, mainly rapid transit. Social uplift programs, he said, meant that highway builders are being asked to "hire the certified poor" in an attempt to tie the poverty program into the highway program.

Another group interested in the highway program is the trucking industry which derives actual profit from the use of highways. Without them it could not survive. Most of these interests are represented by the American Trucking Associations, Inc., head-quartered in Washington. It is a national federation of sixty-four organizations consisting of fifty independent state trucking associations plus the District of Columbia and thirteen "conferences."

ATA claims the industry has grown from 200,000 motor trucks in 1916 to 15.5 million in 1967. It provides "representation and voice" in Washington, but does not attempt in any manner to buy legislation, according to an ATA former general manager. ATA's representations before the Congress are invariably dignified, force-ful, factual—as befits a great American industry, he explains.

Which does not exactly explain why the Truck Operators Non-partisan[!] Committee, an arm of ATA, donated $40,000 to "friendly" congressmen between 1966 and 1968. Of that amount, $29,000 went to ranking committee members who, in 1968, had before them a bill to allow 138,000-pound triple trailer trucks on interstate highways. The limit is 73,280 pounds. Included among the friendly congressmen were George Fallon, who received $1000; John C. Kluczynski, $3000; John Blatnik and William Harsha (R., Ohio), $1000 each; Senate Public Works Committee member the late Everett M. Dirksen (R., Illinois), $2000; Mike Monroney (D., Oklahoma), a member of the Senate Appropriations Com-mittee on Public Works, $2375. Alan Bible (D., Nevada), chairman of the Senate District Committee, received $1000, as did Peter Dominick (R., Colorado), also a member of the committee.

The ATA emerged at the time federal regulations on the trucking industry became law in 1935. ATA is credited by its own spokesmen as the sole lobbyist for the industry at the time the controls were formulated. The trucking industry has two big constant headaches—railroads and freeway critics. From the point of view of the trucking industry, trucks use the streets and highways, suffer size and weight limitations, are taxed, regulated, controlled, and discriminated against. Trucks received 48.5 percent of the federally regulated transportation, railroads 43.5 percent, and inland waterways, airlines, and pipelines shared the remaining 8 percent in 1966. The total bill for that year for all carriers of commerce was $22.4 billion. The trucking industry's share was $11 billion.

Trucking is big business for a number of companies. There are 1298 trucking companies whose annual revenue is $1 million or more per year. The largest of these grossed more than $175 million in 1966. ATA lobbies and testifies before roads subcommittees for more and wider highways and reduced fuel and weight taxes and against farm co-operatives that try to haul their own freight.

Also high on the list of associations interested in promoting more highways is the Portland Cement Association, whose national headquarters are also in Washington, close to the source of Highway Trust Fund revenues. The goals of PCA are simple: to improve and extend the uses of Portland cement and concrete through scientific research and engineering field work.

An example of their scientific research is a report entitled "Major Highway Corridors of North America." It projects major highway needs through the end of the century. The main element of scientific research generated from Wilbur Smith and Associates, an engineering firm in New Haven, Connecticut, an old hand at feasibility studies for highway departments.

The report favors a 128,000-mile Inter-Metropolitan Area network which will:

1. Incorporate nearly every intercity highway route that can reasonably be expected to require upgrading to four or more traffic lanes, with full control of access, during this century.

2. Serve the vast majority of the present and future population and accommodate expected economic growth and development.
3. Provide mainline highway service interconnecting all existing and emerging metropolitan areas on the continent. (This includes Mexico and Canada.)

Explaining public response to freeways in urban areas, the report states: "The response by the public to new freeways in metropolitan areas of Canada, the United States, and Mexico has been overwhelming. That motorists have swarmed to use most freeways built in metropolitan areas during the past quarter-century is a clear sign that the decision to build them was sound. Continuing traffic congestion, however, indicates that demand for such facilities is far from satisfied. . . . Congestion-free driving on all urban freeways should be the goal of federal, state and provincial, and local highway officials. . . . It is clear that the existing mileage of freeways in most metropolitan areas falls far short of present needs. Urban area transportation studies now being conducted in nearly every metropolitan area of Canada and the United States are providing extensive evidence concerning the needs and benefits of urban freeway development. Analyses of these studies indicate that expected increases in motor vehicle ownership, together with continued extension of low-density land uses, justify developing, on the average, about one mile of urban freeway for every 10,000 urban residents. . . . If motor vehicle travel in metropolitan areas is to be well served, if traffic congestion is to be eliminated, and safety is to be significantly improved, then it will be necessary to construct . . . 360 to 420 miles of new urban freeways *per year* in the United States between now and the end of the century."

If highway departments begin such a program in 1970 and build PCA and Wilbur Smith's conservative estimate of 360 miles per year, by the year 2000 our cities would have 10,800 more miles of superhighways than the currently planned 6650 Interstate miles.

These figures mean that the concrete we would pour into our cities alone would equal at least four six-lane highways spanning the width of the United States. Their higher figure of 420 miles per year equals more than five such highways.

The asphalt industry has a stake in highways, too. It is represented by the Asphalt Institute, whose more than fifty oil company members are aware that more than 90 percent of all paved streets and roads in the United States have at least an asphalt surface.

The Automotive Safety Foundation has its own interest in freeways. Its green pamphlet describes the purposes of the foundation as "a non-profit organization working in the public interest to improve the safety, efficiency and convenience of automotive transportation in the United States" with an annual budget of $1,600,000, which it gathers in from automobile manufacturers, petroleum and asphalt, parts and accessories, and rubber tire manufacturers, advertising agencies, media and graphic arts suppliers, steel, automobile finance, insurance interests, major banks, automobile and tire dealers, Portland cement, aluminum, and school bus manufacturers. The foundation boasts that it is created by businessmen, financed by industry, serving industry by serving the public interest. Its executive committee is chaired by J. W. Keener of B. F. Goodrich, while the other officers are Benson Ford of Ford Motor Company, George Russell, General Motors, and J. E. Buchanan, Asphalt Institute. Trustees and officers represent the auto, steel, rubber tire, parts and equipment, banking, petroleum, insurance, cement, credit, and broadcasting industries. It was originally the safety division of the Automobile Manufacturers Association, but was reorganized in 1937.

One of the foundation's divisions, titled Urban Planning and Traffic Department, is concerned with all aspects of the urban or metropolitan problem ranging from ways to get maximum safety and capacity from urban streets to studies of the social and economic factors relating to transportation modes. Other areas include parking, freeways, esthetics, and intergovernmental planning. The Highway Administration, Development and Planning Department is concerned with all aspects of highway development including planning, design, classification, maintenance, laws, administration, future needs, new concepts, finance, and research.

In any typical year, the ASF annual research grants total $700,000. They spend approximately $850,000 distributing these grants, $525,000 of that amount for salaries and wages alone.

Thus, the foundation manages to spend more to administer its programs than it spends on grants. Its reports point to faulty driving as a cause of accidents, not poorly designed cars or highways.

The foundation has distributed some expensively produced books extolling the need and virtues of freeways. One, *Urban Freeway Development in Twenty Major Cities,* states in its introduction: "When the Interstate System is completed in 1972, there will still remain a requirement for considerable additional urban freeway mileage." To support this statement, the foundation points out that there are 1,256,340 automobiles available in New York City and less than one million in Los Angeles. However, there are 6.2 persons per auto in New York compared with 2.6 in Los Angeles and only 0.47 autos per housing unit in New York compared with 1.1 in Los Angeles. "The first example—automobiles available—indicates the sheer magnitude of the number of automobiles dictates a requirement for an extensive highway and freeway system in both cities." It does? Only if the cities decide it is desirable to bring more automobiles into these cities. They might decide to expand other forms of transportation instead.

The discussion continues: "The other examples—persons per automobile and automobiles per housing unit—partly explain the existing extensive mass transit system in New York." A more accurate interpretation of that phrase is that the existing extensive mass transit system in New York partly explains those other examples.

The book illustrates the various types of freeway construction in major cities, the grid, loop and radial, and irregular systems. Each illustrates a city with parks, streams, neighborhoods, and business districts carved into small patches by wide black lines representing freeways. The foundation book also points out that freeway construction, now combined with urban renewal, "replace large sections of existing development with needed facilities." Their statement implies that the "existing development," euphemism for slum housing, is not a needed facility for the persons living in it. Before urban renewal, they simply boasted that they cleared slums to lay much-needed concrete.

Another highway-oriented organization, which wears the mantle of academia, is the Highway Research Board, which is supported by private and public funds. It was founded after World War I as a branch of the National Academy of Sciences when, as the Board brochure puts it, "It became increasingly apparent to many individuals and organizations interested in furthering the transportation progress of the United States that such progress depended primarily upon the improvement of the country's highway system." It was formed after the Bureau of Public Roads, the state highway departments, the American Society of Civil Engineers, and "a number of highway-oriented organizations and educational institutions" pressured the National Research Council to do so. Its purpose is to stimulate highway research and "the Board was established as an arm of the greatly respected private and nonprofit National Academy of Sciences because of the Academy's reputation for objectivity and ability as a scientific body to the government. The Board today, as when established, is therefore a *nongovernmental* organization, although its ties with government on all levels have been strong through the years." State highway departments finance approximately 60 percent of the Board's activities, the BPR 20 percent, and supporting memberships make up the remaining 20 percent. The Board is responsible for a plethora of volumes on highway research, most of it supporting highways. It also doles out the money for such research.

For instance, HRB's progress report through June 1968 shows that Bertram D. Tallamy Associates and Wilbur Smith Associates shared $100,000 to investigate research needs in highway transportation. In addition, Tallamy Associates received $205,128 to study maintenance of way and structures, described as "an intensive study into typical maintenance operations on 28 Interstate test sections."

Some of the studies have social significance. These are allotted small budgets. One such contract provides for studies of payments to persons who have sued highway departments for damages due to noise, pollution, or other environmental factors, in order to provide a "first-class trial memorandum that can be used by the practicing trial lawyer and appraiser on a day-to-day basis." HRB awarded $2500 for that study. Another such study examines legal cases brought by persons displaced from their homes by highways and measures for assisting relocation. This study received a $5000 grant.

Officers of the Board include vice chairmen D. Grant Mickle, president of the Automotive Safety Foundation, and Oscar T. Marzke, of U.S. Steel. Its executive committee in 1968 consisted of Federal Highway Administrator Lowell Bridwell, A. E. Johnson, executive director of AASHO, J. B. McMorran, of New York's Department of Transportation, and a mixture of representatives of engineering firms, auto manufacturers, state highway officials, and the petroleum and steel industries, plus a few university people.

In other words, members of the Highway Research Board can be and often are members of the Automotive Safety Foundation or AASHO or AASHO-ARBA joint committees, state highway departments, federal highway administration, the AMA, AGC, or NHUC, so that public officials become members of groups bent on promoting special interests; in this case, highways. Burch McMorran is a fine example of a public official, now heading up the Department of Transportation in New York, who belongs to AASHO, ARBA, and the Highway Research Board. He has, in fact, been president of ARBA and AASHO.

Mickle is another. He was Deputy Federal Highway Administrator of the Bureau of Public Roads from 1961 to 1964. He was HRB's executive director between 1964 and 1966. He spent eighteen years as ASF's director of traffic engineering. He is also a registered professional engineer, a member and past president of the Institute of Traffic Engineers, a Fellow of the American Society of Civil Engineers, and a life member of the American Public Works Association, thus demonstrating the form of musical chairs played in and out of public office by members of the highway fraternity.

Then, too, there is the American Automobile Association with its eleven million membership. It supports highways more visibly than the guardian of the automobile companies, the Automobile Manufacturers Association, which desperately needs superroads if their products are going to sell. Members are American Motors Corporation, Checker Motors Corporation, Chrysler Corporation, Duplex Division, Warner and Swasey Company, Ford Motor Company, General Motors Corporation, International Harvester Company, Kaiser Jeep Corporation, Mack Trucks, Inc., Walter Motor Truck Company, and White Motor Corporation.

There is no doubt in the minds of AMA members that the country needs more highways. Back in 1961 when George Romney, now Secretary of Housing and Urban Development, was president of American Motors and a director of AMA, his colleague L. L. Colbert from Chrysler, president of AMA, stated, "Our recent published studies of highway economics helped to shape the legislation now moving through Congress and aimed at keeping the construction of the Interstate Highway on schedule and soundly financed." He was referring to an AMA-financed study by Wilbur Smith Associates entitled "Future Highways and Urban Growth," which predicted a need for more highways.

The AMA was originally titled the National Automobile Chamber of Commerce and, true to its belief in the free enterprise system, James J. Nance of Studebaker-Packard told the House Public Works Committee in May of 1955 when the Interstate System was being promoted:

"We have a direct interest in safer, more free-flowing highways. The future of our industry depends on them." Today, the AMA discreetly declines to testify on proposed highway legislation. The organization simply submits a letter or statement for the record of public hearings.

No list would be complete without including the American Petroleum Institute whose membership consists mainly of presidents or vice presidents of U.S. oil companies. They also belong to the Asphalt Institute, since oil is a major component of asphalt pavement. API is interested in promoting more highways to sell more gasoline and to provide asphalt roads for their motor fleets to transport their products.

Other special interest groups include the American Right-of-Way Association, the Roadside Business Association, the National Safety

Council, the National Joint Heavy and Highway Construction Committee, engineering, auto insurance, and lumber firms, and the rubber tire industry. Last, but not least, is a group of 240 men known in inner Washington highway circles as the Road Gang. The membership describes itself as a very informal group of business and government executives, highway engineers and consultants, press and public relations specialists, company representatives and trade association officials from highway transportation and its allied fields located in the District of Columbia. The group meets on Thursdays for lunch for the purpose of promoting fellowship and the interchange of ideas among the Washington highway transportation fraternity, and one of the important traditions of the Road Gang is the lively "round table" sessions often held on current highway transportation issues, *particularly when legislative matters are on the horizon,* according to the Road Gang's semisecret publication which lists its membership by name, affiliation, and address.

Chairman of the 1968 Road Gang was Norman Almquist of American Road Builders Association. Other members include Jesse Buchanan of the Asphalt Institute; Harry Boot, American Trucking Associations; David Buswell, Highway Research Board; William Emmerich, Mobil Oil; John W. Gibbons, Automotive Safety Foundation; Charles Day, Ford Motor Company; Harold Wirth, Firestone Tire and Rubber Company; Elmer Timby of Howard, Needles, Tammen and Bergendoff; R. W. Tupper, Automobile Association of America; Kennard Underwood, Jr., General Motors Corporation; John Plum, U.S. Steel; Robert S. Holmes, ARBA president; W. J. Sears, Rubber Manufacturers Association; J. N. Robertson, former D.C. Highway Director and current treasurer of ARBA; D. Grant Mickle, Automotive Safety Foundation; A. H. Neunabar, Chevron Asphalt; Walter B. McKendrick, Portland Cement Association; John H. King, Automobile Manufacturers Association; John R. Gray, National Asphalt Pavement Association; Vincent Grey, Truck Trailer Manufacturers Association; Myles Goldbranson, International Harvester Company; William C. Hamilton, National Automobile Dealers Association; Richard Creighton, Associated General Contractors of America; Yule Fisher of National Highway Users Conference; E. H. Wallace, Uniroyal; plus Francis Turner, then director of the

Bureau of Public Roads, and Lowell Bridwell, then Federal Highway Administrator. Difficult as it is to obtain a copy of the 1968 Road Gang membership list from ARBA publishers, there are numerous copies available at the Bureau of Public Roads for perusal because numerous federal highway officials belong.

Since 1962, the Road Gang, which began meeting in 1942, has made an award, the P. D. McLean Memorial, to outstanding leaders in the highway field. The first award went to Pyke Johnson, at that time head of the ASF, later with the Highway Research Board. In 1963, John V. Lawrence, then managing director of ATA, received it. In 1964, Norman Damon of ASF received it. In 1965, the Road Gang tipped its hat to an old friend, Congressman George Fallon. In 1966, Federal Highway Administrator Rex Whitton was the recipient, and in 1967, Walter W. Belson of the American Trucking Association's Research Foundation received the coveted award. C. D. Curtiss, former commissioner of the Bureau of Public Roads, received the 1968 award for "outstanding contributions to the advancement of highway transportation in the public interest."

During the 1969 Highway Research Board conference in Washington, the Road Gang held its twenty-sixth annual luncheon meeting. Guest speaker was Congressman Cramer who, it was announced, spoke on the subject, "An Insight to Future Highway Programs and Procedures." Meetings of the Road Gang are closed to outsiders and any person inquiring about the organization is closely scrutinized by ARBA officials. Requests to ARBA for membership lists are denied, even though public officials are members of the organization. Even a request to the Department of Transportation for the list was denied as late as December 1968, despite the fact that DOT officials were listed as members of the organization and the freedom of public information law had been in "effect" for more than a year. Despite the information act and despite the fact that public officials were listed as members and these same public officials had copies of the membership list in their government offices, indeed, they had been invited to join because of their capacity as public officials, DOT took the position that the membership list was not a part of the Transportation Department's information file. Therefore, DOT avoided facing up to the issue of carrying on the public's business within an atmosphere of semisecrecy. Although the public officials who are involved in such commingling of private and public interests may defend themselves on grounds they are serving the public interest, they convey the appearance of breaching their trust to the general public by participating in such organizations.

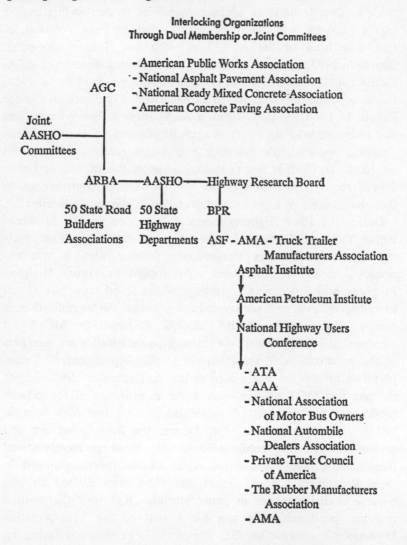

**Interlocking Organizations
Through Dual Membership or Joint Committees**

- American Public Works Association
- National Asphalt Pavement Association
- National Ready Mixed Concrete Association
- American Concrete Paving Association

AGC

Joint
AASHO
Committees

ARBA———AASHO———Highway Research Board

50 State Road   50 State   BPR
Builders   Highway
Associations   Departments   ASF - AMA - Truck Trailer
                                Manufacturers Association
                  Asphalt Institute

                  American Petroleum Institute

                  National Highway Users
                      Conference

                  - ATA
                  - AAA
                  - National Association
                      of Motor Bus Owners
                  - National Autombile
                      Dealers Association
                  - Private Truck Council
                      of America
                  - The Rubber Manufacturers
                      Association
                  - AMA

For instance: J. E. Buchanan of the Asphalt Institute is secretary of the Automotive Safety Foundation and a past president of Materials and Services Division of ARBA. He is also a member of the Road Gang, as are many other members of these or related associations.

"I'm Supposed To Be In The New U.S. Department Of Transportation——If I Can Get To It"

1. Proof Positive — Daily auto congestion on our urban highways such as these Los Angeles commuters are experiencing demonstrates that the system does not work because highways induce their own congestion. Yet we continue to plan and build more of the same. *Air Pollution Control, County of Los Angeles.*

2. Acres and Acres of Concrete—Urban freeways like the Dan Ryan, Eisenhower and Kennedy Expressways which meet in this vast interchange in downtown Chicago are touted by highway promoters as necessary for the revitalization of our cities. In reality, however, they deface cities, encouraging more automobile traffic and remove precious land from the tax base for the sole purpose of moving and storing automobiles.

3. The Stack—Los Angeles has its own version of Times Square (for automobile traffic) in the form of a four-level interchange which joins, clockwise, middle right, the Santa Ana, Hollywood and Pasadena Freeways, a hub from which radiates much of that city's famous sprawl. *Division of Highways, Department of Public Works, State of California.*

4. The Law of Impenetrability—This massive traffic jam occurred in Boston on December 30, 1963, paralyzing the center of the city for five hours. Shortly thereafter public officials approved extension of still more freeways through the heart of this historic city. *Boston Globe.*

5.   Graceful Ribbons of Concrete—From the air, the Interstate Route 10 and State Highway 11 interchange in Los Angeles resemble the bow on a package tied with concrete ribbon. On the ground, it's more like a noose. *Division of Highways, Department of Public Works, State of California.*

6.   Downtown, U.S.A.—Vast areas of our most precious urban land like this section of downtown St. Louis are used for the movement and storage of automobiles. Result: lowered tax base, congestion, pollution, ugliness, transportation strangulation and the destruction of neighborhoods. *General Electric.*

7.   Representatives George Fallon (D. Maryland), left, and Senator Jennings Randolph (D. West Virginia) in white coat turn a spade of sod in 1964 at groundbreaking ceremonies for the American Road Builders Association's new building conveniently located next door to Federal Highway Administration offices. Boyd S. Oberlink, then ARBA president, is in the middle. Retired Army Major General Louis W. Prentiss, then ARBA executive vice president, is between Fallon and Oberlink. Burton F. Miller, ARBA's executive vice president, is at right. *American Road Builders Association.*

8.   A Model for the Nation?—Washington's monuments are steadily being engulfed by freeways and automobiles like this Potomac-Channel crossing that sweeps down on the capital city. Viewing morning rush hour traffic by helicopter, President Nixon stated he was glad he did not have to drive to work.

9.   Historic Georgetown Waterfront—The famous old shipping port, now part of Washington, D.C., is a conglomeration of smelly pollutant-producing factories and the Whitehurst Freeway. D.C. highway officials plan to replace this ugly scene with a new waterfront freeway plus still another Potomac crossing. But there is no money available to develop the waterfront for recreation purposes, as has been advocated by residents.

10.   Congress Amid the Auto Age—The massive Rayburn Office Building, upper right, where many Congressmen work, appears surrounded by freeway clutter in Washington, a direct result of action taken by some occupants of the new office building. Voteless residents of the District of Columbia who have turned down more freeways were overruled by a road-happy Congress.

11.   Mass Exodus—Each weekday evening New York commuters merge bumper to bumper at the entrance to the Queens-Midtown Tunnel for the grueling drive home. Each new such facility encourages still more traffic, which in turn quickly fills all available road space. The highway lobby's answer: more roads. *Triborough Bridge and Tunnel Authority.*

12.   Squeeze, Please—Every weekday evening twelve lanes of automobile traffic converge into two lanes at the entrance to Manhattan's Queens-Midtown Tunnel which connects to the Long Island Expressway. Tunnel promoter Robert Moses points to the resulting congestion as "proof" of the need for still another automobile-attracting tunnel in the neighborhood. *Triborough Bridge and Tunnel Authority.*

13. Big Highway Booster—Representative William Cramer (R. Florida), ranking minority member of the House Public Works Committee, proudly displays the annual award of the American Road Builders Association which he received in 1969 from the highway contractors for his "especially significant contribution to the progress of the national highway program." Cramer demanded that freeways be constructed in the nation's capital despite overwhelming opposition from residents. *American Road Builders Association.*

14. Hurry Up and Wait—The endless stream of bumper-to-bumper traffic on this San Francisco freeway demonstrates a variant on Parkinson's Law, that peak-hour congestion rises to meet road capacity. *National Center for Air Pollution Control.*

15. Safety First—Millions of tax dollars continue to be poured into such "safety" research for automobile travel as this Experimental Route Guidance System which, if installed in our highways, would cost still hundreds of millions of more dollars. Meanwhile, traffic piles up and public transportation systems continue their downward trend without a meaningful financial boost or political commitment.

16. The Daily Commuter Queue—During rush hours there is no need to worry about enforcing the 40-mile-per-hour speed limit posted on these approaches to the San Francisco-Oakland Bay Bridge. *General Electric.*

17. The San Diego Freeway Traverses a Mountain—Thirteen million cubic yards of material were torn from the Santa Monica Mountains to make way for this stretch of Interstate 405, creating the impression of a huge sand pit surrounded by homes and trees. *Division of Highways, Department of Public Works, State of California.*

18. Safety First! — The federal aid highway program's congressional watchdog subcommittee regularly reports on built-in engineering mistakes like this one. The automobile left the roadway, slid along the stone wall and smashed into this huge concrete and metal sign post, which should have been surrounded by a properly installed guardrail, placed on the other side of the wall, or on the wall.

19.   Another Target for the Subcommittee—This guardrail has been placed between trees rather than around them. Instead of offering protection, the guardrail adds to the danger by guiding skidding vehicles into the trees.

20.   Long Island Expressway—One of the earliest examples of what to avoid. Frequent exit and entrance ramps and easy access in densely populated areas result in a slow, serpentine ooze of automobile traffic daily into and out of New York. *Triborough Bridge and Tunnel Authority.*

21.   American Know-How—Despite criticism that superhighways are dangerous and do not belong in the urban scene, money and engineering manpower continue to be channelled into them as, for instance, this central control panel for a television surveillance system in Detroit's freeway system, that costs hundreds of thousands of dollars. *Michigan State Highway Department.*

22.   Acres and Acres of Automobiles—Perhaps appropriately, downtown Detroit resembles a huge used car lot, with a few buildings interspersed between the parking lots. Even the roof of the Motor City's civic center, Cobo Hall, left, is covered with automobiles. Skyscrapers in the foreground fail their civic duty with roofs raised to heights unacceptable for parking cars. *Michigan State Highway Department.*

23.   The Wrong Approach—Running a rapid transit line in the median strip of Chicago's Eisenhower Expressway does not discourage automobiles from entering the city since so long as freeway facilities are provided, people will continue to use them. *General Electric*.

24.   The City is a Parking Lot—Downtown Los Angeles already devotes 60 percent of its land to serving man's master, the automobile. The isolated stretch of parkland at left center almost looks out of place amid the surrounding highways. *General Electric*.

25.   Believe it or Not, by GM—General Motors, which produces a substantial number of buses, actually has a clean, comfortable model that could revolutionize public transportation on our urban streets and highways. This transit coach features extra window space, a lounge type seating arrangement, carpeting, and a floor 14 inches lower than current models with a "kneeling" capability to lower the step height.

26.   Modern Train Transportation—The Department of Transportation is sponsoring improvements in train service to attract riders to the nation's 211,500 miles of railroad tracks in an effort to provide safe, efficient and economical public ground transportation between large metropolitan areas. As a result, these coach passengers on the Pennsy's Metroliner make the trip between New York and Washington in a record two and a half hours. Passengers enjoy telephone, cocktail and snack service enroute. *General Electric.*

27. A Long-overdue Train — Modern, comfortable trains have been providing transportation for residents of Moscow, Montreal and Toronto for years while our cities have been innundated with automobiles and our transportation crisis grows. Residents of San Francisco wised up, cancelled freeway construction, and are now looking forward to riding in streamlined comfort on Bay Area Rapid Transit trains which will soon roll at 90-second intervals at speeds up to 80 miles per hour during rush hours. *General Electric.*

28. For the Future—Vehicles like this model appear futuristic but only because we have for so long allowed quality train and public transportation services to decline while feverishly building highways for automobiles. *General Electric.*

29.   Suburban Pickets—Residents of Takoma Park, a Washington, D.C. suburb, borrowed the Burma Shave sign technique to express their opposition to Maryland State Roads Commissioner John B. Funk's plan to barrel a freeway through their neighborhood. *The Washington Post.*

30.   Venice, City Without Highways—Charming narrow streets and canals make walking and boating in Venice not only necessary but pleasant and rewarding, free from traffic lights, screeching brakes, pedestrian casualties, ugly gas stations, traffic jams and automobile smog.

5. The Road Producers

"It was decided that the association would not register its executive secretary as a lobbyist for it did not appear proper for the officials of the several state highway departments to be represented by a lobbyist, but that the chief administrator of all the state highways departments would maintain a close liaison with their respective congressional delegates . . ."

—A. E. Johnson, executive director,
American Association of State
Highway Officials, 1964

One organization that oversees our highway program in the guise of protecting the public interest is the American Association of State Highway Officials. Founded in 1914, two years before the first Federal Highway Act, AASHO is made up of "heads and other chief directing officials" engaged in administrative work of the various state highway departments. The purpose of the organization, according to its 1964 revised constitution, is "to foster the development, operation and maintenance of a nationwide integrated system of highways to adequately serve the transportation needs of our country." The association also pledges to "counsel with the Congress on highway legislation . . . and to cooperate with other agencies in the consideration and solution of highway problems."

AASHO has two standing committees, one on administration and another on standards. Under these are subcommittees on highway

finance, transport, right-of-way, planning, urban transportation planning, and numerous subcommittees on highway standards such as
its panel on planning and design policies, whose purpose it is to
"investigate available data, pursue studies and recommend policies
for the development of planning and design standards, which will
advance to a maximum degree the utility and safety of highways in
rural and urban areas." Standards are adopted by a two-thirds vote
of member highway departments.

AASHO has four subdivisions, or geographical areas, in the
United States, each represented by a regional vice president. In
addition to these, there are four Regional Associations of State Highway Officials, in the North Atlantic, Southeastern, Mississippi Valley,
and Western states. These organizations do not operate as branches
or divisions of AASHO, but they do co-operate fully with the
national organization.

"Partly by coincidence the boundaries of the four Regional Associations match the four geographical regions of AASHO," the
national organization explains. The Regional Associations, according to AASHO, fill a need for highway administrators, engineers,
and other technical specialists to meet and discuss mutual problems
and exchange views and experiences on such matters as weather,
economics, and load material.

AASHO also has what it labels "special" committees. One of
these, the Joint Committee on Cooperation with the Associated
General Contractors of America, Inc., was formed to "promote
harmonious relations between state highway officials and highway
contractors that are in the public interest . . . to discuss, jointly,
those matters which relate to or affect the actual construction of
highways."

Another special committee, the Joint Committee on Cooperation
with the American Road Builders Association, was formed to "discuss the development and use of highway equipment and materials
and to maintain an effective liaison between the two associations."

AASHO commemorated its fiftieth anniversary in 1964 with publication of a Golden Book. In it, A. E. Johnson, executive director
of the association, explained why, back in 1914, the organization

was formed: "Many highway organizations existed at the time, of which the membership not only included public officials, but also those primarily motivated by the profit incentive, such as professional good roads promoters, highway contractors, equipment and materials producers. . . . State highway administrators felt that there was a definite need for an organization with membership limited to public officials, who had the responsibility of planning and administering the State's highway programs . . . and who would be free from the commercial influences." Yet state highway officials have continued to serve in these profit-oriented organizations.

Commenting upon highway administrators' relationship with their congressmen, Mr. Johnson further reminisced on the early foundations of the association. "It was decided that the association would not register its executive secretary as a lobbyist for it did not appear proper for the officials of the several state highway departments to be represented by a lobbyist, but that the chief administrators of all the state highway departments would maintain a close liaison with their respective congressional delegates. . . . It was to be the duty of the executive secretary to keep the members advised of proposals, developments and actions in order that contracts might be made when the need was indicated. . . . The executive secretary of the association has maintained a close liaison with the appropriate committees and staffs of the Congress and has never lobbied for an action, but has only expressed opinions and given information upon invitation or request, which has been frequent. The association, through this process, has enjoyed immense prestige and respect on Capitol Hill, and many times the executive secretary has been asked to submit legislative language for consideration." In other words, he functions as a lobbyist but does not register as such.

Mr. Johnson was president of AASHO in 1955, during the period of intensive lobbying for the legislation establishing the Interstate System and expansion of our entire highway program. It was at that time that he was, in his own modest words, "the unanimous choice" of the executive committee to succeed the retiring executive secretary of the association, a post he has held continuously since.

While the title has changed to executive director, Mr. Johnson remains the official spokesman for the association.

In addition to state highway officials, the membership of the association includes representatives of the Bureau of Public Roads, and now, the Federal Highway Administrator. Mr. Johnson explained the reason for this mixture of federal and state officials thus: The association is fortunate that all of the men who have headed the Bureau of Public Roads were active in the affairs of the association previously and were its strong supporters. This attitude, he said, has done much to keep the partnership concept operating and to instill a strong spirit of mutual respect and friendship between the state and the Bureau. Then he warned that if a person not friendly to the association were ever to head the Bureau of Public Roads and not co-operate with the states through the association, or disregard association-developed recommendations and standards, the reaction could be serious. On the other hand, he did not explain how the association reacts when, as frequently occurs, member state departments themselves do not adhere to association standards and recommendations.

He also had a few words for members of the public who criticize freeway planning as carried on by the states. "There are several . . . groups wanting a prominent role in highway planning and decision making that have taken little or no interest in highways previously. Part of this is brought about by the glamour of the important program, changing conditions, and, in particular, more emphasis on urban needs. I refer to such groups as architects, landscape architects, and planners. These groups are sometimes referred to as the artistic and creative elements and definitely express ideas regarding highway layouts and esthetics, but have considerable difficulty, at times, agreeing among themselves as to their ideas and how they should be applied to highways."

AASHO president in 1967, E. M. Johnson, chief engineer of the state of Mississippi (no relation to A. E. Johnson), told state highway officials: "On some urban projects it is necessary to have a number of hearings with city and county officials, Chamber of Commerce committees, and groups of citizens. State highway departments recognize these situations and have these hearings or meetings. Such hearings and meetings may or may not be made a part of official records, but the data obtained is effective.

"In less congested areas the necessity for obtaining information on attitudes of the public decreases. Therefore, it would seem to be a waste of manpower, money, and time to have the same hearing requirements for every project.

"Additional reviews and consultations on historical site preservation, recreational area encroachments, conservation, or any other particular would not, in my opinion, eliminate all protests. All of these features, and more, are forcibly brought to the attention of state highway departments, and no one is more anxious to have a happy and satisfied public than the state highway departments and the Bureau of Public Roads. In my opinion, consultations and reviews, ad infinitum, do not add much, if anything, to information pertinent to a highway location and design but only delay needed improvements.

"Beauty is a matter of individual taste, but it is believed that most of the public would be pleased with designs, construction, and maintenance resulting in clean, neat, and well-kept highways blending into the environment. . . . Excessive audits, hearings, inspections, investigations, and record keeping have damaging effects on contractor-engineer relationships, and, in some instances, erode the public confidence in the state highway departments and the Bureau of Public Roads, whether criticisms are justified or not.

"There seems to be a deepening crisis in the highway program, but our mission is to live with it while bending every effort toward reversing trends considered not to be in the best public interest."

Even Senator Randolph, in addressing the fifty-third convention of AASHO in October of 1967, cautioned highway officials that they must listen to the public and weigh the criticisms brought forth at public hearings. "Following the urban riots of this summer, investigators seeking the whys and wherefores of these great catastrophes found that highway construction in the core city was a serious point of complaint," the senator reminded his audience.

"We must know if we are really affording people the opportunity to be heard and have their views considered or whether we are merely going through the motions of listening to their complaints, comments, and criticisms. It is their city through which the highway is to be built. The full range of their interests must be understood and served if we are to give local needs the equal consideration which the law requires."

AASHO encourages member state highway departments to publicize their good works. No one has explained better how this is done than J. H. Kultgen, a member of the Texas Highway Commission, in the pages of AASHO's publication, *American Highways*.

Kultgen explained that the commissioners and members of the department information staff travel extensively in the state, checking local problems, conferring with local groups, and repeatedly telling the highway story.

"We constantly encourage local highway organizations and help local groups prepare their presentations to the commission. At all times we stress the need for a balanced highway program as it relates to the overall economy of Texas. . . . The commissioners and the state highway engineer keep up a year-round public relations campaign to maintain harmonious relationships with Texas legislators, other state departments, and state officials.

"In addition, there is a continuous explanation of the organization of the Highway Department by districts and residencies, stressing the importance of these groups to local economies. The fact that our people become permanent, substantial local citizens with important local payrolls is a strong public relations force.

"A separate but equally important facet of our public relations program is based on the co-operation of the Texas Good Roads Association, which releases a continuing barrage of publicity stressing the fact that the commission is relatively independent and free of political interference."

He described how the commissioners serve or have served in positions of leadership in city and county Chambers of Commerce, the Texas Good Roads Association, the Boy Scouts, the Rotary Club, the Lions Club, various law associations, and church groups . . . while the Texas Highway Department Travel and Information

Division regularly sends out news and feature releases to some 670 Texas newspapers and 50 trade publications, 500 radio stations and 50 television studios. In one year, 761 press releases, 11 radio and TV spots, 295 radio-taped spots, and 2 filmed TV spots were spread throughout the state, he reported.

AASHO thus assumes the pious posture of the one highway officials' organization which truly represents the public highway officials untainted by special interests. It consists of public officials only. It forbids commercial advertising in its official publication. It prohibits commercial exhibits at its meetings, declines invitations to have booths at industry trade shows, and generally resists any good roads promotion group bent on expanding the highway industry market, A. E. Johnson explains. It does allow industry salesmen to attend its annual meetings. But its position is standoffish "to the trade." It can afford to be so, for a substantial number of its members, those public officials of AASHO "above commercial interests" in promoting more highways, are also members of ARBA or joint committees with ARBA and AGC.

In addition, congressmen make the AASHO speaking circuit frequently. No less than four congressmen addressed the fifty-third AASHO convention in 1967. They were Senator Randolph and Representatives George Fallon, John C. Kluczynski, and James C. Cleveland, Republican from New Hampshire, all frequenters of ARBA and AGC meetings also. Senate and House roads subcommittee members know well their home state highway commissioner and none pass up the opportunity to introduce highway officials at congressional hearings. State and county officials know their highway officials, too.

AASHO, directed by Fallon, grabbed the ball when General Prentiss suggested that there should be some post-1972 highway "needs" planning for a program after completion of the IS. This came to fruition in June 1967, when the association told both Senate and House roads subcommittees that, indeed, we needed more highways. AASHO presented a plan that would start more highway construction on expiration of the Interstate System without missing a stroke by continuing the Highway Trust Fund, which was supposed to be retired on completion of the Interstate program, and initiating a new ten-year program while collecting $72 billion in highway taxes to pay for additional concrete and asphalt. Add to this estimate of nonfederally supported construction and the entire post-1972 plan carries a price tag of $210 billion.

The proposal also complains about "the increasing requirements and reviews, some statutory and some by Executive order, that complicate getting a project ready for construction," which were designed to protect the public. AASHO suggested the congressional committees examine these checks and that state highway commissioners be allowed to make many of the decisions instead of complying with regulations that "impede" highway programs. On the other hand, the AASHO proposal stated that "The public's wishes must be cranked into any policy or formula in determining transportation programs and systems."

AASHO even had the audacity to proclaim, "We have now reached the point in the highway program evolution where there is public support for the expenditure of funds to enhance esthetics and to provide for safer highways. Because of the grossly inadequate budgets of the past, and the fierce competition for the highway dollar to furnish more miles of roads, we have not had such public support in the past." Yet it was the billboard and junkyard lobbies along with AASHO, ARBA, and AGC that had squawked the loudest and were most responsible for gutting the Beautification Act. The public supported the measure and wanted it paid for with Highway Trust funds as a legitimate expense of the consequences of highway construction.

Then the AASHO statement turned from the ridiculous to the impossible. After agreeing that it was important and vital to coordinate programs in urban areas and require comprehensive planning, AASHO threatened that ". . . if . . . penalties continue and more complications are introduced, it might cause a reappraisal of the desirability of federal aid in our highway programs, especially in some of our larger states," whereupon the state highway departments threatened to pull away from a 90-percent federally financed program if they were not freed from the harassment of regulations that protect the public's interests.

Finally, the proposal called for "an increase in highway facilities and service in urban areas by adding an urban system that could be termed arterial or thoroughfare system to be selected co-operatively by the states and the urban areas involved and would include urban extensions of state highway and federal-aid system routes," preferably, with at least a two-thirds federal matching ratio. It was little noted at the time, but when AASHO representatives met with the congressional roads subcommittees, after presenting their statements, the state highway officials and congressmen, all public figures, went into executive session, excluding the public from public business.

The overseeing agency for all highway projects financed with federal money is, of course, the Bureau of Public Roads. It works in tandem with those states wishing, but not forced, to participate in federal highway programs. BPR was headed by Francis Turner in 1968 when it was under the aegis of Federal Highway Administrator Lowell Bridwell, a former Washington-based correspondent, specializing in highway interests for Ohio newspapers. The Highway Administrator is directly responsible to the Secretary of Transportation, now former Governor Volpe. The Bureau's Washington offices employ approximately 1800 people and there are 3660 in the field. There are eleven regional offices throughout the United States, each with its own regional administrator, plus a division office in each state capital with several division engineers, so that theoretically federal officials in Washington can keep in touch with grass-roots developments in the nation's highway program and confer with state highway officials.

Yet in 1966, Turner, then BPR chief engineer, explained, "We have delegated to our field officials and division engineers in each of the states almost complete authority to handle our program and to handle all of the details in administration of the job. We could not do it any other way. We have, at any given time, some 20,000 projects in some stage of activity. We have a total engineering force of about 1800 people, including both field and Washington offices, and we could not begin to cope with the number of projects and the diversity of problems that come to us today if we didn't decentralize the decision-making process to the lowest level of the organization as possible. This is done by giving it to our division engineer. He is, of course, supervised by a regional engineer who is attempting to develop consistency of application and interpretation in his particular region."

Turner emphasized that local field BPR people are more familiar with local problems and therefore able to make faster decisions on projects than if all were sent into the Washington Bureau to await a decision. But a few did get to Washington, such as the North Expressway in San Antonio, the Inner Loop through Boston and Cambridge, and the plan to smash through the heart of the District of Columbia.

"The Bureau is an administrating agency charged with carrying out what Congress enacts in the way of law. Whether we agree with it personally or not we have to administer it exactly as Congress wrote it," Turner has commented.

Actually, however, there is no such agency as the Bureau of Public Roads. Instead, there are fifty autonomous state highway departments. For instance, when Minnesota Congressman John Blatnik's watchdog subcommittee discovered that highway officials were building deathtraps and driving hazards into the nation's Interstate Highway System, the lead witness at the hearings explained that the Bureau had published information informing highway officials of the dangers and showing them the correct methods to use, but that local officials had ignored them. When asked why federal funds were not denied to states not complying with the standards, one Bureau official explained that federal officials preferred to let state highway officials correct their own errors. He cited rules and standards adopted by AASHO, to which every highway department belongs, as the guidelines the Bureau preferred to follow in policing states. He explained that association members adopt standards and procedures and "make their own rules." When they are not followed, the Bureau can remind state highway departments that the association made the rules and that they are violating their own rules. Those reminders are often ignored. Our federal highway program is an example of a federal program without federal controls.

As late as November 1965, almost ten years after initiation of the Interstate Highway program, the Bureau of Public Roads confirmed that highway officials in some states were shaving costs by offering less than fair market value for land needed for highways. Highway Administrator Whitton issued a directive to all states warning them that federal aid would be suspended if this practice continues. "It should be unnecessary for anyone to have to bargain with a state in order to receive an offer that represents fair market value or be forced to institute legal action to be fairly compensated."

A BPR spokesman said that new rules had been set up to inform people of their rights in an attempt to "bring more compassion" into the road-building program.

The Bureau's approach has been to place control of the highway program in the hands of the states, including control of outdoor advertising and junkyard landscaping, and scenic easement as well as construction. In this manner, the "state-federal partnership" is assured. Parenthetically, this assures that federal controls will be loosely administered because of the states' muscle, which they exercise through their congressional representatives. For instance, the General Accounting Office, which checks federal expenditures, for years complained that state highway departments were hiring an excessive number of outside consulting engineers for projects when Congress clearly approved the long-range highway program with the proviso that states would staff their departments to do their own design work. New York State's Department of Public Works answer to this charge was typical. A spokesman said that the highway building program could not have been achieved without outside consultants, that sufficient engineers could not have been added to the staff to meet the increased work load. In other words, they simply did not answer the criticisms, and nothing could be done about it until 1966 when the Congress passed highway legislation that provided state highway departments with full authority to avail themselves of the use of private engineering firms. That stopped GAO complaints about the excessive numbers of engineers.

State highway departments handle criticism from within the state
just as cavalierly. For instance, New York State's Public Works District ⚹10 around New York City was audited by the state comptroller
for the period 1961–63 and involved $276.6 million, almost all of
which was highway construction. His report is replete with examples
of sloppy bookkeeping, including "guestimates" of out-of-pocket consultant expenses, questionable pricing of materials and estimates by
the state, and publication of the state's estimated cost of a job before
bidding, a practice the federal government rarely follows. This last
item tells the contractor how much the state is willing to pay for a
job, allowing him to bid just under the state's price whether the
amount is justified or not.

The report found scant evidence of competitive bidding among
contractors, excessive use of outside engineers, and noncompetitive
selection of engineering consultants. The department had not even
made a study to determine whether or not it was more expensive
to use outside consultants.

The report also stated that AASHO recommendations for testing
tolerances was ignored, resulting in both shortages and excessive
concrete and asphalt pourings, some in excess of $10,000. All of
this occurred while J. Burch McMorran was the head of New York
State's Public Works Department.

The Department of Public Works responded to these criticisms
by issuing a manual in March 1964, outlining a uniform method
of record-keeping to be used in all districts thereafter, and in May
1964, began a program of indoctrinating supervising engineers in the
state's procedures and specifications as well as periodic inspection
of bookkeeping methods and records. The department also initiated
a review of its policy of publishing cost estimates prior to awarding
a contract. As for the excessive number of consultants for planning
and designing highways, the department answered that sufficient
engineers could not have been added to the staff to meet the increased
work load that resulted from the stepped-up highway program (which
began with the New York Thruway back in 1950!).

As for sloppy testing practices and controls, shortages and instances
where no inspection was performed, the department stated that for

the most part such criticisms dealt with minor matters and the deviations had no ill effect on the end product.

Within the halls of the state capitol and among state legislators, the game is played slightly differently. In Sacramento, California, for instance, Senate Transportation Committee Chairman Randolph Collier, a Democrat of Yreka and supporter of freeways, swung into action when two assemblymen introduced separate bills that would have provided extra transportation money from a sales tax on gasoline and automobiles. Under the proposed law, the money collected would have been handed back to the governmental body collecting it to be spent on rapid transit, roads, or transportation associated projects.

Collier contacted two auto club lobbyists who literally followed one legislator as he circled the capital to round up votes for his bill. The legislators garnered enough to pass the bills. It was a useless gesture, however, as Collier's committee wiped out the bills before they got to the floor for a vote.

Such legislative proposals that would create new gasoline tax revenues for alternate transportation systems are branded by the freeway lobby as "raids on the Highway Trust Fund."

The California State Highway Department itself and its divisions are no less active in drowning out proposals that threaten freeway construction. Few public officials pursue their professions with the zeal of the highway division engineers. Although Los Angeles traffic jams and smog provide them with the proof of their horrible pudding, they continue to promote more concrete for the county. Robert D. Zaniboni, highway administrative officer of District Seven, wrote in a division highway publication, *How Los Angeles Was Unified by Freeways,* "The challenge to men and machines to move mountains is here. We have a vast area for construction; we have the money and what's planned for the area mostly lies ahead. We've only scratched the surface. . . . Population means money. We're doing things in a big way, money-wise. Look at the construction schedule. Every couple of weeks, it seems, we let a contract for $6 million, $7 million, $5 million. Here's one for

$14 million. That takes a lot of engineering of varied kinds. It's the big time!"

When bills are introduced that threaten to curtail highway construction, the California Highway Division lets loose an armada of lawyers from the Legal Division of the Department of Public Works, whose function is to lobby in the interests of the highway division before individual legislators and committees.

Furthermore, the broad political base of the administrative branch of the state government reaches back to the county level, making it possible for division engineers and other public works officials to bring significant pressure to bear on a legislator in his home district. Division engineers are well aware that their salaries are paid for by gas taxes and aware also that revenue derived from gasoline but used for nonhighway purposes threatens the sinecures of division personnel. District engineers play a dominant role in setting local priorities and the Division of Highways dominates the Highway Commission in Sacramento, which has no staff to evaluate recommendations the division submits.

Two of California's busiest lobbyists are the representatives of the California Trucking Associates and the representative for Gulf Oil, Atlantic-Richfield, Humble Oil, Mobil Oil, Phillips Petroleum, Shell Oil, Standard Oil of California, Union Oil, E. I. duPont de Nemours, and Ethyl Corporation.

The truckers representative is kept busy because freeways, especially in California and other Western states, carry a great deal of freight. The now retired district highway engineer for the Los Angeles region wrote to the Assembly Transportation and Commerce Committee that the freeways of 1980 will carry six times the ton-miles of freight as did those of 1960. ". . . there will be approximately five times as many lane miles of freeway available to carry the load," he explained. "It would appear from this that the freeway system, if constructed, will adequately provide for the freight movement which it might be called upon to handle."

The truckers can mobilize their 2000 members where it really counts, in a legislator's home district. "Our guys locally get together and decide whether to back a certain legislator," their lobbyists explained. "Sometimes it can be pretty important to him."

On highway legislation, the Teamsters Union generally falls in with its usual adversary, the Truckers.

Collier, as chairman of the California Senate Transportation Committee, can promote or kill all transportation bills. This is an example of how he operates: Thomas Rees, a senator for Los Angeles County, introduced a bill to collect taxes on autos in that county for planning and building a rapid transit system. He notified Collier in advance that a planeload of southern California transit supporters would be in Sacramento on the public hearing date to testify for the measure. When they arrived, Collier busied himself and the committee members with other bills and refused to bring up the Rees bill for consideration. The frustrated transit supporters returned to Los Angeles. The next day, the hearing room was packed with auto-club members opposed to the Rees bill. Collier called the bill for hearing and, in light of what he called "overwhelming opposition," kept it in committee.

In 1967, Collier tangled head-on with an assemblyman from Long Beach who introduced a bill to relieve hard-pressed urban transit lines by reducing the tax on diesel fuel burned in urban buses. When it sailed through the Assembly, the highway interests got nervous because it threatened to reduce highway revenue, even if only slightly, and represented what could become a greater demand to reduce highway revenues.

The assemblyman confronted the Senate. He had done his homework, securing the names of eleven of Collier's thirteen-member committee as co-authors. Undaunted, Collier gaveled the bill to death by decreeing at the public hearing that the bill constituted diversion of gas-tax money and would have to be sent to interim study. The assemblyman protested that fifteen or twenty witnesses had made the trip to Sacramento from southern California to testify. Collier offered them a total of five minutes to testify, so the assemblyman asked that the bill be put over to another date, which Collier refused. Finally, he attached it to one of Collier's own pet bills, and passed it out again. But Collier chose to sacrifice his own measure rather than see the bill pass with the attached legislation.

Collier enjoys financial contributions to his political campaigns from representatives of the Associated General Contractors of America, California Portland Cement Company, Monolith Portland Cement of Los Angeles, Southwestern Portland Cement Corporation of Los Angeles, and the American Portland Cement Corporation of Los Angeles, the Motor Car Dealers' Associations of Northern and Southern California, and the Trailer Coach Association, among others.

So popular is the highway program in the Congress that both state and federal highway officials have been able to ignore public criticism by holding the required number of public hearings and simply shelving citizen comments. Most states that had laws restricting the width and other features of highways simply went to their legislative bodies and got enabling legislation removing the restrictions after the 1956 honeypot of 90–10 federal funds became available. State highway departments were vested with enormous power to exercise over land use. And it is not difficult to understand that the District of Columbia's highway program emanates from a congressional ukase, since the Congress is the city's local government. Failure to get the program completed in D.C. might spell halts in other cities.

The same process of ignoring the public criticism of the program has been practiced in every state. BPR regional representatives have concurred with state officials on decisions despite their unpopularity with the public they are supposed to serve. The history of the Grubb-Harvey Interchange in a suburban community outside Wilmington, Delaware, demonstrates again how the engineers brush aside citizen complaints.

In 1957, the Delaware State Highway Department held public hearings limited to the alignment only of proposed I-95 from Farnhurst, Delaware, to the Pennsylvania state line. In 1959, the BPR conditionally approved that portion of I-95, including an interchange at Harvey Road. Final approval of the project was granted in 1962. Public hearings were held in 1964 on the entire project at which time residents of the area complained that the Harvey Road Interchange was unnecessary and detrimental to the community. Residents of the area formed the Grubb-Harvey Interchange Committee.

They argued that no interchange was needed at Harvey Road, a high-crowned, old-fashioned, tree-lined rural road about 25 feet wide. The highway department wanted to widen it to a four-lane high-speed road with a 60-foot right-of-way. The GHIC argued that Harvey Road should be a well-designed, 30-foot-wide road. They argued that the highway department did not study the impact of the interchange on surrounding communities and that there were other I-95 interchanges available, less than three and one-half miles apart, one at Naamans Road, one and one-quarter miles north of the proposed Harvey Road Interchange, another two miles south at Marsh Road, plus another interchange at I-495 near Naamans. Most of all, the committee complained that the highway facility would attract heavy auto and truck traffic into their quiet suburban community and destroy the atmosphere, forcing people to move farther away from the city, thus creating a need for even more roads farther out.

GHIC pointed out that the public hearings of 1957 did not consider the total environment of the neighborhood except the cost of acquiring the land and drainage. Original plans for the interchange called for a full cloverleaf, but officials admitted it was reduced to half because of the short stretch between Grubb-Harvey Road and the next interchange, Naamans Road, which could cause traffic-weaving problems.

Citizens met with the Highway Commission and state engineers to request that the interchange be de-mapped and preparations for bidding on construction contracts be terminated. When no guarantee was forthcoming, residents argued before the Highway Commission in Dover, the state capital, at which time the State Highway Department promised to carry out a formal study of the effects on community life of increased traffic on the proposed access road.

By October 1965, the State Highway Department let preliminary grading contracts for the proposed interchange. GHIC hired a lawyer and brought suit against Delaware highway officials, charging that the Highway Department had acted in a manner arbitrary, capricious, and unreasonable, and that the department had failed to hold public hearings prior to the decision to design and build the interchange. The Highway Department argued that 3236 vehicle trips would have been made on the interchange if it had been in existence in 1964 and would have saved money for Delaware motorists. Worse still, construction had begun on the interchange before the residents took their case to court and therefore public funds had already been spent on the project to the tune of $191,107.07.

As for the public hearings, the Highway Department argued that under section 173 of title 17 of the Delaware Code, the Highway Department was empowered to "plan, designate, establish . . . maintain and provide controlled access facilities . . . whenever the department is of the opinion that traffic conditions, present or future, will justify such special facilities," and that the department was vested with the broadest kind of administrative discretion regarding the location of highways, and that the courts were not to interfere with the exercise of that discretion unless a plain and palpable abuse thereof had been clearly demonstrated. A Wilmington lawyer and counsel for the Highway Department, when asked to predict the residents' chances in court, replied by holding up his hand, forming a zero with his thumb and forefinger. He explained that the Highway Department had been through the freeway battle before—all the way up to the State Supreme Court—and won. He represented the Highway Department in this case. He claimed that the Highway Department had spent nine years planning and evaluating the project in conjunction with the BPR and that public comments had been evaluated as well as the economic, safety, and esthetic aspects of the project and the interests of the traveling public.

Frank Akutowicz, a founder of the GHIC, said, "Not so. The regional offices of the Bureau of Public Roads have tapes of the public hearings on the various sections of the Interstate System.

Nobody had ever listened to the ones on our section of I-95. The Bureau didn't even have a machine to listen to them."

The residents lost when the Court ruled that they had delayed too long in exercising their rights since they were aware of the construction plan in 1964 but did not bring the action to court until 1968, a year after construction had begun on the project.

The residents argued in vain that they did not know or comprehend the total impact the project would have on the community until the summer of 1965, after which they had worked diligently to muster support for the lawsuit. By then, construction was underway.

Yet Lowell K. Bridwell, then Federal Highway Administrator, in testimony before Senator Randolph's subcommittee on roads in May 1968, reassured the congressmen that "many transportation planning programs have established 'citizens advisory committees' which provide an effective communication linkage between the technical staff of the planning process and representatives of local business, civic, and citizen groups. These committees provide for continuous communication between the planning staff and the representative citizenry during the course of the planning work. Thus, the local community is encouraged to contribute to and participate in the planning process from its very inception and maintain its relationship with the continuing planning process." Less than three weeks later, the House roads subcommittee tacked onto the 1968 Federal Highway Act a tyrannical provision that the freeway system in the District of Columbia be completed *regardless* of any court order or existing law, or the fact that District citizenry indicated by 19 to 1 in the primary held that May that they did not want freeways.

To date, the Bureau deludes itself that state highway departments are listening to residents' complaints and actually considering citizens' suggestions concerning freeways. For one thing, Turner's words of 1966 are not idly chosen; the Bureau's function has been to implement congressional intent. Then too, state officials, from governors on down, have dictated that highways be built. In fact, land for highways is a "given" in any study of highway need and planning.

The idea of alternatives or cancellation of the proposed highway construction projects takes on the connotations of denying the Almighty. Highway officials reassure congressmen and state legislators that community participation is being encouraged in carrying out the program, while community representatives storm the barricades of public hearings in protest.

To offset some of this criticism, highway officials have okayed the design concept. Bridwell had this to say of the so-called design concept team, the multidiscipline effort to design Baltimore's expressway: "The design of a highway is an engineering task. . . . The planning and location of a highway facility involves many considerations other than engineering. . . . The team represents engineers, architects, sociologists, urban planners, economists and others. It is charged with examining the highway corridor, and location and design alternatives within it, in the framework of overall community goals and plans. On the basis of its analysis, the team will recommend to the city and the state a program for the development of highways and other community improvements to achieve identifiable opportunities in the broadest range of community values."

The Maryland State Highway Department and the Federal Highway Administration allocated $4.8 million to the design concept team to find out what the Baltimore community already had made clear—that they didn't want the highways. The concept team is supposed to explore the city's entire transportation system, the area through which the highway corridor will pass, to determine the qualities, quantities, and values of its social, economic, structural, historical, and open-space characteristics. Commenting upon this aspect of the team effort, Bridwell said, "This team is spending much of its time talking with and listening to groups and individuals in the corridor, that is, stimulating public participation in the project." But as the highway officials well know, "public participation" is not stimulated nor is it desired, but rather, in the past, opinions have been recorded and ignored. The process is really designed to wear down citizen opposition through sheer exhaustion.

Another section of the team is exploring possibilities of multiple city-busting expressway system, they may convince the Baltimore housing, and school needs. With a little frosting spread on the use of space above, below, and along highways for industrial, populace that it is eating cake rather than tasting gall.

Bridwell went on, "It is and it will continue to be our policy to assist the city to the maximum extent possible provided the city acts to assist itself. . . . In Nashville, Tennessee, a segment of I-40 was routed, early in the 1960s, through a predominantly Negro area adjacent to the university complex containing Fisk University and Meharry Medical College. Land was acquired and cleared for the expressway. Not until last year, apparently, did community leadership coalesce sufficiently to articulate objections to both the route and the planned design of the expressway." Those articulated objections he referred to have been raised since 1957 by Nashville residents, who, when repeatedly ignored, finally brought a lawsuit, charging racial discrimination in locating I-40.

The Nashville I-40 case began in 1956 when a firm of consulting engineers was retained to design a section of the Interstate System from the outskirts of Nashville to a proposed inner loop which was to encircle the business district and the state capitol (designed to dump traffic not at city hall, but, rather, the state house). As designed, no significant residential or commercial displacement would occur, although a small number of white-owned retail stores which served the black community would be taken.

The consultants submitted, along with their proposal, a comprehensive report containing engineering and traffic data, plus facts concerning the impact of the proposed route on neighborhood patterns and structures and the economy of the area traversed by the route. A public hearing was scheduled for May 1957, at which time a completely different route was proposed for the disputed section of I-40. This new route crossed a residential neighborhood to a street containing 80 percent of all black-owned business in the county, turned to take the rear of all the properties along that street, to a point where it formed an interchange with the inner loop. The combined effect of the new highway plus widening of the business street, which would ultimately accompany it, would

be to eliminate all businesses on one side of the street. Here is
the difference in effect between the two routes:

	Original Route	Current Route
Homes affected by right-of-way	320	626
Businesses affected by right-of-way	45	128
Apartment houses affected by right-of-way	8	27
Churches affected by right-of-way	2	6
Schools affected by right-of-way	1	3

The Tennessee State Highway Department claims it held public
hearings on the current route in May 1957. Although no notices
of the hearing appeared in the local newspapers, the highway
department did post notices of the hearing on the "wanted" bulletin
boards of eight branch post offices, none of which were in the
community through which the road would pass. The notice said
the hearing would be held on May 14, 1957. The hearing was
held May 15, 1957. The transcript of the hearing contained no
specific reference to I-40 and consisted of several vague general
statements by public officials about the blessings of limited access
highways followed by a series of replies to questions which were
not included in the transcript. The current route for I-40 received
approval from local, state, and federal agencies late in 1957.
Local residents and businessmen were not notified of the approval.

Meetings were held in the community from time to time to discuss
the route as descriptions began appearing in the newspapers.

At each meeting, objections to the road were raised by local
people. The inevitable response to these objections was the claim
that the routing for I-40 had not been finalized and that all factors
were being considered. Not only black residents, but two black
members of the Metro Government Council were unable to obtain
information about the status of plans or the specific area which
the road would affect.

It was during the three-day court proceedings on the citizens'
lawsuit in 1967 that the original report by the consultants and

the originally proposed route were discovered in the files of the Metropolitan Planning Commission. A review of the minutes of the federal, state, local, and consultant liaison committee meetings following the 1956 submission failed to reveal any mention of the change from the earlier proposal to the present one, although minutes of one meeting in 1956 described the approval by the group of the earlier plan. When the Tennessee Highway Commissioner was questioned in court, he denied ever seeing or hearing of the earlier plan. When confronted with the minutes of the meeting in 1956, which described his participation in the approval of the earlier plan, he conceded that if the minutes indicated his presence, he was probably there, but he denied any recollection of the meeting or the plan.

Judge Gray in District Court in Nashville, Tennessee, concluded that the plaintiffs had failed to prove that the destructive, disruptive, and discriminatory effects of the plan were intentional. As for the public hearings, he concluded that since the hearing was a requirement of the BPR, it was a matter between the federal agency and the state highway department, and that if the federal agency chose to fund highway construction in the absence of this requirement, it was of no concern to the court.

A higher court upheld the lower court decision on the grounds that in spite of the devastating effects of a demonstrably poor plan, too much time and money had been spent to alter the proposal. The Supreme Court refused to hear the case.

Subsequently, the I-40 Steering Committee attended a meeting of Tennessee State Highway officials, Metro Government officials, including Nashville Mayor Beverly Briley, fresh from his job as county judge and highway booster, and federal highway officials, including Lowell Bridwell. Bridwell states that the original route would have interfered with the operation of Baptist Hospital (at that time all white), would have had adverse effects for Centennial Park (which was operating on a racially restricted basis), would have dislocated some business and industrial establishments (virtually all white), and would have caused some residential relocation, most of which would be white.

Turner and Bridwell concurred that "to relocate the route, for which the right-of-way already had been acquired, would cause additional, unwarranted dislocation within the area—and without eliminating that disruption which already had taken place."

The Bureau did, however, attempt to mollify the I-40 Steering Committee by ordering the State Highway Department to redesign the highway "to protect the community and help it in its 'Model Cities' redevelopment" by developing air-rights space in the Fisk University area, avoid property of some businessmen, and provide an underpass at one location to open up access not presently available to certain residents of the area as well as some pedestrian underpasses.

Dr. Flournoy Coles, professor of economics at Fisk University and chairman of the I-40 Steering Committee, says, "There's a pervasive feeling that the people downtown, the leaders of the economic and political power structure, not only don't care but have gone out of their way to bait us." He believes Mayor Briley is secretly laughing at blacks for accepting the promises he made to gain their votes. Briley piously explains, "When I talked to the state highway boys, I wasn't so sure the road should go where they said. But I got the idea that they weren't going to voluntarily change this—they were too committed. And I have no authority to tell them what to do." And, despite statutory regulations contained in the 1956 Highway Act which call for public hearings and BPR assurances that state highway departments weigh public responses to proposed highway plans, the case of I-40 joined the long list of examples of meaningless public hearings.

Bridwell concluded his testimony before Senator Randolph with these reassuring words: "I hope my testimony has made clear to the committee our deep concern with both the environmental and operational aspects of the program we administer. These are real, practical concerns to us." So much so that he established an Environmental Development Division in BPR's Office of Right-of-Way and Location. To head it up, he selected Harold King, an employee of the Bureau for eleven years and division engineer for Connecticut since 1966. Before that, King was with the New

York State Department of Public Works, working on bridges and
road design in the Albany area.

Mr. King explains his job this way. "As Connecticut division
engineer, I tried to incorporate human aspects into highways such
as the beautification program, improved design concepts in the
Interstate System such as joint development and alignment inde-
pendence that would employ maximum use of land in highway
corridors in cities." King sees his job as twofold. First, to improve
the total environment of the area any new highway goes through,
mainly by encouraging state highway departments to purchase
additional land for adjacent parks and housing or commercial
interests, and, secondly, to put to work all the land over, under,
and beside sections under construction. This means employing air
rights. He said that in Connecticut, the State Highway Department
was reserving land within the right-of-way for mass transit. He
also wants to promote the return of land to the tax roll by employing "cut and cover." In this manner, highways in cities
could be cut deep into the ground and covered over for other uses.

As an example of joint-use-joint-development, he cited a project
in Omaha, Nebraska, which involved an elevated multilane expressway. King said highway officials would attempt to utilize the land
over, under, and beside the expressway. He suggested that parking
lots could flank each side of the highway, and car dealer show-
rooms and offices could be built underneath. He hypothesized
that the local city government might wish to put a police or fire
department near such a facility or choose any alternative that meets
BPR standards. "We do think our image, the highway industry
as a whole, can be improved by bringing the human values—
establishing human values—to the factors that are unqualifiable—
that is, social, as well as economic factors of the highway," he
stated.

Despite King's talk about human values, there exists among
BPR employees an atmosphere of bewilderment and anger over
public criticism of the roads program. In cities where highway
engineers have taken a roasting in the past few years, BPR engineers repeatedly claim that they are the whipping boys because of

urban unrest, which they feel they have been blamed for unjustly. For those who believe that freeway construction exacerbates unrest and adds to the pickle our cities are in, they have an explanation that is very popular within the BPR. They cite experiments which show that when rats are raised in a crowded environment, they become neurotic. Bureau officials have stated this is exactly why we are experiencing urban unrest and that we need more roads out into the countryside to disperse the population. They state that the high density of our cities is causing "urban problems." This notion is popular on Capitol Hill, too, particularly among highway promoters, who have written off the city as a salvageable place to live and are thinking in terms of population growth funneled to "new towns." They earnestly believe this to be the wave of the future. They stubbornly cling to the notion that imposition of a gigantic highway system on an established city can only benefit that city.

Bureau officials and congressmen will not admit that people who are challenging freeway construction have an intelligent point of view to get across—that highways can do more harm than good. Sammie Abbott, Washington's most vocal freeway critic, is summarily dismissed at the Bureau as a fanatic. As for the flight into fancy over our crowded cities, they should do their homework. They would find that most European cities are much more densely populated than ours. In fact, the densest cities we have are along the Atlantic seaboard between Boston and Washington. The 150 counties that make up this Atlantic urban area contain 67,690 square miles and 43 million people. If this area were developed to the density of the western Netherlands, the number of people would be tripled. Perhaps it is just that our urban land looks more filled up than European cities. Filled up with the clutter of automobiles, gas stations, and billboards. European cities may some day match us on this score, but we certainly got a good head start on them.

The skeptic who challenges the validity of the highway program or asks if this is what communities really want, a total environmental shift to accommodate automobiles, is met with a barrage of statistics and tons of research reports. Most of them purport to prove that highways are essential to our health, economy, safety, and national defense, despite the evidence to the contrary. Great tomes on the benefits of highways have been produced by universities across the country as well as research and engineering firms that have flourished since enactment of the 1956 Highway Act.

The federal government supplies millions of dollars for this sort of "research" each year. It does so by allocating 1½ percent of the annual Trust Fund billions to research and planning. Another big chunk comes from the trucking and auto industry, asphalt and cement interests bent on forcing the public to perpetuate a market for their products. The states also fund research from their own separate funds. Before 1964, any of the 1½ percent federal funds not spent on research and planning automatically reverted to construction funds, which the states could use.

Between 1958 and 1963, $342 million in federal money was spent researching and planning. The lion's share, roughly two thirds, went for what the BPR considers planning. By 1962, highway laws declared that it was in the national interest to encourage and promote all forms of transportation systems, not just highways, in a manner "that will serve the states and local communities efficiently and effectively," and that after July 1965, no federal highway project would be approved by the federal government in any urban area unless the project was based upon a continuing comprehensive transportation planning process carried on co-operatively by state and local communities. This portion of the Highway Act was designed to get highway officials to consider factors other than merely the construction of roads in urban areas and to encourage other forms of transportation, particularly public transportation.

But the wording of the law was not specific enough, and in 1963 the Congress specified that federal research and planning money should be used for development as well as research and could not revert to construction if not spent. The federal kitty for research and planning has grown to a total of $876 million, with the same heavy emphasis on planning. By 1968, 20 percent of the funds went into research while 80 percent supported planning. Yet we still see the Road Gang building freeways in a way that shows how oblivious they are to effects on neighborhoods, on people. We see poor research on the need for more highways and the effects proposed subway systems will have on providing the public with transportation.

The vagueness of the wording of the laws lingers on. Planning can mean almost anything. According to the BPR, the following activities are considered planning: administration and control of highways, road inventory, mapping, volume counts, vehicle classification, truck weighing, other and specific traffic studies, highway statistics, speed and traffic service studies. And so, the planning money plans—more highways. After all, it is the only form of ground transportation for which there is money set aside in the form of a trust fund. Certainly highway departments would not study and promote rapid transit, rapid rail, or monorail systems, for that is not their job. Their job is to build highways. The federal government has spent twice as much money on such research and "planning" as it has on all aspects of mass transportation.

The stacks of the Bureau of Public Roads library groan under the weight of highway research reports, most of which are sponsored by federal-state grants. One such AASHO-BPR financed study was reported in the spring of 1968. The research, gathered by Chilton Research Services and National Analysts, Incorporated, was devoted to determining "whether or not existing procedures for allocation of resources for highways are responsive to public attitudes and to determine the relationship among attitudes and behavior of the public relating to transportation of people." In other words, whether people objected to spending a vast amount of money on highways, and why or why not.

The researchers concluded that the automobile is the most significant mode of transportation for the American family. By "significant" they meant that motoring "is a way of life, an extremely important part of the social and cultural environment and of everyday life. It is the most frequently used form of transportation, is most important in work, social and community affairs, and will become increasingly more important. . . . Attitudes toward highway planning were generally positive, but not as clear-cut . . . there was a marked separation of attitudes toward roads and highways and attitudes toward the auto—these are two completely different dimensions in the individual's attitudinal set." On the other hand, Chilton found that persons clearly identified public transportation as a mode of transportation and a public facility. They attributed this difference to the fact that a person considers his automobile to be a personal possession and the highways as public facilities.

This was borne out in their research, which they claim showed that the public is overwhelmingly for more automobile travel and highways. This could well be true because the respondents were not asked to think in terms of the effect highways have on the land they traverse. They were asked only about the automobile and its immediate needs.

Chilton did ask persons to evaluate statements ranging from "The automobile is the best form of transportation invented by man" to "The automobile is the worst form of transportation invented by man." Regionally, the East clearly expressed the least favorable attitude in evaluating the social role of the automobile and agreed most that the automobile is not worth the disadvantages of being a deadly weapon, injurious to health, and a bad system of transportation.

Easterners and Southerners agreed strongly that highways in urban areas are ugly. Attitudes toward highways were more favorable in the North Central and Western regions.

Chilton also found that persons living in large Eastern metropolitan areas most favored pumping money into public transportation and that these residents were more likely to be critical of highway planning and the auto's role in our society. But, overall, most respondents favored both improved public and private transportation and agreed that highway planners were doing a good job. With this "data," the highway officials declared that the automobile continued to be the favored choice for transportation. They did not crow about some sections of the study. For instance, Question

28 stated, "The auto pollutes air, creates traffic, demolishes property, and kills people. Is the contribution the auto makes to our way of life worth this?" Respondents answered 85 percent yes, 15 percent no to the question. When asked why the automobile was worth all of this, almost 50 percent answered that it was because it was *the only form of transportation available.*

6. Congress—Protectors of the Public Trust

"Government is a trust, and the officers of the government are trustees; and both the trust and the trustees are created for the benefit of the people."

—Henry Clay, 1829

The trustees of the federal highway program are the congressional subcommittees that oversee funding and progress of the program. There are three such subcommittees.

One is Congressman Blatnik's "watchdog" subcommittee, an offshoot of the House Public Works Committee. It was established in 1959 to monitor the federal highway program. Chairman Blatnik has undertaken in-depth investigations of the program that have revealed wrongdoing, corruption, ineptness, and laxity.

The first such investigation was undertaken in 1960 to determine whether the highway program, touted as a crucial defense measure, was contributing to our national defense. The investigation revealed that although the Army, Air Force, Corps of Engineers, and Navy all had weapons or other essential items that exceeded 14 feet in height when loaded on transporters, the vertical minimum clearance was set at 14 feet for the Interstate System. The Department of Defense had not even been consulted.

The same investigation revealed that as early as 1954, the size of the Atlas missile, which exceeds the 14-foot minimum, was well established and the difficulties of transporting the weapon from California to Cape Kennedy were known in 1956 when the Interstate System was launched. Yet neither highway nor defense officials bothered to learn what these difficulties were.

It was not until four years after passage of the 1956 Highway Act that a standard was worked out with the military establishing a vertical clearance of 16 feet. During those four years, more than 2200 bridges or structures had been built to the obsolete standard. The subcommittee concluded that liaison between the Department of Defense and the Bureau of Public Roads had been inadequate. But this inadequacy actually suggested that there was little real concern either within or without the halls of the Congress for the defense role the highway system would play, since labeling the system vital to our defense was simply a "sweetening" device to gain support for the program back in 1956.

Subsequent investigations conducted by the special committee through 1966 uncovered graft, collusion, conflicts of interest, nepotism, or fraud in Florida, West Virginia, Oklahoma, Arizona, and Louisiana. Investigations into land acquisition and other practices in Massachusetts resulted in indictments of nearly a score of persons. In fact, shortcomings were found in right-of-way acquisition practices in twenty states. By 1966, the Interstate System was 44 percent completed, 19,000 miles were open to traffic, and the cost of the project had mushroomed from the original estimate of $27 billion to $46.8 billion.

Illegal practices spilled over into the petroleum industry, too. Late in November 1965, some members of that industry were exposed for participating in some hanky-panky in the highway program when eighteen petroleum products manufacturers and seventeen individuals were fined a total of $2 million by a United States District Court for conspiring to fix the price of road oil (used in asphalt) sold to the state of Missouri. They included American Oil of Chicago; Phillips Petroleum, Oklahoma; Socony Mobil Oil, New York; Skelly Oil, Oklahoma; Shell Oil, New York; Sinclair Refining, New York; Kerr-McGee Oil, Oklahoma; American

Petrofina, Texas; Union Asphalt and Road Oils, Missouri; Apco Oil, Oklahoma; Delta Refining, Texas; Missouri Petroleum Products, Missouri; Rock Hill Asphalt and Construction, Missouri; Allied Materials Corporation, Oklahoma; Sanders Petroleum, Missouri; Trinidad Asphalt Manufacturing Co., Missouri; Wilshire Oil, New York; and Hydrocarbons Specialties, Inc., Missouri.

In September 1966, Socony, Mobil, Skelly, American Petrofina, Union Asphalt and Road, American, Phillips Petroleum, Apco, and Wilshire Oil companies were again indicted along with Colorado Oil and Gas of Colorado and Consumer Cooperative, Kansas City, Missouri, for price fixing $12 million worth of liquid asphalt sold to the state of Kansas between 1959 and 1965. All but Wilshire pleaded no contest.

Then, in the second week in June of 1967, the federal government announced it had not planned any harsh penalties against states that failed to meet the 1969 deadline for compliance with new highway safety standards (10 percent cut in federal aid for states failing to enforce and create an effective safety program by December 31, 1968, including highway construction, design, and maintenance). That same week, Joseph Linko appeared before Congressman Blatnik's special roads subcommittee.

Joe Linko had spent four years trying to get New York highway officials to listen to him as he explained and showed pictures of highway hazards on expressways in his native New York City. Finally, he appealed to the subcommittee. For several days Linko appeared before the subcommittee and explained with the aid of colored slides how huge signs, too close to the roadway, were supported by massive concrete and steel structures which demolish an auto and its passengers when hit; badly placed light poles, many mounted on formidable concrete bases; guard rails that guide a skidding driver into abutments, instead of helping him slide around such obstacles; aluminum guard rails that snap like toothpicks when hit; trees planted too close to the roadway with guard rails running behind them (in one case a guard rail was placed in front of a group of trees and then trees were planted in front of the guard rail), and too many dangerous gore areas. Gore areas are those Y-shaped forks in expressways which often are not well lighted nor adequately equipped with directions. They can confuse the motorist, who often does not make the decision to go left or right until it is too late to avoid an accident.

Linko is a television repairman. As he described to the subcommittee members some of the conditions which were depicted in his slides, he stated several times that "This book I studied said that this was not the way to design an expressway." The book he so diligently studied was a publication of the Bureau of Public Roads on safe highway designs.

His slides included numerous pictures of automobiles that were demolished on impact with some of these state-designed-and-placed road hazards.

Congressman Blatnik issued several statements during the hearings. "It has been astonishing to learn that these hazards are as widespread as they are dangerous. They exist from coast to coast. . . . It has been shown that not only would it not have cost more to construct some of these projects safely, but in many cases they could have been built more safely for much less money. . . . Somewhere the people responsible for design have subordinated safety to other considerations. . . . Again and again we have found, for reasons that seem completely unaccountable, that the findings of research and experience are simply not being fully utilized by those who design and build our roads."

Mr. Linko estimated that he had spent $3500 of his own money over the four years gathering evidence and attempting to persuade highway officials and engineers that he indeed had a point. Representative Blatnik said of Linko that he "has compiled a report that would do credit to the most qualified traffic engineers. Indeed, he has brought to this subject matter a layman's eye view that might well be given urgent attention by our highway design, traffic and safety engineers alike."

Highway engineers scoffed.

An editorial appearing in the June 1967 issue of *Engineering*

News-Record demonstrated the spirit of contempt with which some of them received the criticism:

> Rep. John A. Blatnik (D., Minn.), chairman of the public works investigating subcommittee that has been holding hearings on the relationship between highway design and highway accidents, professed "astonishment" at the facts revealed by such expert witnesses as a TV repairman from the Bronx. It is hoped that as the hearings continue, Representative Blatnik's committee will get a broader picture of all that is known and all that is being done about highway safety.

In July 1968, one year after Blatnik's subcommittee heard Joe Linko describe hazardous highway construction practices, the subcommittee heard from additional witnesses who described examples of freeways that were improperly built and signs that failed their basic purpose of communicating information. Most examples involved the newest interstate highways.

The hearings produced evidence that it is not a lack of technological or scientific information that accounts for most deficiencies, but rather what was described as a "failure to apply what is known." Such features as undersized signs, dropped lanes, left-hand exits, and peculiar geometric configurations abounded in testimony presented, including movies of confused truck and auto drivers. In other words, not only are state and federal highway officials failing to remedy past mistakes, they continue to make new ones while a few congressmen sputter about the situation.

In addition to the "watchdog" subcommittee, the highway program falls under the aegis of the Senate Public Works Committee, chaired by Jennings Randolph. This committee also has jurisdiction over flood control and rivers and harbors; public buildings and grounds; economic development; air and water pollution, and roads.

Randolph chairs the roads subcommittee of this panel. Ironically, eight of its thirteen members belong to the subcommittee on air and water pollution. The members of the roads subcommittee in 1968 were Democrats Ernest Gruening, Alaska; B. Everett Jordan, North Carolina; Birch Bayh, Indiana; Joseph M. Montoya, New

Mexico; Stephen M. Young, Ohio; Joseph D. Tydings, Maryland; William B. Spong, Jr., Virginia; and Republicans John Sherman Cooper, Kentucky; Hiram L. Fong, Hawaii; J. Caleb Boggs, Delaware; Len B. Jordan, Idaho; and Howard H. Baker, Jr., Tennessee.

Federal highway legislation is enacted in even-numbered years. In the spring of 1968, the roads subcommittee was scheduled to formulate legislation for the 1968 Highway Act which would spell out the amount of money from the Trust Fund to be authorized for highway construction for 1970–74. But before that was considered, Senator Randolph held hearings on the development of snags in urban freeways in Nashville, Washington, D.C., New York, Baltimore, New Orleans, San Antonio, San Francisco, Philadelphia, Detroit, Chicago, and Cleveland, of which he was more than painfully aware. Senator Randolph was also aware of that General Accounting Office report on progress, or lack of progress, in mapping out I-696 in Detroit, I-494 in Chicago, I-83, I-70N, and I-95 in Baltimore, I-478 (Lower Manhattan Expressway), I-78, I-278, I-495, and I-678 in New York City, and I-280, I-80, and I-480 in San Francisco and the fact that the Bureau took the position that these segments could be deleted. All ran into citizen opposition and were still only squiggles on a map.

Was there a better solution to building the freeways in cities so that local citizens wouldn't object so much, the subcommittee wondered. Randolph invited the vice president of Urban America, William Slayton, to testify on what was wrong with the manner in which freeways were being built and why the public wasn't happy about them. He also invited representatives of the American Institute of Architects, the National Society of Professional Engineers, the American Road Builders Association, American Society of Civil Engineers, Consulting Engineers Council, and American Institute of Consulting Engineers, AASHO, and several state public officials in the transportation field.

Randolph set the tone of the hearings by announcing that the purpose of the hearings was to investigate the disputes surrounding a number of urban highway projects. To that end, he introduced for the record a statement he had made recently in the Senate pertaining to highways. In it he had stressed that urban highways are a basic element in the transportation skeleton of the city and affect the growth and development of the area. He said highway planning must take into account the social, economic, ecological, demographic, esthetic, and other factors which constitute the total environment of the city. He pointed out that the committee would hear from five categories of witnesses, among them those who have the political responsibility for decisions at the local level.

William Slayton of Urban America testified to committee members that often the urban freeway is simply routed on a map through the cheapest land available in the city. Consequently, when social and environmental costs result in rerouting and a more expensive urban highway, the additional money is considered an "extra." Slayton stressed that the highway program should include all the costs of building an urban highway, including the cost of disrupting the community, removing land from the tax base, dissecting parks and playgrounds, and removing housing.

"The old way, the single-purpose way, is not only easier, it is cheaper—millions cheaper. And those millions, we are frequently reminded, mean miles added or subtracted from the highway system. . . . The application of rigorous and realistic accounting might lead to the conclusion, in some cases, that certain urban highways were uneconomical to build and that alternatives should be explored—perhaps better utilization of existing highways, perhaps the strengthening of other modes of transportation," he said.

He reminded the subcommittee that although the 1962 Federal Highway Act called for establishment of a comprehensive transportation plan by 1965, it was no secret that the only money available for such planning was from the 1½ percent of highway funds for research and planning and that only *highway* planning, not comprehensive, systemic planning, had resulted from that provision of the 1962 Act.

"I think it was really a mistake to talk about comprehensive transportation planning which resulted in comprehensive urban highway planning and not to recognize that highways are but one element of the whole planning process. . . . We found greater difficulty in persuading the metropolitan areas to crank in more than highway planning as part of their transportation planning. We found it difficult to persuade them that they ought to take a look at mass transportation systems, rapid transit and so forth, in planning the area. These ought to be included; it ought not be just highways."

Idaho's Senator Jordan asked Slayton how mistakes of the past could be repaired and if we had to live with the mistakes of the past. Slayton replied that he thought we would begin to correct mistakes by introducing new forms of transportation and perhaps "redoing" some of the painful expressway examples of the past. He cited as examples the Embarcadero in San Francisco and Boston's inner city expressways. Yet no one discussed the plans for Boston's proposed Inner Belt which had become controversial.

Next, Robert Durham from the American Institute of Architects told roads committee members that "we have subjected America's communities to the greatest ping-pong game in history. As an architect in Seattle I have watched the public being passed back and forth between the State Highway Department and the Bureau of Public Roads, and when you go and question a certain alignment the local engineer says, 'No, that is the federal government. You ought to go see them.'

"So somebody takes a trip to Washington and it only takes so many trips from Seattle to Washington to wear a community out, not only financially, but psychologically."

Senator Randolph interrupted Durham and answered his charge by stating that the federal government has within each state people "who are able to act. There is in each state, for example, a person from the Bureau of Public Roads."

Durham responded: "Well, I have sat with the chief of the Highway Department and the governor and the representative of the Bureau of Public Roads and I have seen the ping-pong game in action on the local level, and I might suggest Seattle's history with laying a twelve-lane freeway right down across our city that took out 5000 houses and in which the local community tried to stimulate the idea that perhaps this twelve-lane section should become a great open plaza, and the ping-pong game went on until Seattle gave up. . . . It seems to us that we could improve our system so that we are able to make such a thing as a highway through the center of a city an asset and not a twelve-lane ditch as we finally ended up in our city."

Durham charged that most pitched highway battles in urban areas were due to a lack of sophistication on the part of design engineers, who were mainly interested in moving automobile traffic. He stressed that local citizens should have more influence in highway planning.

The roads subcommittee had long been aware of another point of contention between highway builders and urban residents that stemmed from the fact that every dime that accrues to the Highway Trust Fund is returned in the form of concrete only to the exclusion of other modes of transportation. No Trust Fund money has ever been available for beautification or environmental improvements, housing or parkland for recreation in the cities. Highway interests and the Congress argue that Trust Fund money is for roads only and, besides, there isn't enough for all the roads they want to build. They state that it isn't that engineers are insensitive to the other needs of the community, in the form of better housing, better schools, better recreational facilities . . . it's just that the community has been unwilling to pay for these extras. It is just as true, however, that the highway interests have been just as unwilling to release Highway Trust Fund money for them either. They have not considered that they must provide housing for people displaced by a freeway nor worried about the school district that gets cut in two by construction of a superhighway or any of the other effects wrought down on a city as a direct result of constructing a highway project.

Instead, the kind of thinking that permeates the entire highway program was best exemplified by a witness introduced by none other than Congressman Fallon before the Senate subcommittee, a friend and neighbor, Edward J. Donnelly, of the J. E. Greiner Engineering Company of Baltimore. Fallon said the company had done some outstanding engineering work and that Greiner was particularly outstanding in designing highways. Donnelly was made co-chairman of the Baltimore design concept team "which will develop not only the highways in urban areas, but must consider a wide range of urban problems, and must take into account a wide range of factors related to the urban environment," Fallon explained.

Donnelly, an engineer, began by saying that of all of the professions, none is more deeply involved or more closely identified with the urban highway program than the engineering profession.

He told them what they wanted to hear—that engineers must take into account a multitude of factors which combine to make up the total environment of the city. As examples, he cited population densities, land uses in the affected neighborhoods, socioeconomic patterns, circulation patterns of people, preservation of historical sites, and preservation of esthetic vistas. He got down to specifics and plugged for the urban design concept team. He said that the two most difficult problems that face highway builders are finding new housing for displaced families and getting the money to pay for all of the aspects of highway planning that design teams suggest. He even went so far as to state that engineers as a group had demonstrated their ability to consider all of the environmental factors when they constructed a highway. The fly in the ointment, according to him, has been the fact that in the past there was no money to pay for anything but construction on a miles-per-dollar basis. Then he added, as if this were the fault of the paying public, "Hopefully, in the face of our cities' rapidly mounting environmental problems, the public's attitude is changing, and new policies relating to environmental needs and costs are emerging."

But Donnelly warned the committee members that Trust Fund money won't be sufficient for the added "ancillary beneficial and necessary improvements" inherent in better designed roads. He suggested the public pay *more* money into the Highway Trust Fund for more highways and provide separate revenue for environmental improvements.

Next, the subcommittee members heard Norman Klein, an

architect with Skidmore, Owings and Merrill, a member of the Baltimore design team also. He discussed the setup of the design team and its goals. He also addressed himself to the question of funding, which Donnelly had discussed. Klein urged that funds be committed for all of the programs involved in the team effort—not just the road—including the private sector, other public agencies, and the Bureau. He predicted that fulfillment of the entire project, with its housing, parks, community services, alternate modes of transportation, and other features, would cost at least three times the $300 million allocated for the highway.

Senator Jordan said that highway transportation represents only one medium of transportation and he asked if anyone was in the business of providing overall transportation planning for urban areas which include other forms such as surface, rail, subway, air, and water. He asked Klein: "Would you agree with me that the time is not far off when we no longer can afford the luxury of providing highway facilities for one man to drive one automobile to and from his job, polluting the air as he goes?" Klein agreed.

The next witness was Professor Ian McHarg of the Landscape, Architecture and Regional Planning Department of the University of Pennsylvania. His statement was brief and was summed up in his closing remark. "I think the problem about highways is [that] we permit engineers to have a profound effect upon cities and, in fact, design them." He was profusely thanked for appearing, hustled off stage, and the hearings recessed for the day.

As the hearings continued, the subcommittee received suggestions that one of the problems with transportation in this country is that the only kind of transportation medium with a big fund to finance it and a huge bureaucracy to implement it is highways, and that perhaps if there were other congressional committees set up for other modes such as the very committee hearing these suggestions, perhaps the public would begin to get changes.

The subcommittee also heard that in 1907 a horse-drawn vehicle could traverse New York City's streets at an average speed of 11.5 miles per hour. By 1966, motor vehicles make the same trip at the rate of 8.5 miles per hour.

The subcommittee heard that one horrible consequence of the impact of the federally aided highway program on the cities was a new financial burden on the city as the result of increased traffic volumes, enforced subsidy of the motor vehicle by the city, despite pressing demands to spend money for other purposes. The federal-aid program in turn made scarcer still the financial resources of the cities by fostering an outflowing of the affluent to the suburban areas, taking their purchasing power, revenue-generating activities, and real estate holdings beyond the central city's tax reach and stifled attempts to encourage alternate modes of transportation. The congressmen were told that maintenance costs of these superhighways was becoming astronomical and all out of proportion to their initial cost and benefit to motorists.

The roads subcommittee members asked for recommendations and they got them. They were told to provide the money to build the different kinds of transportation systems that comprehensive planning showed were needed for cities to provide money for multidevelopment projects such as educational, recreational, housing, and commercial centers, to give more money to relocatees, to develop and pay for high design standards in urban areas with Highway Trust Funds, and to reduce air pollution. They were urged to provide federal money for street improvements, traffic control device installations, off-street parking, and commercial loading and unloading facilities insofar as their need has been generated by federal-aid highway construction, and to broaden the concept of cost-benefit ratios limited to road user factors so that community values and urban objectives are included.

They were also told that cities are reluctant to veto an interstate project and lose the 90 percent federal funding or have the project shifted to the ABC program and end up on a 50–50 percent matching basis.

After hearing all that, the committee members turned to a familiar face, Rex Whitton. Whitton traced the history of the expressway system in Kansas City. After the city planning commission made a study of the city's expressway "needs," the city council, Missouri State Highway Commission, and BPR had approved the proposed system. The study was financed by the State Highway Commission and BPR. Whitton explained how smoothly the project advanced due to close co-operation with other agencies, for instance, urban renewal. He said that in some instances the urban renewal agency bought up additional property which it sold to the Highway Department for the expressway system! He said that by 1967 more than 42 miles of the total 98.8 miles recommended in the 1951 study were completed and the remainder was either under construction or being designed.

"All of this work to date in Kansas City has been accomplished with an absolute minimum of local resistance and protest. This I attribute to the complete co-operation between the local city, state, and federal officials, and the joint efforts of the federal highway and urban renewal officials." But Whitton's glowing report was not unanimous.

John Kohl, a former executive secretary of the highway division of the National Research Council and member of the Highway Research Board at the National Academy of Sciences, once cited the Kansas City expressway system as a poor example of highway planning in an urban area. He said that engineers and planners justified the cost and disruption to the city caused by building the project strictly on the basis of the amount of time the motorist would save traveling in, out, and around the city. He added, wryly, that engineers no longer are allowed to justify freeway systems solely on the basis of travel time saved.

Whitton went on to enumerate the myriad of conferences held since 1956 on the problems of highway building in the city; conferences, incidentally, which paid lip service only to the problems beginning to pile up as the result of freeway construction in cities. In 1958, it was the Sagamore Conference, attended by highway engineers, city managers, planners, university professors, architects, landscape artists, etc. They even published a pamphlet full of recommendations on sensitivity of constructing urban freeways as a result of the conference.

The Sagamore Conference spawned four regional conferences across the country, where the gospel was more widely dispersed.

After that, it was Hershey, Pennsylvania, in 1962, ". . . at which time architects, landscape architects, and city planners of national reputation spoke on freeway location and design in urban areas." The word went out again to highway administrators, engineers, and others interested in urban expressways. Yet, still another meeting was needed, this time in colonial Williamsburg, Virginia, in 1965. Ironically enough, restored Williamsburg has no automobiles, only pedestrians, a few horse-drawn carriages, and an efficient public bus system, in keeping with its eighteenth-century theme. One can only speculate on the recommendations that might come forth if the conference had been held at rush hour in Manhattan, downtown Boston, Watts, or even Kansas City with its yet unfinished system of expressways.

At any rate, the Williamsburg "resolves" urged that metropolitan areas adopt regional planning, that planning agencies emphasize the identification and evaluation of urban goals and values in a comprehensive transportation plan, that these plans be directed toward upgrading the city, that transportation values such as safety, comfort, convenience, economy, beauty are a part of total community values. The resolves also called for improving the operation of arterial and collector street systems to their maximum capacity and efficiency; distribution of planning studies to civic, business, and other organizations. Also mouthed was that old saw, "equitable" sharing of financial responsibility for the continuing transportation planning process. But the only change that occurred as a result of these resolves was the length of the list of conferences.

Whitton, in his testimony, complimented the Congress "which so wisely provided for the requirement of continuing comprehensive and co-operative transportation planning as a prerequisite for the approval of urban highway projects in cities of over 50,000 after July 1, 1965." He pointed out that the law says transportation planning, not just highway planning, and that he believed that the automobile and transit, whether bus, rail, or both, are complementary services and that transportation planning must be based on and related to land-use planning and to economic, social, and cultural objectives of the community and its people. Words but no music.

This is the same Whitton who, as Federal Highway Administrator had heard from residents in Newark, Seattle, Westchester County, Boston, and other areas who were tired of having highway engineers decide their community objectives.

Senator Randolph said that it was important to get the information to the local people. "We have to have consultation with the local people, if they themselves are to feel that they have a stake in this program." He added that "sometimes it is the very abruptness of highway development which really shakes them. I think that we can guard against that to a degree if we try to provide a cushion of time and discussion and encourage those people to participate." He simply would not consider the prospect that a community that was against a highway should not have to have it.

Another witness, Mayor John F. Shelley of San Francisco, had a different message for the committee, which was presented by Maurice Shean, federal legislative representative for San Francisco. He told how San Franciscans reacted to the Embarcadero freeway. It was first conceived as a one-deck, six-lane elevated with an underpass under the Plaza at the Ferry Building. Subsequently, the predicted 1980 "traffic demand" forced the six-lane structure to be expanded to eight lanes, double-decked to avoid taking more land. The structure was so large that it became known among critics as the concrete monster. A last-minute effort to have the elevated structure lowered into a short subway in front of the Ferry Building at the foot of Market Street was squelched when both BPR and the State Highway Department refused to pay the extra $11 million this solution would have then cost.

The city's Board of Supervisors was unwilling to finance the $11 million either, so they endorsed the project as planned. But the people raised hell, and in one of the wildest San Francisco Board meetings on record, by a vote of 6 to 5, members chose to keep the view and stop the project.

Shelley also told the committee, "The trouble may also arise from the demonstrated inefficiency of the freeway in handling one type of movement which is of major significance to a concentrated urban core area—the daily home-to-work and work-to-home movement

in and out of metropolitan downtown areas. . . . Proposed new
freeways are regarded by many as rivers of noise, exhaust gas,
and constant never-ceasing motion; 'a river to be kept away from
my door.' " He talked about the need for "integration and construction of parking facilities with roads to induce cars to keep out
of our most dense sections. Here we must look to the day when the
use of private automobiles in our central districts can, to a great
extent, be supplanted by transit vehicles, publicly owned minicars,
and may other possibilities that today's technology—not tomorrow's
—makes possible. . . . Expenditures should be made to give these
urban core areas like San Francisco first-class passenger transportation independent of vehicular traffic. . . . Transit should be given a
'legup' to take its rightful place as the basic passenger mover in
high-density areas. . . . There just is not enough money or space
available to allow every motorist who thinks he wants to drive
downtown to be able to do so unless he is prepared to pay his just
share such as tolls, parking charges, delays, and inconvenience." Nor
did Shelley forget the inner city dweller when he said, "It is of no
use to spend hundreds of millions of dollars to 'get there' if, in the
process, the 'there' is destroyed. In our central cities we must, at
all cost, preserve the value of 'there.' "

Mayor Shelley's statement was not questioned by the senators.

J. D. Braman, mayor of Seattle, appeared and told the committee bluntly, among other things, that there must be equitable
funding of all forms of transportation, including nonhighway needs,
and that the transportation decisions of each city must be made at
the local level, "for only then will we be assured that people affected have the means by which they can make their views
effectively known."

Then he hit them hard. He pointed out that superhighways in
cities disgorge thousands of automobiles per hour into a metropolis
and increase downtown congestion, sweeping into the hearts of our
cities, eating up real estate, compressing people, cars, and services
into ever narrower confines. The convenience of the highway puts
more people into cars or makes it possible for them to move into

newer, more remote suburbs, where public transportation cannot possibly serve them.

"All this traffic makes the highway planner secure in the belief that his highway is a success, and he starts construction on another highway while planning yet another. He claims their use as proof that the American public will not be enticed from their automobiles, and bases his arguments against any other mode of travel on the love affair between the American male and his private car," Mayor Braman declared.

Next came representatives of AASHO, including then president John O. Morton, Burch McMorran, and A. E. Johnson. McMorran was described by Morton as Commissioner of Transportation for the state of New York and head of the AASHO Committee on Urban Transportation Planning, Socioeconomic and Environmental Factors. Morton explained that McMorran's AASHO committee prepares programs including city planners, economists, sociologists, federal, state, and county officials, representatives of various design professions, and other specialists involved in the "nebulous" and complex urban picture.

It is interesting to note that until 1966 the committee headed by McMorran was designated simply as the subcommittee on Urban Transportation Planning. After 1966, it was embellished to include not only Transportation Planning but Socioeconomic and Environmental Factors. In fact, there wasn't even an Urban Transportation Planning Committee before 1960, two years after the much touted Sagamore Conference. And embellishment of the committee title and its concerns did not occur until eight years after the Sagamore Conference, four years after the Hershey Conference, and one year after the Williamsburg Conference, suggesting a foot-dragging attitude on the part of state highway officials toward some of the total impact aspects of the gigantic highway construction programs ongoing in our cities.

Then Morton launched into his prepared statement. He dragged out the Sagamore, Hershey, and Williamsburg conferences again, living "proof" that engineers are listening to criticism and doing their damnedest to make highways beautiful, sensitive, and func-

tional. Then, despite the fact that it was contradictory, he said that
early in the program (this would be about the time of the first conference, at Sagamore) "it also became very evident that we now had
many people wanting to get into the act now that the program was
so big, important, and glamorous, and involved so much
money. . . . We began to hear immediately from many instant
and self-proclaimed highway experts where they had not been in
evidence before." He was careful not to specify who these inter-
lopers were, but the inference was that they were architects, planners, economists, and citizens at public hearings objecting to the
engineers' plans and pointing out pitfalls in selected routes—the
same speech other AASHO members had cranked out numerous
times before.

He went on to say that regardless of charges that highway
planners and engineers are insensitive to social and economic and
esthetic values, and that they are single-purpose people wanting to
pave over the whole city, highway engineers have no such tenden-
cies and "do take a sense of pride in our accomplishments in
producing attractive facilities that fit harmoniously into the socioeconomic structure."

He added that some of the factors that have caused controversy
in the past have been a sincere fear that the highway would en-
croach upon historic areas, parks, vistas, and the like, or that the
highway would cause serious human problems, but in some instances, he said, problems seemed to degenerate into opposition to
highways per se voiced in the most sensational, vocal, and unco-
operative manner.

AASHO's testimony revealed the ossified attitude of highway
officials toward people who oppose highway construction. Such opponents are labeled as unco-operative, obstructionists, or sensation
and publicity seekers; they are never considered as concerned private citizens with a point of view that happens to disagree with the
aims and purposes of the Highway Department.

To prove that highway officials are sensitive to the public, Morton
cited the case of the Baltimore design concept team, with its philosophy of citizen participation. On the other hand, the Department of

Transportation's inclination to let citizens pass judgment on location and design of highways would simply stop the program, he said. He said that local authorities and neighborhood residents should have something to say about a highway project, but that public hearings were the proper place for citizen participation. To allow citizens any more voice than they now have at public hearings "would fragment authority and complicate the approval of projects," Morton explained. In other words, the highways will be built, whether or not the public wants them. State highway departments have been paying lip service to citizen comments at public hearings and then have gone right ahead and planned exactly what they intended to do before the hearings were held. They did not want this procedure altered.

Mr. McMorran concurred: "Senator [Randolph], I think that the local people certainly should have a great deal to say and should be given every chance to voice their feelings in the matter. Sometimes, though, it gets to the point where certain groups want complete, absolute veto power, which is hard to go along with, because it stops the project." "Certain groups" like Miss Collier, whom he booted out of the Reuben-Deyo House to make room for an interchange.

The next witness was Burton Miller, executive vice president of Chairman Randolph's former fraternity, the ARBA. He introduced Elmer Timby, president of ARBA's engineering division, a consultant to state highway departments, and member, as is Whitton, of Howard, Needles, Tammen and Bergendoff.

Timby reiterated the story of the great contribution highways were supposed to have made to the economy and growth of the nation—opening up new land beyond the city, clearing slum buildings and improving the land adjacent to the highway. He repeated the argument that the highway is required even for public transportation—bus transit—in urban areas, and commented on how important the relocation of displaced families had become. He did not remind the committee members that his organization ARBA had testified against relocation payment for displaced businesses and families at the time hearings were held on *that* legislation.

According to Timby, ARBA supported the joint development

concept, which he claimed can stimulate other local programs to provide cities with parks, playgrounds, open space, and other improvements, and commercial and residential redevelopment, by combining them with freeway construction. In this manner, he claimed, the freeway adds to the community.

"The highway engineer is much maligned," Timby argued. "Highway officials have generally been in the forefront of progressive thinking. They have been particularly aware of the importance of co-ordinated urban planning. Too often, the cities have been slow in realizing the necessity of joining with the highway officials in planning the development of new transportation facilities. . . . The American Road Builders Association, over a long period of years, has concerned itself with the problem of communication between the highway agencies and the general public. . . . It is a necessary function of any public service agency. . . . In our humble opinion, and with the single exception of our educational system, there is no government program which, when measured by service to all citizens, by value contributed to economic development, and by contributions to increases in standard of living, can even begin to compare with the highway program. Transportation, efficient, service-giving, and convenient, is as essential to the economic health of America as is the circulatory system to the body of a world's champion."

The problem with that old chestnut is that if the champ's body develops the clots in his circulation that are analogous to the traffic jams inherent in our highway system, he will drop dead.

Randolph assiduously questioned Timby about public hearings, the conduct of which is a function of state and federal highway officials, not contractors. The senator wanted to know if sufficient opportunity was offered to persons wishing to present their point of view. "Is there enough time to let them know we really want them or do we say 'Yes, yes, yes' and shut them off with a very brief hearing?" he asked.

Which is a strange question, since there is no need for ARBA to concern itself with the conduct and purposes of public hearings on highway projects. The question to the contractors' spokesman suggests that there is some confusion in Randolph's mind as to the conduct of public hearings since he asked private industry to comment on the performance of public officials. Such questioning further suggests that the role of the public hearing is also blurred in his mind, and that he does not realize that the hearings are to further the citizens' role in the decision process rather than to further the aims of the highway industry.

Timby reassured the senator that highway departments advertise public hearings, normally thirty days before, and print maps of the proposed roads. Incredibly, he could not recall any hearing that had ended before everyone had been heard.

Randolph then asked if each person's viewpoint is really considered, studied, and evaluated. Timby assured him that all were evaluated.

Randolph commented that there was some difference of opinion about this. Then, leaning forward slightly toward ARBA's representative, he asked, "Do you have any suggestions for change in procedure? Do we need to do anything from the standpoint of rewriting the law in reference to the impact, the positive impact which we know the highway has in the urban area? Can we do a better job?"

This was a spectacle—a federal legislator asking a representative of a special interest group for specific legislation to help the group perpetuate its own interest in the name of a public program and the public good.

Timby answered carefully. He said that transcripts of all public hearings are forwarded to the BPR, where they get additional consideration.

Randolph lauded Burton Miller's promotion to executive vice president following the retirement of General Prentiss, and expressed the hope that "there will be a continued exchange of thought with the subcommittee on roads by the ARBA, as in the past."

The lead-off witness of the second portion of the hearings was Senator Jacob Javits (R., New York). He told committee members what they did not want to hear. Javits said, "Funds must be reallocated from urban highways to urban mass transit systems. . . .

Our national priorities are misplaced. Highways are not the most efficient way to move people between suburbs and central cities, between home and job. Yet the federal government is spending more than $4 billion a year on highways and less than $200 million on urban transit. . . . As the National Advisory Commission on Civil Disorders noted in its report, most new jobs are not being created in central cities, near the Negro ghettos. Instead, they are likely to occur in the suburbs and in outlying areas of the city . . . it is crucial that inexpensive transportation be available, which will permit the residents of the ghettos to reach new job locations. Urban highways are not the answer to this need. There must be improved rapid mass transportation linking slums and suburbs— and we must be prepared to pay for such mass transit systems. . . . For too long, we have accommodated the development of our cities to the needs of automobiles and to the requirements of engineering." Javits suggested that highway funds pay for various types of transportation, not just highways.

Randolph quickly retorted that AASHO's report on future highway needs estimates that $260 billion will have to be spent by 1985 to meet future highway needs alone, suggesting that there would not be enough money left over for any other type of transportation, particularly from the Highway Trust Fund. Charles B. Rangel of New York's State Assembly supported Javits' argument. He added, "As services have moved from the cities, so have industries relocated themselves. The federally aided roads have served as a vehicle for employers to escape the heavy tax burdens imposed by local governments. They take with them employment opportunities, which in most cases, for a variety of reasons, cannot be followed by the inner city residents. Thus, the under- and unemployed numbers increase, causing frustration that usually manifests its symptoms during the summer months. . . .

"We must determine priorities, it is said—even essential programs for the future of the cities, and through them, of the suburbs and countryside as well, are being cut. If this is true, then every penny being put into highways is being subtracted from the most urgent tasks for the welfare and strength of our country. In light of what

I have already said, this amounts to putting last things first—and with a vengeance, on a planned basis." Senator Randolph made no response.

Highway critics leveled with the subcommittee. Planning consultant Harry Boswell said that if the Interstate System were completed that day, within a year the ingenuity of the automobile manufacturers would have the system jammed.

Other critics said that highway officials are scornful of joint development concepts such as houses, parks, schools, and ancillary community services that should be explored as part of a highway project. Typically, highway officials react to joint development concepts with a flip "Is this a highway funding project or is this a special project?" When, at public hearings, citizens tell engineers they must consider human values, the engineers explain that the "human values" can adapt themselves after the bulldozers are through.

All of this was followed by a statement from John Volpe, then a contractor, former president of AGC, governor of Massachusetts, still a Republican vice-presidential hopeful, and chairman of the Governors' Conference. He stated that 80 percent of all families in the United States own a car and that we have urban sprawl and that we are dependent on the automobile for travel, leading to a pressing need for more highways in the future. He did not like the idea of the Highway Trust Fund financing fringe parking facilities. As for our urban freeway problems, he suggested that the federal government beef up a new arterial highway program in the cities by providing more money for roads after completion of the Interstate System.

Senator Jordan of Idaho asked, "Now, as we make these arterial city streets more attractive for travel by automobile, are we not going to invite more people to move into the city and compound the problem in other ways besides transportation?" Volpe disagreed, saying, "I can only envision what might have happened and what could have happened if President Eisenhower and the Congress in 1956 had not decided to proceed with this system; we would really be bogged down now and bogged down very badly. So that, I would say that although these improved facilities do invite supposedly more travel, that more travel was coming anyway. It is a question of where are we going to put it?"

On the next-to-last day of the hearings, Senator Randolph observed that the hearings had crystallized two critical points in highway location in urban areas, for which purpose the hearings were held: (1) Displacement and dislocation suffered by individuals from a large public works project, which the government should be concerned with; and (2) the problem of highway location and design plus decision making in the process. He pointedly omitted the suggestion made time and again by witnesses that automobile travel on highways was not answering our desperate transportation needs in urban areas, that Highway Trust Fund money should support other modes of transportation, and that comments brought forth by citizens at public hearings were being ignored.

Then federal governmental agency representatives appeared. The first was Charles Haar, of the Department of Housing and Urban Development, who said, among other things, that "It is difficult for the poor central city resident without an automobile to persuade himself that a new superhighway which he will not use, but which requires him to pull up roots and find a new home, is a beneficial improvement—particularly if the alternative modes of transportation he depends upon, buses or subways, give increasingly poorer service at higher costs. It is difficult for those driving in congested areas to understand how more and better highways which serve only to add more vehicles to city streets will benefit them. It is difficult for the suburban housewife in a one-car family to be enthusiastic about new highways, when she and her children are stranded with no alternative means of transportation while her husband is using the car to go to work." He listed alternate forms of transportation for urban areas. He continued with a direct slap at the powerful highway lobby and highways-only philosophy. "This new technology [for other transit modes] is viable—much of it right now. But implementation of these new systems of transportation cannot be made a reality as long as present institutional obstacles are permitted to overshadow the needs of the citizenry."

Randolph said that $2.2 billion was being spent annually on urban highways, $132 million on other forms of transportation, and $874 million on housing and community development. "Now, does this make possible the urban strengthening of our society within those dollar figures? What do those figures say to you?" Randolph asked.

Haar snapped back that they address themselves to the national priorities as determined by appropriations. Randolph then went tangentially off to discuss the design concept team without pursuing the subject further.

Alan Boyd, then Transportation Secretary, testified that the design concept team was valuable, along with joint use projects, and expanded and improved relocation assistance programs. "It would be naïve, however," he said, "to assume that these proposals will meet the objections raised to certain urban segments of the Interstate System. In many cities, portions of the Interstate System have become so entangled with deep political and social forces that we cannot expect the alleviation of immediate problems to resolve the controversies."

Armed with information developed at the preliminary hearings, Senator Randolph's committee considered the 1968 Federal Highway Act in June of that year. Two organizations sent familiar faces back for these hearings, Burton Miller for ARBA, and John O. Morton and A. E. Johnson for AASHO. He also invited representatives from the National Parking Association, Associated General Contractors, lumber manufacturers, mayors, AAA, Roadside Business Association, National Safety Council, International Association of Chiefs of Police, Inc., and the National Joint Heavy and Highway Construction Committee, and Secretary Boyd and Highway Administrator Bridwell.

Senator Randolph opened the hearings with a brief explanation of the proposed highway legislation for 1968. The legislation authorized funds for the ABC system, forest highways, roads and trails, covered the schedule for completion of the Interstate System, and funded and authorized the program called TOPICS. TOPICS was designed to improve the capacity and safety operation of existing urban streets. The bill gave authority to states to use federal-aid funds to establish fringe parking facilities, relocation assistance, and improved relocation programs. It also included consideration of advance acquisition of rights-of-way plus highway safety and beautification proposals. The proposed legislation provided, among other things, authorized funding of $18.25 billion for the Interstate System to be spent between 1970 and 1974, extending the completion date of the system to 1974. It earmarked $2 billion for the ABC system for 1970 and 1971, and $1.25 million for the TOPICS program, to be spent between 1970 and 1974. It authorized funding money from the general treasury for highway beautification and provided for the right to acquire right-of-way seven years in advance of constructing a project, as well as the right to acquire land outside a central business district along a federally aided highway land for fringe parking on a 75–25 percent ratio with the states.

Senator Mike Monroney, from the oil-producing state of Oklahoma, proposed the federal Highway Trust Fund be extended from 1972 to 1985 intact to provide funds for additional construction on existing and new roads.

Senator Randolph took the opportunity to remind Monroney that he planned to introduce legislation establishing an airport trust fund similar to the Highway Trust Fund, presumably to line up support of the aviation-minded Oklahoma legislator.

Monroney was followed by John W. Long, president of the National Parking Association, who opposed Trust Fund financing for fringe parking areas on the grounds that suburbanites would not bring their cars downtown to park.

Next came AASHO spokesman John O. Morton, accompanied by A. E. Johnson. They argued against the parking provision because members of AASHO do not believe the Trust Fund money was adequate to support any programs other than highway construction, particularly because estimates of projected highway needs exceed funds.

AASHO was also against section 4(f) of the 1966 Transportation Act which directs the Secretary of Transportation to consult with the Secretaries of Interior, Housing and Urban Development, and Agriculture, and with the states in developing transportation plans and programs that are directed toward maintaining or enhancing the natural beauty of the land traversed. That clause said: "the Secretary shall not approve any program or project which requires the use of any land from a public park, recreation area, wildlife and waterfowl refuge, or historic site unless (1) there is no feasible and prudent alternative to the use of such land, and (2) such program includes all possible planning to minimize harm to such park, recreation area, wildlife and waterfowl refuge, or historic site resulting from such use."

AASHO lamented this section as "a delaying factor in getting the program completed." And the state highway officials were unhappy that Department of Transportation lawyers were attempting to force highway engineers to weigh the contents of public hearings. The lawyers were doing so by proposing that two separate public hearings be held before engineers could settle on a specific route for a new freeway, the first to be held before the route location is approved and a second one before design of the highway is approved. AASHO commented, "Some of the material being drafted relative to double public hearings would allow dissidents, through legal procedures, to tie up highway projects almost indefinitely." In other words, it would give a community a legal lever to stop a highway project if it didn't want it. The association complained that the provision was being used to slow down the highway program and encroached on the authority and responsibility of state highway departments.

AASHO described DOT's lawyers as "nonhighway oriented" and complained that "the procedures go into complete detail and would overlegalize every component of the public hearing procedure."

Morton said that the state highway departments were becoming extremely exercised over the complications and details that were being spelled out at the federal level and the encroachments upon prerogatives and responsibilities that the states had assigned to their highway commissions in carrying out their highway responsibilities. He called for a clear delineation of state functions separate from federal. In other words, the federal money was welcome but he did not like the idea that the Department of Transportation was pressuring the Bureau of Public Roads to enforce federal controls.

Then he launched into AASHO's post-1975 program. He began by reciting population figures—that by 2000 there would be 275 million Americans. He said that people were driving an average of 4600 miles per year, a figure which he predicted would increase. Rail freight traffic between cities, on the other hand, had decreased from 57 percent to 44 percent between 1950 and 1966 so that over-the-road heavy hauling truck traffic would increase also. This proved, he explained, that although there was a need for other modes of transportation in certain areas and for certain specific purposes, the highways would continue to be a major form of transportation and there would be a great demand for them. He predicted that the present motor vehicle registration figure of 95 million would shoot up to 150 million by 1990 while vehicle miles traveled would increase from the present one billion to one and one-half trillion by then, whereas "on the other hand, the 700,000 miles plus on the state highway systems would probably increase to something in excess of 800,000 miles."

He proceeded to the "advantages" of highways of the future, complete with utilization of air space over highways, around highways, and under highways. He talked, too, of improving the safety and capacity of some present highways.

As for advance acquisition of land for highways, AASHO recommended that a $100-million revolving fund be set up in the Trust Fund to buy rights-of-way. And for urban areas, he said, "In order that the central city may remain a dominant part of the urban metropolitan area, it is necessary that adequate transportation into and out of the central city be provided." He asserted that "There is only about 5 percent of the present 233 metropolitan areas where mass rail transit would be applicable, and we cannot foresee in the near future a change in this condition."

AASHO stressed the need for relieving the urban traffic crisis by pouring more money into upgrading existing streets.

Then Senator John Sherman Cooper asked, "I note that you all have pointed out that highway transportation will remain dominant, but in your consideration of its development in the urban areas, have you been able to give consideration to alternate types of transportation which I don't say would limit the development of the arterial street system within the city but might limit the development of great highways running through the cities?" The AASHO representative stated that highways and other modes of transportation must supplement each other.

Cooper hammered away: "Of course, as you know, there are some people in this country, and a growing number, I think, and this is reflected in newspaper editorials and conservation articles, who think that highway engineers and highway commissions like to build, and therefore they put these highways through cities and cause the problems that you have been offering recommendations toward alleviating. That, it seems to me, makes it important that this whole problem of service to these urban areas and providing methods of ingress and egress has to be considered in relationship to, if not alternate forms of transportation, at least mixed forms of transportation."

All in all, AASHO's official statement favored new legislation which would continue the Trust Fund until 1985, at which time it would have yielded an additional $60 billion. It wanted provisions for a new federal-aid system of metropolitan arterial streets for urban areas instead of spending money on the TOPICS program. It wanted to force the Secretary of Transportation to come to an agreement with all state highway departments on the location of the remaining miles of the Interstate System before December 31, 1969, with a penalty that would deny federal 90 percent matching money if agreements were not reached. This, of course, was designed to force a decision on the location of certain freeways currently being held up by citizen complaints.

Here, too, the statement predicted that most of the new highway mileage after completion of the Interstate System would occur in expanding suburbs.

Burton F. Miller testified for ARBA. He expressed concern that "innovations" proposed in the legislation by DOT and the Federal Highway Administration would deplete the Highway Trust Fund when all of the money was needed for more mileage. Miller urged that ABC funds be increased to reflect the increased cost of construction. He proposed that all safety and beautification programs directly involved with highway construction be financed from the Trust Fund only if the fund received new revenues to augment such expenses. Safety measures more directly related to autos and drivers, he said, should not be financed from the Trust Fund. Forest highways and public land roads should be paid from the general treasury too. ARBA believed fringe parking definitely should not be financed from the Highway Trust Fund. ARBA also could not support extension of the Davis-Bacon Act to construction of the ABC system because it would involve "a tremendous amount of paperwork and red tape . . . and we are having enough difficulty now in complying with the interstate phases of the Davis-Bacon, and we urge you not to extend this law to the ABC system."

John de Lorenzi testified for the American Automobile Association. He urged that $4 billion should be authorized each year through fiscal 1974 for the Interstate System and that the system completion deadline should be extended to June 1975. Incentives should be provided, he said, instead of penalties, for states still not participating in the beautification program. He asked for a revolving $100-million-per-year fund for advance land acquisition and general treasury funding for the TOPICS program instead of highway trust funding. (The AAA has consistently taken the position that the safety program be paid from the general fund.) Senator Cooper commented that he thought the funds for it should come from the Highway Trust Fund. AAA took the position that money spent on safety meant less Interstate completed. Cooper said, "But here we have a problem of death and injuries on our highways and all I hear is, 'Well, if you put this in there we can't build more highways for more people to get killed on.' I wonder what our relative values are. What does it mean?"

AAA's legal counsel C. R. Gray answered, "It means stretching out the program." De Lorenzi claimed that the Interstate System itself is a safety system and repeated the familiar cliché that when the system is completed it will save about 8000 lives annually "because it is the safest highway system yet devised. By completing the Interstate System on time we are saving lives."

Cooper replied to this, "What about those portions of the Interstate which we discussed when we had the safety bill before us which are deathtraps now? . . . Would you favor going ahead and correcting those now, or would you want to use that money to continue construction of the interstate program?"

De Lorenzi replied that to his knowledge there were funds available to correct such situations and that the funds didn't have to come out of the Interstate program. Then the conversation switched to AAA's position that the cost of fringe parking should be treated as capital investment by rapid transit. Senator Bayh pointed out that transit systems have been and are in financial difficulty and that some way must be found to make them appealing to users.

De Lorenzi argued that there have been no studies to demonstrate that fringe parking would pull people off roads and be a benefit to the highway user.

Bayh rejoined, "Is there not already enough evidence, because of the rapidly growing numbers of motor vehicles on the highways, to know that if in ten years nothing is done our roads will be so crowded that we are not going to be able to get to work in the morning? Isn't it a worth-while goal to find means by which there can be more rapid conveyance and fewer vehicles, even if there must be a collection point, if you want to call it that?"

De Lorenzi said that we are not necessarily going to reach the point where roads are overcrowded. He offered, incredibly, Los Angeles as an example of a city with constantly increasing traffic but a freeway system "in good shape." He added that the Interstate System is not yet completed, and suggested that when it was, it probably would be able to handle traffic jams, implying that traffic jams occurred because the system was not complete.

One of the last to testify was Howard Pyle, president of the National Safety Council. He was most concerned with that portion of the bill devoted to safety programs. He related some highway statistics for the senators. For instance, in the past five years, a quarter of a million persons were killed and nine million disabled by highway accidents at a cost of $45 billion. The first four months of 1968 saw an increase of 5 percent in traffic fatalities over 1967; a larger percentage of white persons died in car crashes, while deaths of pedestrians were nearly twice as high for nonwhites, and accident rates for nonwhites are increasing faster than the rates for whites. The Air Force experienced 70 percent more deaths in private, off-duty motor vehicle accidents in the United States in 1967 than resulted from enemy action in Vietnam.

Over in the House, Congressman Kluczynski held hearings before his roads subcommittee on the upcoming 1968 Federal Highway Act. So fanatic is the thinking of some members of this committee that it had tacked onto the 1968 bill the mandate to build freeways in the District of Columbia.

It would be difficult to describe Kluczynski's committee as sympathetic to *any* criticism of freeways. An example of the attitude in his shop is the view of Audrey Warren, clerk of the subcommittee, who explains away the more than 50,000 persons who die each year on highways by saying that the 50 states, divided into the total number of deaths, "means only about 1000 for each state." As for the damage freeways inflict upon cities, she explains, it is necessary to entice people out of the city anyway, particularly to new towns and out West so they will have space to drive their automobiles. The auto must be kept useful because to shut down the auto industry would throw people out of work.

Richard Sullivan, chief counsel for the House Public Works Committee, has best expressed the thinking of the majority of the House roads subcommittee members. He was asked whether or not the committee ever undertook studies to determine the economic soundness of the highway program and whether it was benefiting the public. He answered, "There is no need to justify this program, the benefits are obvious." He explained that the General Accounting Office and the Bureau of Public Roads keep a check on the program, and besides, in addition to the benefit to the construction industry, the highway program links up cities, makes it possible for people to move all over the country, and moves goods. He cited shopping centers at interchanges and beltways as economic progress and said the highways provide "ingress and egress" to these areas. Then, too, he added, there are the national defense aspects of building the system—to move troops and goods quickly in wartime. He stressed that most members of the House Public Works Committee are intractable in their position that the Highway Trust Fund must be preserved for highway construction only.

Kluczynski's colleagues on the roads subcommittee in 1968 included Democrats John A. Blatnik, Robert E. Jones (Alabama), Frank M. Clark (Pennsylvania), Ed Edmondson (Oklahoma), Arnold Olsen (Montana), James C. Wright, Jr. (Texas), Robert Everett (Tennessee), Richard D. McCarthy (New York), James J. Howard (New Jersey), Ray Roberts (Texas), and William Jennings Bryan Dorn (South Carolina). Republicans included William C. Cramer, William H. Harsha (Ohio), James C. Cleveland, Don H. Clausen (California), Robert C. McEwen (New York), Fred Schwengel (Iowa), Robert V. Denney (Nebraska), Roger H. Zion (Indiana), and Jack H. McDonald (Michigan).

These subcommittee members were told by witnesses that they should consider a new highway program when the Interstate System is completed, that contractors were suffering from cutbacks in the program, that the highway industry and the people it employs need to be sure there will be plenty of money so they can keep in business and provide jobs. Governor Volpe appeared and stated that another 41,000 miles of Interstate would be needed by 1985. The ATA testified that it was time to put bigger and heavier trucks on the Interstate highways, particularly triple-trailers. Some state highway departments made pleas for specific additional mileage on the Interstate. For instance, if they have their way, Mobile, Alabama, will have to find space somewhere for six more miles of superhighways; Delaware, 103.3 miles, 17.5 of it in the Wilmington area; and Michigan, 750 miles, fifteen of which will be squeezed into the Detroit area.

One witness, Congressman Jonathan Bingham of New York, didn't ask for more highways, however. He jolted the subcommittee by stating, "The current imbalance in our transportation investment is due in part to the financial machinery we established in 1956 for highway funding. The Highway Trust Fund has produced an annual account that gets larger every year and that must be spent for highways without any consideration of the priority of highway construction and improvement in relation to other national needs. . . . No other public works program has received such automatic and unquestioned funding, practically insulated from congressional review."

Bingham suggested the Highway Trust Fund be renamed the Transportation Trust Fund so money could be available for other modes of transportation. Chairman Kluczynski commented, "I am not opposed to mass transportation. I do not think any member of this subcommittee is opposed to mass transportation. I do not favor changing the Highway Trust Fund to the Transportation Trust Fund."

Congressman Clausen asked Bingham, "Do you believe that we should tax the transit commuters to build highways?" in an obvious reference to the old argument that highway users alone are paying for highways and not mass transit.

Bingham answered, "I think we should use whatever taxes we have available for whatever purposes are most important. The way you put the question makes it sound very harsh, but, in principle, all of our federal taxes should go to the general fund and then should be allocated in the scale of priorities that the Congress determines the most urgent."

Congressman Cleveland challenged the need for mass transit. He referred to AASHO's current study which claims that people are happy with highways and autos and want more. But Bingham replied that he had received overwhelming support for mass transit from a questionnaire he sent his constituents.

The Senate and House subcommittees reported out their own bills. Kluczynski's bill demanded completion of the proposed freeway system in the District of Columbia, extended the deadline for the Interstate System through June 1974, added 3000 more Interstate System miles, authorized $6.2 billion for the interstate program in the two extra years, reduced the Secretary of Transportation's authority to disapprove highways that infringe on parkland, allowed for higher relocation payments to displacees, and limited federal funds for fringe parking. Both major newspapers in Washington hailed the House's decision to tack the mandate for D.C. freeways onto the Federal Highway Act as a stroke of genius. Congressman Natcher crowed that unless all proposed Washington freeways were built there would be no Washington subway, which he seemed to forget had been ordered by the Congress.

When the bill went before the whole House, Cramer offered an amendment to halt the beautification portion and won, 211–145. After the bill left the House Public Works Committee, it had already diluted authority to preserve parkland by inserting the provision that highways be built on parkland if local officials have first done all possible planning, including "consideration of alternatives." Cramer then offered an amendment that shrank DOT's authority even further by limiting the Secretary's jurisdiction to federal parkland only. The House adopted Cramer's proposal, 62–32.

The Senate version provided for increased payments to displaced families and businesses and strengthened the requirement that highway planning conform to comprehensive city planning, including urban expert teams. It also contained a proviso establishing fringe parking and authorizing $2.6 billion for the ABC system in 1970 and 1971, $3.6 billion for the Interstate System each of those years, money for TOPICS, safety, and beautification. It contained no directive to build freeways in the District of Columbia. The bill passed the Senate and went to conference.

The final bill authorized a total of $21 billion for federally aided highways over the next five years, when the Interstate System is scheduled to be completed, ordered the District of Columbia to build its freeway system, no matter what courts or citizens said, added a trimmed-down 1500 miles to the Interstate System, limited the Secretary of Transportation's authority to veto highways that take parkland or historic areas, provided money for TOPICS, beautification, safety, and fringe parking, and extended the Davis-Bacon prevailing wage law to all federal-aid highway programs.

The bill was debated on the Senate floor. Senator Dominick (R., Colorado) and Senator Mansfield (D., Montana), expressed concern for District parkland if the city had to build the freeway system so ordered by the House provision; Senators Cooper and Jordan of Idaho bravely spoke against the precedent of the Congress ordering specific highways to be built in a city. Senator Ralph Yarborough (D., Texas) questioned the wisdom of changing the Transportation Secretary's authority to veto highway plans that take parkland, historic sites, or wildlife refuges. Yarborough cited San Antonio's North Expressway as an example of such a highway, but Senator Randolph assured him that the Secretary would still retain authority to prevent parkland from being paved over. In fact, Randolph said, "We are not going to allow that." The Senate voted on the bill shortly thereafter. It passed 60 to 6 with 27 members absent. Those senators voting against the bill were Edward Brooke (R., Massachusetts), Clifford Case (R., New Jersey), John Sherman Cooper, Jacob Javits, Thomas Kuchel (R., California), John Williams (R., Delaware). Senator Joseph Clark (D., Pennsylvania), although absent, left word that he would have voted against the bill.

As District residents and conservationists groaned over the "compromise" bill, Chairman Randolph explained that he was not at all pleased with the District freeway mandate, but it was the price for getting any bill at all. That was a specious argument since there was no pressing need to pass a highway bill in 1968: money had been authorized and appropriated through 1969 and the bill could easily have been recommitted. But politicians are reluctant to trim a fat pork-barrel bill in an election year, and so the bill went to President Johnson for his signature.

He was deluged with letters and telegrams urging him to pocket veto the bill while the Congress adjourned for the Democratic National Convention. District of Columbia Mayor Washington and a majority of the City Council urged a veto. Neither DOT nor Interior could support the bill. Senator Mike Mansfield questioned the highway engineering credentials of the House Public Works Committee and what "special qualities" they had that enabled them to confidently demand specific freeways for a city. Senator Cooper argued that it was bad precedent for the Congress to tell the city what to build and where.

Both Washington newspapers hailed the bill and urged the President to sign it. The New York *Times* denounced the bill and advised a veto.

On the very day the pocket veto would go into effect if the bill was not signed, Senator Randolph, fearing the President would allow it to expire, hustled to the White House and pleaded with Mr. Johnson to sign the bill. The President flew to the Texas White House that night at ten P.M. and took along the unsigned bill. By midnight, Texas time, he signed it.

He did so with a proviso that the District City Council, with the help of the Department of Transportation, come up with its own freeway plan. He refused to direct Secretary Boyd to allocate money for the freeways as planned in the bill. The President said that the directive from the Congress to build them "is inconsistent with a basic tenet of sound urban development." President Johnson said he would have vetoed the bill, except that he felt the 1956 Federal Highway Act overruled the right of Congress to draw specific highway plans. Not happy that the bill authorized $21.5 billion in concrete in the next five years, the Washington *Post* moaned that "The burden that the President's action places on Mayor Washington, the City Council and other agencies is extremely heavy . . . and everyone involved with freeways and with planning must be kept under the greatest possible pressure" or the city will lose both freeways and subways and die of automobile strangulation!

It is interesting to note that Senator Randolph addressed the Texas Heavy Highway Contractors meeting in Austin in September, shortly after the bill squeaked by with the President's signature, and he told his audience of highway contractors: "It should be recognized that we must concentrate on efforts to reduce unnecessary demand for highway construction, for the simple reason that under no set of foreseeable circumstances can we possibly build all the roads we must have; anything, therefore, which relieves the demand for construction by alternate solutions should be given positive consideration."

Yet he staunchly defended the Highway Trust Fund when Senator Javits suggested it be opened to use by alternate modes of transportation, and he was a prime mover in securing the President's signature on a bill calling for $21.5 billion more concrete. Since his election to the Senate, Randolph has piously and consistently suggested that the public is interested in improving its education system and that there are other priorities, after which he goes after another huge highway authorization. Thus, he can appear to be a victim of circumstances, and when the highway program blows up in the face of its proponents, he can point back to a long history of I Told You So speeches.

Part of the reason the highway program goes rolling along as it does is because it is a state-run program with virtually no federal controls, fed by the zeal of congressmen with little vision and much greed. Several roads subcommittee members, critical of the federal highway program, have suggested that Kluczynski's tubular vision pertaining to freeways stems from the influence of the Public Works Committee staff, particularly Audrey Warren and Counsel Sullivan. This pro-freeway attitude crosses party lines. Ranking minority member Cramer has flatly stated, "Cities can plan around the highways." He is, after all, the one member who has most often expressed concern that a halt to the freeway program in the nation's capital could mean a halt in cities across the country. But Congressman McCarthy argues that to direct construction of specific freeways in the District of Columbia could establish a bad precedent for every other city. His argument falls on deaf ears.

And only a handful of congressmen seemed concerned about the amendment that diluted the Transportation Secretary's power to protect parkland from the bulldozers. As Congressman McCarthy sees it, the 1968 law permits any freeway, airport, railroad line, or any other type of transportation facility to be constructed through areas of historic or natural importance simply on the basis that an engineer has given "consideration of alternatives." If so, the engineer will make a determination which formerly the Secretary made. McCarthy asked, "What does it mean when an engineer states that he has 'considered' an alternative? It could mean he has given all of five minutes' thought to an alternative but remains firmly convinced that the route through a park is best because it is the straightest line or requires the least land acquisition costs. Ironically, it is just such barreling through that has caused bitter controversy in New Orleans, Washington, and San Francisco, magnifying opposition to urban freeways. Yet the House and Senate Public Works committees insisted on softening the Secretary's mandate over parkland because highway officials complained that such power was slowing down the highway program in urban areas. Their intent is clearly to ignore the wishes of the local community and they now have the nod from the Congress to do so."

Senator Randolph stated that the amendment will actually strengthen the position of the Secretary of Transportation. Chief clerk and staff director Richard Royce explained that Randolph meant that the new directive will allow local officials to make the determination. He said that the urban freeway hearings held by the Senate roads subcommittee made it clear that many times people in old-age homes, colleges, and neighborhoods were being displaced for highways when perhaps it would have been better to reroute through nearby parkland and that the local community officials will make the choice whether to relocate people or take parks!

Another factor that keeps the program rolling along is the grease provided by campaign contributions. Congressman Fallon, a big highway booster, was crass enough to list a 1966 $500 campaign contribution from the Committee for Action of Bellevue, Washington, a front for heavy construction and paving contractors. That year, Senator Robert P. Griffin (R., Michigan) received $14,000 from the committee and when he won re-election, was assigned to the Senate Public Works Committee.

All such publicly acknowledged campaign contributions have been described by some voices on Capitol Hill as only the peak of the iceberg. They speculate that most campaign contributions are funneled into coffers of congressional candidates through local party organizations, particularly in big cities, where the sources can remain anonymous.

The law states that a congressman must disclose the source of his campaign funds only if he has "knowledge or consent" that they are being spent on his campaign. Any congressman can, and most do, claim that those private interests which donate heavily to his campaign did so without his knowledge or consent, obviating the need to reveal them. Also, contributions from organizations within a candidate's state need not be filed, only funds that come from outside the state. Therefore, a special interest group can channel funds into a state political committee from which it is poured into a local campaign without ever turning up except as a lump sum donation to a state committee.

Then, too, many congressmen are partners in law firms in their districts and can receive contributions as fees to their firms. The Greyhound Bus Lines retained the law firm of Kimble, Schapiro, Stevens, Harsha & Harsha of Portsmouth, Ohio. One of the Harshas is Representative William H. Harsha, Jr., R., member of the House Public Works Roads subcommittee. Greyhound is vitally interested in legislation that would allow larger and heavier vehicles on our interstate highways.

Proponents of reforming the nebulous system of campaign contributions have labored long and produced a House Committee on Standards of Official Conduct. Its 1968 vice chairman Charles Halleck (R., Indiana) received $500 from truckers between 1966 and 1968. Spokesman for the truckers, Frank Grimm, explained, "We do what we can for those on the committees who might help us."

In 1968, Congressman Fred Schwengel wrote the ethics committee chairman, Melvin Price (D., Illinois), calling attention to the generous contributions from truckers to members of the House and Senate Public Works and related committees. He suggested that every member of the Congress be given a chance to publicly disavow the intent stated by the spokesman for the truck lobby. He also plugged for passage of a law that would penalize those who seek to unduly influence members of the Congress.

Price responded that filing a list of campaign contributions with the Clerk of the House, along with attendant newspaper publicity, amount to sufficient warning for congressmen to take whatever steps they feel are necessary if they need to publicly disavow any inference that they were influenced by such a contribution. Furthermore, it is improper to conclude that by accepting the contribution, the recipient agreed to conditions established by the contributor, he cautioned.

As for any new ethics legislation, Price suggested that if there were any overwhelming public sentiment in this direction or any possibility that current campaign contribution conduct could be "injurious to the . . . public's confidence in the Congress," corrective legislation might be in order. Apparently the Congress does enjoy the confidence of the public. It is for this reason that the handful of congressmen in both the Senate and House who would like to reform our federal highway program, and they do not necessarily agree on the method, believe that if desirable changes can be made in our highway program, they will be brought about through public scrutiny of the merits of the highway program, rather than by congressional reform.

7. A Road Test for Our Highway Program

"It is the position of the State highway administrators that the automobile may not be the most efficient form of transportation under all conditions in terms of dollars and cents, but that the highway program should continue in accordance with highway needs and the public's desires in the matter."

—AASHO Progress Report to the
House and Senate Public Works Committees
concerning future highway needs, June 1968

The car-borne American would probably be shocked to learn that when he signs a contract for a new $3000 automobile, he is in fact committing himself to spend $11,000 for 3500 pounds of steel, glass, and plastic to be moved 100,000 miles over a period of ten years. That is one of the conclusions of a recent BPR study on Auto Operating Costs.

The American driver would probably be even more shocked to learn how much his highways really cost. But highway-cost information is not given in the study. The only reference to this expense is the calculation that it costs an average of 11 cents per mile to operate a four-door sedan and that of this amount, state and federal taxes for highways take 1.2 cents. It certainly doesn't sound like much.

The $11,000 total averages out this way for the ten-year period: Besides the initial cost of the car, there is $2230 for 7000 gallons of gasoline; $1415 for insurance; $1763 for maintenance and repairs; $1800 for parking and tolls; and $1172 for federal and state taxes for highways. Even if a car has a series of owners, overall operating costs remain about the same as for a single owner for the ten-year period. If a person trades in every year, he pays an additional $8420 in depreciation.

The BPR study carefully notes that the $11,000 total does not include interest or financing charges. In 1968, approximately 70 percent of all new cars sold were financed through banks, finance companies, and other credit institutions. That year, Americans borrowed $33 billion to buy cars and paid $2.5 billion for the money.

The Bureau study emphasized that the public was only too glad to pay the 1.2 cents per mile for highways: "Most motorists seem willing to pay the costs of an adequate highway system and would be willing to agree that a 1960 Ford, on a modern safe highway, gives more satisfactory transportation than a 1967 Cadillac on a congested, outdated road. . . . The new Interstate routes are whetting the appetite of the motorist for more of the same. . . . Nothing seems to discourage the motorist enough to make him want to, or even be willing, to give up his car. The developing pattern of shopping centers, residential areas, and employment centers tends to make the automobile nearly indispensable to most households, and despite congestion and expense, it remains an important part of recreational activity."

Such reasoning is like arguing that people must prefer cancer because it is so prevalent. The motorist's willingness to pay gasoline and other highway taxes may be the price he must pay to be able to move about at all. When highway promoters argue the public's "willingness" to pay road taxes, they imply that the motorist is exercising some choice among modes of travel when he decides to make a trip. Often, this is simply not the case. Meanwhile, the gas and oil taxes pile into the Highway Trust Fund.

Before 1956, all federal gasoline and oil taxes went into the general treasury, and federal aid to road construction came from the general fund, where roads competed with a long list of other needs. Since July 1956, however, the Highway Trust Fund has been the sole repository for revenues from the taxes imposed on gasoline and other items used in motor vehicle transport, on the theory that this will guarantee that only road users will be paying for roads. A National Highway Users Conference booklet on the Trust Fund carefully states that "from these receipts have been made all expenditures for the Federal share of the cost of the Federal-State highway projects." But not one cent of Highway Trust Fund money is spent on other federal-aid road projects such as forest development roads and trails, which are built for recreation and lumber interests, or for forest highways, or for parks and trails roads, parkways, or public-land roads. In 1968, the House and Senate Public Works committees felt free to authorize more than half a billion dollars for such roads. Since their costs must come from the general fund, such other roads must compete for their funding in Congress. Not so the remainder of our gigantic IS and ABC highway program, however. They are guaranteed funding from the Highway Trust Fund, which is inviolable for any other purpose.

In 1968, the Highway Trust Fund accumulated $4.5 billion. Since the money cannot be spent on anything but highway construction, that is where it will go. Attempts to divert Trust Fund money to any other purpose are referred to as "raids" on the fund. There have been numerous attempts, none successful. Between 1956 and 1967, $31.92 billion in federal tax revenues have poured into the Highway Trust Fund. The Treasury Department estimates that total receipts through September 1972 will reach $57.88 billion—twice the cost of the U.S. moon-landing program.

But the billions of dollars spent annually by the federal government on roads are only about one third the entire amount spent for all roads in the United States. In 1968, when the total road program cost $15 billion, the Trust Fund revenues contributed almost $5 billion and the states contributed $10 billion. Each state collects its own gas, oil, license, and other auto-related fees, which it uses to "match" federal money for roads. Despite claims that only "users" pay for roads, it is a fiscal fact that 26 percent of total roads costs in 46 standard metropolitan statistical areas in 1965 were being funded from general revenue, property taxes, or assessments and miscellaneous sources. On a state-wide basis, the amount of revenue derived from nonuser sources totaled close to 20 percent per state.

Highway lobbyists counter that highways have contributed immensely to the economic growth of the country, and state and federal officials and politicians insist that highways save everybody money. Volumes have been written on the economics of highway building or, rather, on the economics that should go into calculating the benefits and costs of building highways.

There are several very important factors to consider in evaluating the merits of constructing a highway. One of these is the need for the facility. This is determined by what engineers call traffic volume forecast predictions—estimates of what future traffic volumes will be, based mainly upon population growth figures and the current and past automobile traffic volumes.

In addition to determining the need for a highway facility, highway planners often calculate, as a separate exercise, the economic factors related to actually building the facility. Engineers and economists use a "benefit-cost" formula which is supposed to crank in such factors as time, fuel, and oil saved, wear and tear on autos, and reduced accident rate, all in terms of dollars that can be saved by improving or constructing a particular highway. They stack this "benefit" total up against the cost of building the highway, which they calculate in terms of the price of acquiring the land, the actual cost of construction, labor, etc. When the calculated total of gains equals or is greater than the total costs, the undertaking is considered to be economically feasible. But many economists—and, from the highway engineers' viewpoint, far too many highway critics—point out that highway planners don't really evaluate the *total* cost of proposed facilities. Planners don't consider such items as the cost of air pollution that will be generated from use of the facility or social disruption, caused by displacement of people, destruction of businesses, and the like. Engineers also tend to count as benefits some items which are not benefits at all. For instance, they often count as pluses the increased land values that attend the opening of a new highway facility. But they ignore the decreased land values that so often develop as a consequence of road construction. For instance, a freeway reaching from the city far into the countryside can re-distribute *total* land values by bringing a large new supply of land within the urban land market. Thus, the benefit does not accrue to the people of the metropolitan area as a whole. Rather, a few, often politicians, benefit, while the many suffer. The few include land-owners holding property strategically located near road paths such as some Fort Worth ranchers described in the New York *Times.*

Two new interstate highways and a related loop around Fort Worth opened large ranching areas to development. In addition, a Dallas-Fort Worth Regional Airport is on the drawing boards that will require building $50 million of additional roads. The price of raw land for the airport has jumped from $1059 per acre in 1967 to $5000 per acre in 1969. Land with road frontage may command $10,000 an acre.

President Roosevelt addressed himself to this very point on January 12, 1944, when he sent the Congress his message outlining a national system of interregional highways. The last paragraph of the President's message stated:

> It hardly seems fair that the hazard of an engineering survey should greatly enrich one man and give no profit to his neighbor, who may have had a right-of-way which was equally good. After all, why should the hazard of engineering give one private citizen an enormous profit? If there is to be an unearned profit, why should it not accrue to the Government—State or Federal, or both?

Interchange sites make money for speculators, too. A developer or speculator picks up a large tract of land cheap along a proposed highway and announces he will build a shopping center. He then pushes for an interchange at his location. Then he sells his land, at a profit, to someone who develops the shopping center, or builds one himself, justifying the need for the interchange, which the public pays for. Meanwhile, other speculators buy up land around the interchange and farther out, and as the new highway presses out and connects with older roads, new housing developments spring up and businessmen established in the shopping center hope to heaven that enough people will move to the new area to justify their investment in the new shopping center. Such developments are considered by engineers as stimulators of the economy. Yet merchants in the new shops and home builders will not prosper simply because the highway is there. They will prosper only if enough people demand new homes and goods and have the money to pay for them.

Highway proponents boast that such highway projects expand the economy by providing more jobs, bigger metropolitan areas, and expanded industry. To hear them tell it, it was highways that created the United States economic boom since World War II, not population growth, increased demand for goods, or expanded technology.

For example, a study done in Kentucky around 1960 produced the conclusion that an IBM plant had located in Lexington because of an improved highway facility. But a closer look showed that while there had been apparent gain for some landowners and Kentucky businessmen, and possibly the labor force in the area, the highway per se had not created the demand for the electronic typewriters being produced at the new plant. IBM would just as surely have put the plant someplace else if it had not gone to Lexington, Richard Zettel, research economist at the University of California, pointed out. He noted the broad claims that highways contribute to the national defense, improve our education system, facilitate essential government services, increase land values, foster medical care, and promote just about anything anyone might regard as salutary. Such arguments are used by politicians and highway lobbyists to prove that everybody benefits from highways and that everyone should pay for them, not only motorists. Commenting on the Highway Trust Fund, Zettel sarcastically pointed out to a meeting of the American Society of Civil Engineers, in 1961, that, using the same sort of "logic," one might argue that steel should be subsidized to enhance national defense, or that since electricity is essential to the operation of our schools, or that since telephone service is a boon to effective police and fire protection, perhaps there should be special taxes to support all of these enterprises too.

Even when engineers tote up the benefits in terms of savings to motorists, they can be wide of the mark, according to Tillo Kuhn, economist, at Toronto's York University. For instance, the savings in motor-vehicle operating costs can be relatively accurately estimated. Wear and tear on tires, savings in fuel consumption and the like can be calculated in terms of dollars. But to calculate the savings in time, fewer accidents, comfort, speed, and convenience in the same terms, i.e., dollars, with any degree of accuracy, is not so easy. For instance, time has a different value for each person and it also varies for each person throughout the day. Unfortunately, the most reliable and objectively determined factors, dollars saved in wear and tear on vehicle and fuel savings, etc., can account for less than 5 percent of the total benefits, as calculated by engineers, while they can tack on as much as 95 percent of the remainder from their supply of rather subjective factors such as convenience, time saved, etc. Thus, economic justification for building a freeway can be heavily weighted with subjective factors. Those freeways in Kansas City, Missouri, were justified mainly on grounds that they would save motorists time and this is still one of the most popular arguments engineers use today to justify building a freeway. Economically, the argument doesn't stand up. The engineer's argument is demolished when congestion rises on the new freeway and motoring speed drops drastically, eliminating any time savings.

However, according to BPR highway research engineer Robley Winfrey, the benefit-cost analysis isn't all that important. In fact, it isn't even done on every project! He admits that an economic analysis of a proposed project does not really determine whether or not the highway should be built. Winfrey explains that the traffic volume forecast is probably the most important premise, because the *basic objective of highway improvements is to facilitate the flow of vehicular traffic.* Other Bureau officials explain that no economic analysis at all is made on projects "when it is clear that the facility is needed." Clear to highway engineers, that is.

Winfrey claims "nonmarket" benefits from highways; one he cites is that highways make it possible for buses to take children to school and thus reduce the number of school buildings needed. This is patently absurd. It is just this suburban sprawl, with its miles of highways, housing developments, and shopping centers, that has forced schools to provide transportation for students. The money spent for bussing is money that cannot be spent for needed staff, improved plant and equipment, and has nothing to do with reducing the number of school buildings.

Winfrey explains that highway departments pour data into a computer and are able to produce an "analysis" of a proposed project within an hour. Any trained person can do this, he says. "Of course, we must assume that the analyst is completely objective," he cautions. But he admits that there are many "unquantifiable" ingredients such as air pollution, noise, and other social effects that remain unmeasured. So the analyst falls back on his old stand-by, traffic forecasts.

As for public opinion, Winfrey echoes what has become the standard line of highway officials faced by irate citizens. His philosophy: "The public should be heard but it doesn't mean you have to follow what they say. Engineers are professionals just like lawyers and doctors. Does the community make the laws? Do you take a vote in the community to see if you need an operation?" he asks. He believes the public should be invited to comment on proposals. But he says that the engineers really know what is best for the community.

This arrogant belief is shared by most highway officials, who automatically turn to their future traffic volume projections to convince skeptics and justify their proposals.

While the state highway department computers grind out economic analyses, Tillo Kuhn has investigated the economics of San Francisco's often proposed Western Freeway. He postulates that if motorists paid a 30-cent toll charge for use of the facility, based on 1961 gas taxes and license fees of 6.4 cents, the 30-cent toll charge would be equivalent to a 50-cent tax on a gallon of gasoline. He argues that if users of the freeway knew the road was costing them an amount equal to 50 cents in tax alone on a gallon of gasoline, they would not use it.

Kuhn argues that the full costs and gains of a freeway should include the price of the automobile, cost of parking, feeder trips to and from the freeway, as compared with the same trip by some other mode. Then add the costs of running the freeway, the cost of owning and operating and maintaining a car, the private and public costs of storing the vehicle, plus the costs to the public of providing the feeder roads. He says there should be some price tag assigned to the initial reduced congestion on local streets that planners claim will follow the opening of the facility. Also cranked into the analyses should be the overall efficiency and performance of California highways and the national network of interstate highways. He calculated that the cost for the Western Freeway over twenty years would be $170 million but that it would only generate $31 million in revenue.

He argues that just because revenues accrue from gasoline and oil burned up on California's other roads, it is ridiculous to assume that these taxes represent users' demand for the Western Freeway. Some highway officials were arguing that if the Western Freeway were not built, the Bayshore Freeway would have to be expanded or another facility built at greater cost. Kuhn compares this logic with the student who tells his father that it is economically sound for the father to buy an $8000 sports car because otherwise he will have to buy his son a Rolls Royce. There is no proof that expansion of the Bayshore or Western Freeway is economically justified, he argues. "The presumption that absolute needs exist for projects that happen to be proposed pervades much of current highway thinking," he points out. He calls highways monopolistic and declares that highway authorities exercise more power than private monopolists, who at least are threatened by potential competition. The hue and cry of the highway promoters is that the public must want more highways, since they use them and seem willing to pay the cost. He says that passengers should be given a choice of modes before the taxes collected are interpreted as a vote in support of highways. As the study by the Highway Research Board has indicated, almost half of the 80 percent of respondents who said they used autos for all their trips also said this was so because they had no other means of getting around.

Yet, highway officials continue to state that people are ravenous for more highways and that they can't supply roads to the motoring public fast enough. Such fuzzy reasoning and research are not limited to highway officials. Offhanded claims are standard in the trucking industry. A prime example was the way that trucking interests tried, in 1968, to force passage of a bill that would allow bigger and heavier trailer trucks on interstate highways.

Controls on the size and weight of vehicles on the Interstate System were written into the 1956 Highway Act. They carried limits of 18,000 pounds on a single axle, and 32,000 pounds for a tandem axle or a total gross weight of 73,280 pounds. Also, vehicles were limited to a width of 96 inches (8 feet). However, when the 1956 Act was passed, some states were allowing trucks on their highways that exceeded those limits. So a "grandfather clause" was included allowing larger trucks on the Interstate System in those states which were permitting larger trucks on their highways at that time. Thus, all size and weight restrictions were frozen in 1956 at whatever level, state or federal, was the maximum for each state. Rhode Island and Connecticut could allow trucks 102 inches wide on their Interstate roads, and Hawaii could allow its maximum 108-inch wide trucks to use its interstate highways. In addition, eighteen states with single-axle load limits greater than the 18,000-pound limit and eighteen states with tandem-axle limits greater than 32,000 pounds and seventeen states with total weight maximums greater than 73,280 pounds could put them on the Interstate System. All other states required trucks to conform to the limits of the 1956 Act. There have never been any such restrictions on any of the federally aided portions of the ABC system of highways.

In the spring of 1968, the Senate Public Works Committee unanimously reported out the bill the truckers wanted that would relax the federal limitations on the width of trucks to 102 inches, raised the single-axle load to 20,000 pounds and the tandem-axle load to 34,000 pounds with a formula for determining the total gross weight depending upon the length of the vehicle and a maximum of 105,500 pounds.

Senator Randolph introduced the legislation in the Senate before a handful of his colleagues, stressing that the proposed regulations applied to the Interstate System only "and will not in and of itself result in any larger or heavier vehicles operating on that system."

He said this was so because the legislation was merely "permissive" in that it allowed but did not order the states to permit larger vehicles on the Interstate System. Randolph admitted that the older roads on the ABC system and particularly old bridges would not support heavier and bigger vehicles, a point the Department of Transportation made. He waved away any reservations about the safety aspects of the legislation with the statement that there appeared to be no "safety involvement" in the proposed increases. Several senators expressed concern that most long-haul trucks begin and end their trips on the older roads. It is interesting to note here that the largest and safest system, the Interstate System, has weight and size limits while the ABC system, which comprises 88 percent of all of our other roads and which is less capable of handling larger and heavier vehicles, has no controls whatsoever! Roads designed to lower standards can and do carry heavier and larger vehicles than the Interstate System. DOT had suggested that the proposed standards be applied to all federally aided highways. That idea got nowhere. And while Randolph could stand in the Senate and state that "We must never allow safety to be relegated to a secondary position," not one conclusive study was presented to ascertain the safety implications of large vehicles on our highways nor was there any evidence that anyone had conducted any studies on the safety aspects of the proposed limits. Except the truckers. They claimed that truck drivers have the safest driving records. Figures from the National Safety Council for 1966 show that trucks represented only 16.1 percent of all registered motor vehicles and of that number, only 10.9 were involved in accidents. Automobiles that same year accounted for 81.3 percent of registered motor vehicles, 85.5 percent of which were involved in accidents. The American Trucking Association cites these figures to congressional committees to demonstrate their safety record. Yet an Interstate Commerce Commission Bureau of Motor Carrier Safety report of 1966 on truck accidents revealed that in 13,575 car-truck collisions, only 25 truck drivers were killed while 964 automobile drivers or passengers were killed. According to these figures, for every truck-car collision in which 1 truck driver was killed, 38 automobile riders were killed.

ATA explains that intercity trucks are so designed that in most collisions with passenger cars the total impact is below the position of the truck driver as he sits in his cab, which means that few truck drivers are killed but that car passengers are vulnerable. Then, too, the truckers point out, in a collision a truck is so much larger than the passenger car that the opportunity of being killed by hitting a truck is greater for the lighter vehicle, plus the fact that generally there is only one person in the truck while the car may have five or six occupants. Yet ATA pressed long and hard to secure the legislation that would allow bigger trucks on the highways.

The trucking industry said it needed permission to put bigger trucks on the roads in order to maintain a healthy competition with other modes of goods transporters and that larger trucks would accomplish this. Truckers saw it as an opportunity to up their profits by $250 million annually.

Senator John Sherman Cooper expressed reservations about the extra pounding the pavement would take as a result of these heavier loads. He cited BPR tests which showed that the impact of the new limits for a single axle would be 50 percent greater than the current limit. Randolph admitted that no one knew what effect the heavier trucks were having on roads in states where they had been allowed. No research has been conducted to determine how much more it actually costs to maintain roads that take an increased pounding of pavement from heavier trucks. It would also appear that longer trucks could not negotiate sharp turns in urban areas. Asked if the BPR was studying the effects of larger trucks, an engineer in the Bureau stated that in Oregon, Idaho, and Nevada, Bureau personnel were "observing" how triple-bottom trailers 98 to 104 feet long were negotiating ramps, city intersections, and their ability to brake effectively.

The bill passed the Senate by a voice vote, with seven senators present.

It did not fare so well in the House, where it was sponsored by Congressman Kluczynski. There, Congressmen William Moorhead

(D., Pennsylvania), Robert McEwen (R., New York), along with Schwengel, McCarthy, and Cleveland distributed a dissertation by Dr. John W. Fuller II on the subject of increased weights and sizes of trucks on the Interstate System, which he wrote while employed as a transport economist for the Western Highway Institute, arm of the ATA.

Fuller's study showed that the requested new size limits would net truckers a saving of $250 million annually, but that it would cost $282 million annually to adjust highway width, repair roadbeds, and widen bridges, and $750 million annually for social costs such as increased accidents and diversion of railroad freight to bigger trucks. State highway officials have documented that a large number of bridges and miles of pavement on non-Interstate roads could not take the pounding of heavier loads caused by bigger trucks. This is important because trucks must use these roads to get on and off the Interstate System and deliver to their destination, which is not necessarily on the system.

Seeing that so many questions remained unanswered concerning the proposed legislation, and particularly interested in the safety factors of the Senate bill, Congressman Schwengel contacted the Federal Highway Administration's newly established National Highway Safety Bureau. He was chagrined to discover that the bureau was not investigating safety factors of larger vehicles on all federally aided highways but was, rather, awarding grants to study such items as the safety of gas tank caps on Volkswagens and windshield defrosting requirements.

The truckers' bill was not reported out of the House Public Works Committee in 1968, but the truckers renewed their efforts again in 1969.

Apparently, truckers justify the need for highways with one argument while highway engineers use another. As Mr. Winfrey explained it, the justification for building any particular freeway is based, in the main, on projected future traffic volumes. Even these statistics sometimes blow up in the faces of the analysts. Nowhere have the engineers been more embarrassed by their traffic volume projections than in the nation's capital.

In 1944, officials in Washington, from President Roosevelt on down, expressed concern that with the end of World War II, the amount of traffic, particularly by automobile, entering and leaving the District of Columbia would increase rapidly to unmanageable proportions unless bold plans were initiated to facilitate the ever growing flow of people, goods, and autos.

The engineering firms of J. E. Greiner and De Leuw Cather, together with the District of Columbia Highway Department and the federal government, issued a report with recommendations on the transportation needs of the nation's capital that year. In those days, Washington had an efficient bus and trolley system.

The engineer consultants determined that the transportation needs of the city would best be served by modifying the trolley system, "the most economical means, both in cost and in use of space, of moving large numbers of people on surface streets in urban areas," to an expanded system of streetcar subways. The D.C. Highway Department had stated as early as 1941, "We are convinced that with rapid, direct, and comfortable service, mass transportation can and should supplant much of the individual vehicular service into the central business area." The engineers' report concluded that "It will be unnecessary to resort to expensive elevated or depressed highways on rights-of-way requiring the demolition of buildings because the wide streets will accommodate a sufficient number of traffic lanes to serve adequately the business and federal areas."

The strong emphasis on the streetcar system was a consequence of studies which showed that the increasing flow of automobiles entering the city was creating more congestion, making it difficult to reach downtown business retail areas, consuming time of both auto *and* public transport riders, increasing the cost of delivering merchandise, and severely straining parking facilities. The study forecast that these conditions would grow worse faster when the war ended and more autos became available. The result would be a serious loss of business to merchants in the central city, followed by a decline in property values and decreased intake of taxes. Merchants would abandon the heart of the city for less congested outlying areas, which would lead to further decentralization of residential areas. The study also made clear that it would be physically and economically impossible to supply inexpensive and convenient parking for everyone who wanted to drive everywhere downtown. Department stores would have to provide three to four times as much floor area for parking as for retail activity if all customers arrived by car. Office buildings would have to provide parking space equal to the office space to accommodate workers' automobiles. And even if the parking spaces were made available, enough streets could not be provided to carry the number of vehicles involved, the engineers determined. The study pointed out, too, that land values in downtown areas were too high to make one-level parking profitable; also that such parking areas in a retail zone created "dead" frontages between stores. Hence, the emphasis on expanding the trolley system into a streetcar-subway system.

The study showed that by 1940, 63 percent of Washington's workers in the central business and government districts were using transportation other than private automobiles to get to work. Roughly 15 percent were walking and 48 percent were using public transit, while only 37 percent made the trip by automobile, and it was taking the transit patron ten minutes longer to get to work than the average motorist. Construction of a streetcar-subway system, the study said, "will reduce traveling time from a large portion of the city by at least this amount. [With the construction of a trolley subway] the number of workers who will be induced to leave their automobiles at home should materially relieve problems of parking and street traffic congestion," the engineers predicted.

The study emphasized that auto traffic was stabbing at the heart of the city and pointed out that the prosperity of the Washington downtown business area depended on the easy movement of people, not vehicles, and that indeed vehicles should be discouraged from entering the center city. As for cross-town traffic, the study proposed controlling it by means of a beltway made up of existing streets. The planners emphasized that the number of persons who walk to work should be maintained and even increased by protecting the attractiveness of the residential neighborhoods immediately adjacent to the business district, where most walkers originate. "The pedestrian is the most economical user of street space, using approximately $\frac{1}{13}$th as much room as the transit passenger and $\frac{1}{200}$th as much room as the average driver or automobile rider. He requires no parking facilities, and no capital investment for a transit vehicle to carry him," was the way the report put it.

The main point of the study was that it was important to segregate different types of traffic and encourage the most economical modes. Thus, an expanded streetcar-subway system would be channeled separately from automobiles. Pedestrians would have easy access to the streetcar and bus systems unimpeded by automobiles, and new buildings would provide entrances for trucks, phasing out curb deliveries, a basic source of congestion.

The study carried a final caveat that if Washington's transportation problems continued unchecked, more people would turn to the private automobile, "a trend which threatens to explode the city," and that traffic congestion would result in mass exodus of both retail and government facilities from the city, which trend "could easily assume disastrous proportions." As sensible as the proposals were, the Congress provided no money to pay for their implementation, and nothing much happened. Reason had had its brief day. The Congress did take one step in 1944: It authorized the National Interstate Highway System and its original 40,000 miles of highways. Although no money was to be forthcoming until the 1950s for the vast highway scheme, the D.C. Highway Department and engineering firms immediately shifted gears to meet the new emphasis on roads.

In 1946, just two years after they submitted their report on public transportation and warning of the consequences of increased emphasis on the use of automobiles, the very same firms of Greiner and De Leuw Cather issued still another study of Washington's transportation needs. This time they found that "The backbone of the proposed facilities is a system of expressways serving all parts of the District and connecting with existing and proposed highways of this type in Maryland and Virginia." Improved public transportation should consist of buses on expressways, the new report suggested!

The fears expressed in the previous report about the deleterious effects of more automobiles entering the downtown business district had disappeared. Instead the report predicted that, "improved highways will stimulate trips to the central business district both from the metropolitan area and from distant cities. Most of the additional population in the metropolitan area, moreover, will depend on some form of transportation, whereas one person in seven walked to work in 1940." The same facts which two years earlier had been presented to support dire warnings somehow were transformed into assets. To those familiar with their 1944 report, the authors explained that the difficulty of providing parking facilities for automobiles would keep the number of cars entering the central business district from causing deterioration of the core city, the disaster they had predicted in 1944. They underestimated the shrewdness of future parking barons.

Pulling out all the stops to make their new case for an expressway system, the engineers perorated about the high toll of traffic accidents, which, for one seven-week period, had reached an average of one traffic crash an hour. What was needed, they suggested, was more enforcement and education, plus engineering know-how—implying more and better expressways.

The report argued: "The effectiveness of Enforcement in preventing accidents is limited by natural aversion for restrictions. Education, likewise, depends upon acceptance of ideas not readily absorbed by such accident-prone groups as the very young and the very old. Engineering, on the other hand, is popular because it is done *for* the public rather than *to* the public. Good engineering, with the help of Enforcement and Education, can make travel in both public and private conveyances not only safer but also easier and faster." (History did not bear out the convictions of the engineers. In 1940, 5.9 of every 1000 Washington residents was killed or injured in an auto accident. In 1964, after $400 million had been spent on highway improvements, the city's toll of persons killed or injured in traffic accidents was 13.6 per 1000 residents.)

The engineers had no difficulty explaining why they were promoting the expressway system. The reason was "promulgation of the National Interstate Highway System comprising some 40,000 miles of principal highways." Other cities were planning them, some had a few, why not Washington? Interestingly enough, in discussing interstate expressways being planned for the District of Columbia to connect Richmond, Pittsburgh, Baltimore, and Charleston, the engineers noted that "As these routes penetrate the metropolitan area of Washington they will properly serve more and more of the urban traffic and less proportionately that moving between cities." So they knew there would develop mostly local, not interstate, traffic as far back as the mid-forties, long before these same highway promoters labored before congressional committees to convince them of the need for a highway system for interstate traffic.

The 1946 report did say that most of the streetcars should be retained "because of the streetcar's economy of operation on heavy traffic routes as well as for its efficiency in use of street space." Yet, the report warned, people cannot be forced to use public transit just to postpone the day of reckoning for the city's street system. The report explained that as the volume of all traffic climbs, buses and streetcars would move at slower and slower speeds, tempting more people to desert transit and turn to the automobile for transportation. Therefore, new highways had to be built to accommodate this inevitable auto traffic. Inherent in this argument was the assumption that increased traffic would be in the form of automobile traffic only.

The report did not point out that just as increased traffic volume cuts the speed of streetcars and buses, it also cuts auto speed.

The total land area of the District of Columbia is limited to 62.5 square miles, or 40,000 acres. By 1961, the District's central business district, consisting of 1.8 square miles, was squeezing in 92,000 cars per day. At that time, New York City, with a downtown area 50 percent larger, accommodated 79,000 cars. The nation's capital by 1964 was the leader in freeway mileage, per square miles and per capita, among the twelve largest U.S. urban areas, *including Los Angeles.* By 1965, Washington had received over $500 million for major highway projects, while its trolley-car transit system had received not money but orders to dismantle. All trolley lines ceased operation and most tracks were taken up by 1962.

In 1960, traffic congestion had grown so bad that the House and Senate District committees declared, "Washington, like every other large American city, has been suffering from steadily worsening traffic congestion. For more than a decade after World War II, there was a steady decline in transit ridership, and a rapid increase in the number of private automobiles on the streets and highways. The Highway Departments of the District of Columbia, Maryland, and Virginia have never been able to catch up with this increase in traffic, nor does it appear likely that they can do so in the near future. Furthermore, it is becoming increasingly evident that any attempt to meet the area's transportation needs by highways and private automobiles alone will wreck the city—it will demolish residential neighborhoods, violate parks and playgrounds, desecrate the monumental portions of the nation's capital, and remove much valuable property from the tax rolls." To meet the coming disaster, Congress established the National Capital Transportation Agency with the statutory mandate to chart "a balanced transportation system" of highways and rapid transit, with special attention on the early development of a subway. All this triggered more expansive freeway plans within the D.C. Highway Department to the tune of $846 million. But NCTA recommended a less ambitious highway program of $688 million, plus a $681 million metropolitan subway system. Highway promoters reacted by accusing the NCTA of trying to "kill" freeways to "sell" subways. In May 1963, President Kennedy requested the D.C. commissioners to make a complete reappraisal of D.C.'s freeway program in light of NCTA recommendations. It was never made. Instead, the D.C. Highway Department expanded its proposed highway program by still another $127 million until by 1965 it had swollen to $960 million. Meanwhile, NCTA's proposed subway shrank to less than $400 million.

What has happened to Washington as more freeways have been constructed in and around the metropolitan area? Contrary to his hopes, the Washington retailer has discovered that the new highways have been draining customers to the suburbs. Between 1946 and

1963, the city of Washington lost one fourth of its retail establishments and retail sales in 1963 were no higher than they had been fifteen years before. The city reached its peak in population in 1947 when 920,000 persons lived within the District of Columbia. In 1968, the population was 820,000. During the same 1948–63 period, however, suburban Maryland and Virginia increased from 493,000 to 1,534,000, an increase of 200 percent growth in suburban sprawl. Retail sales in suburban Maryland and Virginia increased by 300 percent. Washington's share of the total area retail sales shrank from 75 percent in 1948 to 42 percent by 1963. In 1910, it had been estimated that 52 percent of the land in the District of Columbia was taxable. But by 1964, taxable land in the District had dwindled to 35 percent.

At the heart of the nation's capital, the central business district, more than 60 percent of the land is devoted currently to the moving and storage of automobiles. This means that more than half of the most valuable land within the city is being utilized for automobiles. Within this 1152-acre area, streets and alleys already pre-empt 48 percent of the space, due largely to the heritage of the L'Enfant Plan. Another 157 acres, or 14 percent, are devoted to off-street parking. In 1940, there were 18,000 off-street parking spaces in the area. By 1964, there were 47,976 spaces where formerly homes and offices stood. Owners of the land, upon which buildings formerly stood, were encouraged to convert to parking lots when their buildings deteriorated. By removing the "improvement" on the land and converting to open-space parking lots, the owner's taxes were reduced. High central city employment and ample highways into the area assured the owner of property in the central business district a guaranteed income from the rental of his space.

Unaccountably, the city-based business community joined the clamor for more freeways "to stimulate sagging sales in the core city." Retailers blame a steady decline in downtown retail sales on traffic congestion, which they believed would be remedied by more roads—and inadequate parking facilities. But a study conducted in 1961 showed that there were at least 10,000 parking spaces *vacant* in downtown Washington at all hours of the day.

Furthermore, from 10 A.M. until 6 P.M., 80 percent of all occupied parking spaces were filled by cars that were used for driving to work. Only 4 percent were occupied by shoppers and 2.5 percent by tourists, the two groups businessmen wish to accommodate. The businessmen had been had.

The same survey resulted in a prediction that 33,524 off-street parking spaces would be needed by 1971. In June 1965, there were already 51,422 spaces, 50 percent more than the forecast need for 1971. Yet, as the number of parking spaces increased, retail sales in Washington's central business district decreased from $421 million in 1948 to $407 million in 1963. Clearly, constructing freeways and creating parking spaces in the downtown area do not guarantee increased retail sales.

By 1964, Washington had 142 miles of freeways, including four additional bridges. Stately trees had been cut down to widen and promote "free-flowing" traffic on many of L'Enfant's existing streets. But that was not enough to satisfy the D.C. and Maryland and Virginia highway departments, all of whom were relatively affluent as the result of accumulated revenue from the Highway Trust Fund earmarked for roads in and around the nation's capital.

The District Highway Department proposed 38 lanes of new freeways entering and leaving the nation's capital with a capability of dumping another 40,000 automobiles into the city every hour. The highway engineers insisted the "necessary" 38 lanes of freeways would not be competitive with public transportation, but would be "complementary" to a "balanced" transportation system. And they insisted that their traffic volume forecasting studies verified the need for all the freeways. None of their statements were true. To begin with, from 1941 through 1948, more than 65 percent of commuters working in downtown Washington used public transit. But as new bridges and highways opened and downtown parking increased, trolley riding rapidly fell off. By 1965, only one third of the peak-hour riders to the downtown area used public transit (by then, buses only). The remainder rode in automobiles, averaging less than two persons per car. Between 1946 and 1964, metropolitan Washington's population grew more than 70 percent.

In the same time span, the area's transit passengers declined 57 percent and the daily vehicular traffic entering and leaving Washington increased almost 200 percent.

Cities with populations and commuters far greater than Washington's found in the early 1960s that with comprehensive rapid transit systems they needed fewer highways than Washington already has. For instance, downtown Chicago, smaller in area than the District of Columbia central business district, had 50 percent more people entering at the rush hour in 1962, but barely one third the number of automobiles as D.C. More than 80 percent of Chicago's commuters used public transit. Since then, two expressways have been opened in Chicago: the Dan Ryan Expressway, extending straight south from the central business district, and the Stevenson Expressway, extending southwest from the central business district. Bus ridership has remained at about the 1962 level, but both transit and commuter rail patronage have each dropped by 8000 passengers per rush hour while the number of automobiles entering the central business district increased 5 percent.

In 1960, downtown New York had 700,000 more peak-hour commuters than Washington. More than 90 percent of these used public transit.

Surely if D.C. highway officials, who proclaimed that they wanted a balanced transportation system, were sincere, they would not have advocated 38 additional freeway lanes from the suburbs to the central city with a capability of draining up to 68,000 future riders from the still disputed rapid transit system.* A cursory examination of their traffic forecast figures which predicted that an ever increasing tide of automobiles would descend on downtown D.C. makes them highly questionable.

When the circumferential Capital Beltway was completed in August 1964, traffic from neighboring Montgomery County to Washington dropped sharply. Elsewhere, even in corridors where new freeways had been built, arterial traffic was lagging far behind the

* Urban freeways can carry 2000 vehicles per lane per hour. Of the 38 radial freeway lanes proposed, 18 would be inbound, 18, outbound, and 2, reversible. Average car occupancy is 1.7 persons.

highway engineers' predictions of a few years before. In 1964, Washington's newest bridge, the Theodore Roosevelt, was completed. It was built to accommodate "ever increasing volumes of traffic across the Potomac," according to highway engineers' sloganeering. The new bridge connected Virginia and mid-city Washington. By March 1965, average weekday traffic on the Virginia-Washington bridges was almost 2000 less than it had been a year before. Traffic on one, Memorial Bridge, was at its lowest point in eleven years. On all Potomac River crossings, which include bridges between the city and Maryland, traffic in March 1965 was 111,-000 less per day than had been forecast for 1965 only six years before.

As the true transportation picture became clear to residents of the District as more and more businesses and homes were bulldozed out to make room for more superhighways, citizen protest erupted sharply. Politically conservative and liberal citizen and civic associations alike argued before the National Capital Planning Commission and congressional committees, picketed the offices of the District commissioners, and, in the process, found a mutual bond with suburban communities, which were also threatened by the ambitious highway programs of the surrounding Virginia and Maryland highway departments. Money in large and small amounts poured into a war chest to finance the lawsuit that finally halted the onslaught of the engineers and invoked the rage of the House roads subcommittee, which ultimately ordered the roads to be built.

Who was right, the highway engineers or the citizens? Residents protested that the new highways would only attract more autos into already car-choked D.C. and that the engineers' plans were extravagant, both in the amount of facilities their system would impose on the city and the cost. For example, the 4.3-mile North Central Freeway was estimated by engineers to cost $130 million, roughly $20 million more than the new, much criticized and ostentatious House Rayburn Office Building on Capitol Hill. Furthermore, D.C. Highway Department figures showed that the elaborate freeway plan would consume 700 acres of the District's land, reducing further an already inadequate tax base, and so displace 15,000 residents. Justification for this grandiose highway network has always been based on the D.C. Highway Department doctrine that Washington confronts ever mounting traffic demands. Proof of these demands is based on District, Maryland, and Virginia highway department traffic forecast studies completed in 1959. Their forecast encompassed traffic projections for 1965 and 1980 and is the basis for both the embryonic subway system and the proposed freeway system for the nation's capital. The three basic ingredients in the forecast were population, employment, and travel times, which they poured into a "gravity model" forecasting system. A comparison of highway department forecast figures for 1965 and actual traffic figures for that year reveal that the highway engineers exaggerated actual traffic demand by 40 percent or 406,780 autos per day, the equivalent of 38 freeway lanes, the exact number of lanes in their proposed network. It is interesting to note that actual traffic counts were 25 percent higher in 1965 than had been forecast in the two traffic corridors which had experienced wider lanes and construction of expressways, indicating that the facilities induce traffic beyond the calculations of the engineers.

The most striking difference between the traffic forecast and actual traffic count occurred between northwest Washington and adjacent Montgomery County in Maryland. There, actual traffic was less than half the predicted amount. It was, in fact, 239,179 vehicles per day below the forecast count, the equivalent of 19 freeway lanes. In fact, a comparison of total traffic counts in 1965 with predicted figures derived in 1955 revealed that the principal traffic growth in the decade occurred in traffic corridors in which most of the new highway construction was located. Likewise, it is important to note also that predicted traffic increases did *not* occur where segments of the freeway system were not yet built. The highway engineers' own gravity model forecasting system shows that freeways *generate their own demand* and that if they are not built, forecasted traffic increases will not materialize.

The engineers assumed that all suburbanite trips were into the city. However, they neglected to consider the process by which suburbs "mature." It works this way: Initially, in a new suburb, residents go to established areas for work, shopping, schools, and recreation. As the area matures, however, and increases in density, it acquires its own shopping centers, schools, et cetera. Inevitably, regardless of the transportation system, the relative need or desire to travel to the central city declines. In absolute numbers, the trips to the central city may increase, but never in proportion to increases in suburban population.

One Bureau of Public Roads official expressed this point by claiming that because Washington's freeway system was stalled, traffic was increasing in the surrounding suburbs, implying that such cross-suburb trips would be made into the city if expressways were available.

Beyond the obvious flaws in the gravity model forecast used to predict future traffic increases are simply the socioeconomic factors related to the segments of the proposed system. The highly controversial North Central Freeway, which was planned to extend from the heart of the city through black and integrated neighborhoods out to white affluent Montgomery County in Maryland, is a case in point. The proposed freeway was studied and planned for by, again, the J. E. Greiner Company for the D.C. and Maryland highway departments at a cost of $350,000. The neighborhood through which this segment was planned contains numerous industries providing 2920 jobs. These include several major employers occupying new plants. The firms displaced are expected to move to suburban locations if they must move, since there are few suitable sites left in the city for their relocation. But the virtue of the new freeway would be its ability to reduce travel time and cost for commuters traveling to the central business district and federal employment areas, according to Greiner engineers. The fact that increasingly black communities are proposed as freeway paths for white suburban commuters sparked the militant movement's interest in the Washington battle. Greiner predicted that the central business district would "benefit materially" from a north central freeway as access improved for the "rapidly growing, high-income groups in the Montgomery County portion of the Washington suburbs." Profits would also soar, they predicted, in the county's

suburban business districts of Wheaton and Silver Spring, due to
increased accessibility. To back up their claims, Greiner included
projections of expected increases in District retail sales in 1980
over 1958, and assumed an additional 15 percent increase in sales
for the period that would be exclusively due to the presence of
the North Central Freeway. Such claims, as specious as they were,
helped enlist the support of the suburban business community.

However, the study was contradictory in that it contained data
which showed both a decline from 1954 to 1958 in sales of 0.4
percent, and a drop in the central business district's share of the
area's retail sales from 20 percent to 16 percent. It showed also
that from 1948 to 1967 the District's retail sales had remained
constant at $1.4 billion but the District's share of the metropolitan
area's sales dropped from 75 percent to 42 percent during the
same period. Even if the D.C. population were to grow at the
report's estimated 16 percent, there would be no reason to assume
a much greater increase in central business district sales. The route
chosen for the freeway would involve a tax loss of $594,710 an-
nually, but the report stated that "it is reasonable to forecast a
significant increase in land values." Yet the report did not sub-
stantiate this claim with studies of occupied adjacent land. This is
the same freeway which had begun in the "Wisconsin corridor" of
white affluent northwest Washington and was later shifted eastward
to predominantly black neighborhoods. (The arterial which presently carries heavy volumes of auto traffic through Washington and
into wealthy Montgomery County is Wisconsin Avenue.) But the
tug-of-war over location of the freeway has gone on for a decade.
In May 1962, the Bureau of Public Roads issued a report on the
corridor. Numerous studies and extensive analysis had led the
Bureau to conclude that because of "right-of-way problems, tremendous cost and other difficulties involved in urban highway
construction . . . existing arterial streets must remain the bulwark
of the urban transportation system." The study concluded further
that efficient traffic signal progression, some grade separations, bus
turnoffs, a ban on curb parking, and a few other simple measures
could speed an average of 60,000 to 80,000 cars a day, nonstop, up

and down existing Wisconsin Avenue at 25 to 30 miles per hour. (D.C. Highway Department traffic forecasts predicted that 58,000 automobiles would materialize for this corridor by 1980. This is the basis upon which it has insisted for ten years that the freeway is essential.)

The D.C. Highway Department turned thumbs down on the BPR study, arguing that although their proposal would be cheaper than the freeway, it would cost the city more for these improvements than the 10 percent they would have to spend for an interstate freeway, financed 90 percent by federal money.

Each proposed segment of the freeway system for the nation's capital can be questioned on several points. For instance, engineers from De Leuw Cather have again studied Washington's highway program. They recommended a route for the north-leg east section of the Inner Loop that affected housing, which was rated 92 percent sound, 6 percent deteriorating, and 2 percent dilapidated. They concluded that 78.7 acres of parkland would be required for the recommended routes. This included a public golf course. The report suggested that a public lake located nearby be filled in for a new golf course, which would "produce approximately the same acreage of land as now exists, deducting the proposed freeway right of way." The route would also demolish a school. The engineers suggested taking an additional fifty housing units nearby for its replacement. The study contained no estimate of the amount of tax loss the city would bear as the result of constructing this segment of the highway system, nor the relocation problems of those persons displaced by their proposed school relocation.

When the Arthur D. Little Company reviewed the proposed plans in 1966, they concluded that the approach of the D.C., Maryland, and Virginia highway departments had taken to provide a transportation system for the region was "biased toward the freeway and parkway system proposed. It implicitly assumes that freeways and parkways will be the basis for additions to the transportation system." Furthermore, Arthur D. Little said of the Highway Departments' proposed plan: "The currently proposed system would give Washington a freeway plan which is more dominated by radial routes than most American metropolitan areas of comparable size. No less than nine new or enlarged radial routes are presently planned. Radial freeways carry two distinct disadvantages. First, they provide maximum competition with rail rapid-transit. Second, they make solution of the automobile problem at the center more difficult. Some radial freeways are necessary; however, an excessive number may not provide the best approach for coping with growing transportation needs."

A. D. Little researchers determined that the Interstate System could draw considerable volumes of traffic to the Inner Loop. They estimated that only a small portion of traffic using the loop would be destined for the area within it, however.

All of the criticisms leveled against the D.C. Highway Department were dismissed by department officials, congressmen, and the Washington *Post* and *Evening Star* as delaying tactics and of no consequence. The Little report was issued in March of 1966, at about the same time the Washington *Post* contracted with Louis Harris Associates to conduct a sample poll of the Washington metropolitan area on twenty separate issues, including crime, education, ghettos, jobs, more public transportation, and better and wider roads. The results of that poll revealed that of the total sampled, *more public transportation* was given the highest priority among the twenty issues and fared better than 2 to 1 over roads. District residents chose public transportation over more roads by almost 4 to 1. But the biggest surprise of the poll showed that of the four surrounding suburban areas, three rated public transportation as their issue of highest priority. In these three suburban communities, public transportation improvements were preferred 2 to 1 over roads. And in the fourth community, where public transportation was rated second highest in priority, the ratio was 3 to 1 over more roads. Related to this question was the issue of more parking facilities, which both the Congress and highway interests champion. It received one of the *lowest* priority ratings among the twenty items, rated as of less importance than thirteen other items and tied with two others. While certain portions of the survey appeared in the Washington *Post, the results of the questions on transportation did not.*

Despite this demonstration of community-wide support for public transit, plus the overwhelming acceptance in suburban areas for bond issues to help pay for metropolitan Washington's proposed rapid transit system, and the 19 to 1 vote *against* freeways demonstrated by D.C. voters in the May 1968 primary, newspapers, local politicians, and members of the Congress continue to demand more superhighways for the nation's capital on the fraudulent grounds that suburban communities are in need of, and support, building more freeways from the surrounding areas into the city core.

Most of the costly studies cited by the highway departments as justification for the highway program have been made by consulting firms that earn most of their money working for highway agencies and other construction agencies, and telling them what they want to hear. It comes as no surprise that their reports support freeway construction.

In D.C. it so happened that when three consultants who have not worked primarily for highway agencies were commissioned to evaluate Washington's freeway plans, their conclusions were highly critical. These include the A. D. Little report, an earlier report by the Institute of Public Administration, and a report by the Washington Center for Metropolitan Studies. As Henry Bain of the Washington Center said in 1967, "One of the remarkable things about the highway system currently being proposed by the civil engineers is that it *won't work*. That is, the proposed freeways will be seriously congested during the morning and evening rush hours, and perhaps during busy periods on weekends and at other times. The engineers have never denied this. Presumably their strategy is to get as many freeways built as the public will now tolerate, and then to use the congestion on these as an argument for building still more. This could go on indefinitely. . . . If the engineers ever made some predictions on the assumption that these highways would not be built, they would find that the avalanche of traffic which they are always predicting simply would not take place."

The traffic that appears when a facility is built is either generated or induced. Population, distribution of homes, places of employment, retail stores, churches, and other points of origin and destination, income, auto ownership, number of dwelling units per acre of land, and other social and physical factors generate traffic. The characteristics of transportation facilities and service available, i.e., highways, parking, and public transportation, in terms of cost, speed, comfort, and convenience, induce travel.

This is how it works. An increase in traffic at a time when population is growing and there is little change in the transportation system may be said to be generated by population growth. On the other hand, an increase in traffic following the opening of a new transportation facility at a time when little or no new urban development is taking place may be explained as induced by the new facility. People tend to take advantage of the new opportunity to travel speedily by making trips they would not otherwise have attempted, particularly for shopping, social, or recreational purposes. This accounts for the fact that new expressways often get congested shortly after they are opened.

In 1962, Anthony Downs, then director of retail analysis for the Real Estate Research Corporation in Chicago, postulated a law of peak-hour expressway congestion which addresses itself to this aspect of the relationship between superhighways and the traffic they bear. His law states that on urban commuter expressways, peak-hour traffic congestion will rise to meet maximum capacity, an adaptation of Parkinson's Law.

He explored the effects upon an auto-highway transportation system when a new expressway opens connecting the downtown business district with outlying suburban areas. This road is a non-stop, limited-access highway with multiple lanes in each direction. Assume that the total number of commuters and automobile owners remains constant. The following changes occur: For all auto commuters, the opened expressway results in reduced peak-hour traffic congestion on many previously existing streets as large numbers of commuters switch to the new expressway. Gradually the time required for commuting on the expressway rises as more cars fill it, until peak-hour congestion increases; whereas the time required on alternate routes falls. When the two become identical, equilibrium is restored. While rush-hour level on the alternate roads is now lower, rush-hour level of congestion on the expressway almost always exceeds its designed optimal capacity. Assume the new road is designed to move 6000 cars per hour past a given point at 50 miles per hour. At optimum operating time, 6000 cars are traveling at 50 mph, but this is faster than speeds on alternate roads, so others will enter the expressway because of this speed advantage and more will join until speeds on all routes are identical. Furthermore, above speeds of 35 to 40 miles per hour, drivers tend to allow themselves more room for braking and therefore fewer will pass a given point at a given moment.* The overall effect of the new

4-lane highway maximum vehicles/hr. per lane	
1500	35–40 mph
1250	40–45 mph
1000	45–50 mph

facility is to merely reduce the duration of peak-hour congestion. If a city with a new expressway also has buses, the buses at first can move quicker too, although not as fast as automobiles, since they must stop to pick up and discharge passengers. Because of this time lag between bus and auto trips on the expressway, many bus passengers will be lured onto the expressway with their automobiles, contributing to congestion on the expressway and declining revenue for the bus company. In a city with fixed rail public transportation, the expressway has the same effect except for one difference. Since the path of the fixed rail is segregated, commuters riding the rail do not share the reduction in travel time that the bus and auto users get on the expressway. Consequently, many commuters who formerly used segregated track transit shift to automobiles for both peak-hour and nonpeak-hour travel.

In Chicago, the Chicago and Northwestern Railway, often cited in recent years as a model of commuter service modernization, was making a small profit on its suburban passenger service business before two new expressways opened in late 1960. Each superroad paralleled a set of existing Chicago and Northwestern tracks connecting downtown Chicago with outlying areas. Within three months

* See Wilbur Smith, Theodore Watson, Frederick Hurd, *Traffic Engineering* (McGraw-Hill, 1955), p. 382.

after these two expressways opened, the railroad's suburban passenger traffic declined 9.6 percent and resulted in an overall change from a profit to a loss. (Passenger service had been steadily rising in the months before the expressways opened.)

But the blessings of the freeway are transitory. As more and more people start using their automobiles to commute to work, traffic congestion begins to return to the level existing before the expressway improved traffic conditions and the original situation can never return because the new expressway has lured away many former riders of track transit.

The situation is reinforced if motor registration and auto ownership increase, whether or not population increases. Actually, the number of persons entering the central business district of large cities has remained constant or declined slightly, while the number of automobiles entering the area has increased.

One of the most recent traffic forecast projections in defense of a highway system was offered in November of 1968 by Automotive Safety Foundation graduate Lloyd Rivard who periodically supplies figures to defend the D.C. Highway Department's lavish freeway proposals. It is an example of a facility inducing its own capacity to justify building still another. In his November 1968 presentation, Rivard pleaded for, among other proposals, construction of the controversial Three Sisters Bridge. He argued that the existing bridges would reach their capacity by 1977, at which time the new bridge would be needed.

Peak-hour daily traffic volumes on the Potomac bridges had been increasing at a fairly even rate of 3 percent per year from 1945 to 1962. Suddenly, the rate jumped to 10 percent per year. What happened in 1962 to account for the drastic increase in rate of growth of cross-Potomac travel? Two more Potomac bridges were completed that year, connecting the Virginia and Maryland portions of the Capital Beltway. Rivard estimates that these two new bridges will reach their capacity by 1970, stepping up the demand on the other bridges. Where is the traffic coming from that is filling up those two new bridges? There was no sharp increase in the rate at which the population was growing, nor was there any

major shift in employment centers from one side of the river to the
other that might account for so sharp an increase in the rate of
growth of bridge traffic volumes. Nor did automobile registration
increase sharply in 1962 when the increased growth rate began. What
could account for the increase is the fact that people were more
frequently utilizing the autos they already owned to make more
cross-river trips because the two new bridges provided more facilities for such automobile trips. Thus, people were *induced* to use
their automobiles by the opening of the two facilities. Then, too,
new apartment complexes near the beltway began advertising that
with the new bridges employees in established work centers could
live in the new apartments and drive to work across the Potomac
via these facilities in the same time it was currently taking them to
work, twenty minutes, half an hour, or whatever time. People were
induced to shift bedrooms from one location to another, near the
beltway. This is an example of "induced" traffic whereby people
shift around and move farther away because a new facility initially
allows them to get around faster. They will make home-to-work trips
which, while longer in miles, take less time via the new high-speed
highways, until congestion builds up and equilibrium is restored.
Rivard's figures show that the two bridges will induce a steady
increase in trans-Potomac traffic, which will reach a figure equal
to their own capacity eight years from the date they opened. Apply-
ing Downs's theory that congestion rises to meet peak-hour capacity,
by 1970, the capacity of both bridges having been met, the onset
of congestion will choke off some of the traffic increase which will
then proceed at a lower rate, unless another bridge is built, at which
time disequilibrium will occur and the process will begin all over
again.

The Verrazano-Narrows Bridge from Staten Island to Brooklyn
is another example. Completed late in 1964, the bridge contained
space for two decks. The upper deck was connected to freeways on
the Staten Island and Brooklyn sides while the lower deck remained
to be connected by 1980, according to the engineering firm of
Madigan-Hyland, Inc., when the upper deck would reach capacity,
given as some 25 million automobiles per year. Upon dedication,

Robert Moses stated, "It is a structure of superlatives, a creation of imagination, art, architecture, and engineering. Its scale, magnitude, and beauty will fire the mind of every stranger and bring a tear to every returning native eye," to say nothing of the air pollution in the eye of the New York taxpayer. According to Triborough officials, 2954 families were displaced by construction of the bridge.

Just twenty days short of three years after the opening of the bridge, Triborough issued a brochure containing dire warnings that "Traffic Volumes Are 5 Years Ahead of Original Estimates" . . . "Traffic Volumes Will Congest the Present Bridge Roadways by 1970."

The pamphlet explains, "The bridge was planned not only to link Staten Island and Brooklyn, but also to provide for the bypassing of Manhattan by New Jersey and Long Island motorists, and to remove some traffic from Manhattan's congested streets. Surveys show that the bridge is providing this service, but traffic to and from Staten Island and Brooklyn is far greater than anticipated, due partly to the growth of Staten Island and also to the mobility afforded neighboring areas by this easily accessible crossing. Substantial traffic from more distant points of Long Island and New Jersey also finds the bridge convenient. . . . It is now apparent that congestion, accompanied by operational difficulties, will occur in peak periods as early as 1970 . . . unless additional capacity is provided." All this is followed by more charts and maps of the bridge and area and more text justifying connecting the second deck. No actual peak-hour traffic figures are included, however. Deputy Chief Engineer George Schoepfer says they "are not readily available." The brochure ends on this optimistic note: "The world's greatest bridge will be ready for the future." Does this statement imply that they will add still a third deck when Downs's law of congestion fills the second deck? They offer no assurance that at some future date both decks will not reach capacity, justifying a need for even more bridge facilities.

Why were these bridge forecasts so far short of actual traffic? The brochure admits that some of the traffic is induced—the facility is handy, seducing more people to it. They, of course, point to its increased traffic volumes as proof of its popularity—it's what the public wants. But what alternatives are offered at a competitive level? Even the Brooklyn-Staten Island ferry, which formerly provided the connecting link where now the bridge stands, was closed the day the bridge opened. Madigan-Hyland engineers estimated that 96 percent of the *vehicles* using the ferry would switch to the bridge, so it was closed down! Unfortunately for the many ferry passengers, they had to find wheels in order to make the crossing henceforth. When asked why bridge engineers were so wide of the mark in forecasting the need for a second deck, a BPR engineer suggested that it is entirely possible that they did know traffic would increase at a faster rate than first announced, but may have feared that the public would not believe them and would not want to embark on this expenditure, prudently looking ahead to the total cost. The public might react by saying that it was a huge monument to engineering. The Narrows Bridge is an excellent example of the methods used by highway engineers. They get public funds committed to a project before it dawns on people that the system is just too costly to build. Once it is constructed, the engineers begin arguing for still a larger facility or more links in the system, based, again, on "future" traffic volume projections, which always fill up the facility. But if you ask for the traffic figures to justify, say, the second deck of the Narrows Bridge, you are told they "are not readily available." In other words, just take their word for it, that second deck is needed. After all, they employ experts such as engineers from Madigan-Hyland, and Madigan-Hyland studied the Lower Manhattan Expressway.

While one of the major justifications for building the Verrazano-Narrows Bridge was supposed to be to divert traffic from Manhattan, the proposed Lower Manhattan Expressway was being planned smack across densely populated New York City for the same reason —to alleviate Manhattan congestion. Bureau of Public Roads officials justified the $150 million it would have cost for the 1.5-mile segment of the highway on grounds that it was a vital link in metropolitan New York City's $3 billion arterial system. But at the same time, they admitted it was not vital to the operation of the Interstate System.

One official suggested that the $100-million-a-mile expressway might be justified economically on grounds that if the present stopping and starting that traffic experiences at grade crossings were eliminated, fuel costs would be lowered. Fewer gears would be shifted, and 11-mile-an-hour speeds could be changed to 40-mile-per-hour speeds if the expressway was built. This, coupled with the tremendous volumes of traffic the facility would handle, might generate enough savings to motorists to justify the cost, he suggested, a reassuring consolation to the neighborhood residents who fought the project for so long.

But building more freeway lanes in New York City will not alleviate congestion and certainly is not an economical way to move people. If all present railroad commuters were to drive into Manhattan in private cars, the area would need fifty additional lanes of tunnels or bridges estimated to cost $5 billion. At the time he was campaigning for his bond issue, Governor Rockefeller admitted that the state bought the failing Long Island Railroad for $65 million when it discovered that the cost of replacing its capacity with highway capacity would be more than $2 billion. A rail line uses one fourth the land required for a six-lane freeway but can accommodate five times as many people. Yet New York keeps planning more highway facilities and the governor's own bond issue provides the state with 25 percent less money for public transit than for highways. And he is governor of a state where more than 65 percent of the population lives in urban areas.

The controversial expressway system the design concept team is poring over in Baltimore, which the Bureau of Public Roads has stated is not necessary for the successful completion of the Interstate System, displaced 4100 families. It also slices through a stream-valley park, historic Federal Hill, and Fell's Point, the waterfront neighborhood containing original houses dating from 1732. Jerome Wolff, chairman-director of Maryland's State Roads Commission until he joined Vice President Agnew's staff, explained that the city needs the expressway system "because it's essential to the economic viability of the city. We're putting highways through because we fervently believe that highways will be a boon to the city." He does not submit any figures or studies to support his fervent belief. Closer, perhaps, to the generator of momentum for the highways is a remark made by Walter Addison, a state deputy engineer. "Other urban centers have highways—Baltimore needs one to be competitive." Actually, however, the spark that generates the need for this $376 million highway system is Baltimore's share of the 90–10 money it sends to Washington every year in the form of gas and oil taxes. The pressure has been on for years to build more highways in Baltimore, so that Maryland's portion of the Highway Trust Fund will be returned to the state. Each state has three years to "obligate" the money, to come up with highway projects, and Congress rejuvenates state highway departments with new funds every two years. Therefore, engineers must keep planning at a respectable pace to keep up the conversion of cash into concrete. As one official in the Bureau's budget office says, "It's 90–10 money—no state is going to return any." And so far, none has. When San Francisco turned thumbs down on freeway construction in 1966, its portion of the funds simply reverted to the state of California and made it possible for highway engineers to plan more interstate mileage for Los Angeles.

The Federal Highway Act of 1966 called for a study of relocation problems. So a highway relocation assistance study was conducted by BPR in all the states. It revealed the following: Between 1967 and 1970, highway construction in the United States will displace 168,519 individuals, families, businesses, farmers, and nonprofit organizations. Approximately 77 percent of these are located in urban areas. According to the Bureau estimate, the vast bulk will involve residences. They figure that 146,950 persons or families will be removed and 16,679 businesses and nonprofit organizations. The rest, 4890, are farms to be taken. Each state highway department chief submitted an estimate of the number of relocations his department expected to encounter between 1967 and 1970, based upon the number and location of projects each state anticipated constructing within the three-year span. Bureau officials admit the figures are low. In fact, the Bureau questioned the low estimates turned in by some states, but the states insisted the figures are correct.

"The greater numbers of those displaced will result from Interstate highway improvement," according to the study; approximately 92,000 residence units and businesses, farms and nonprofit organizations. The federal-aid state primary system will remove 65,000 more. The remainder will be caught in the secondary road projects.

The legislation establishing relocation payments and assistance to persons in the path of a highway was passed in 1962. From that date on, some state highway departments were actually offering people both financial and advisory assistance to find new residences. Others were not, since they did not have the state legislation requiring them to participate in the program. Consequently, the records of actual displacement even from the time the 1962 legislation was enacted is subject to question. However, Bureau officials concede that the period between April 1, 1965, and October 1, 1966, provide the federal agency with the most accurate account of displacement that they think occurred during that time. The report states that during that eighteen-month period, 49,605 persons were moved and 3065 businesses, farms, and nonprofit organizations were relocated.

The study also tells something about who can expect to be removed by state highway departments by 1970. Almost 23,000 dwelling units are valued under $6000; 40,096 are valued between $6001 and $15,000, while the balance, 23,161 units, are valued at over $15,000. Rental value, according to the study, means $6000 unit rents for under $60 per month, $6000 to $15,000 rent for $60 to $110 a month, the remainder at more than $110 a month. Also, 60,776 tenants will be displaced and, of these, 25,294 will be persons from dwelling units of $60 per month or less. "Many of the state highway departments reported that a major difficulty in relocating low- or moderate-income families is the shortage of low-rent housing, either public or private," the study pointed out.

The study shows that of 16,679 projected nonresidential displacements, 11,951 are urban located. More than 6000 of the total will experience relocation expenses beyond the $3000 limit, 967 of them more than $25,000.

The study estimates that relocation payments from 1967 to 1970 will be approximately $178 million out of a *$15-billion-annual* road-building program.

The 1962 Act establishing the relocation assistance advice and payment states that the Bureau of Public Works shall not require a state to pay relocation payments where not authorized by state law. Payments are prorated as follows:

Interstate   federal payment 90 percent   state payment 10 percent
Primary   federal payment 50 percent   state payment 50 percent
Secondary   federal payment 50 percent   state payment 50 percent

Since the money comes from the Highway Trust Fund and state highway funds, relocation payments reduce the amount of money available to construct more roads, so they are unpopular with highway interests which have always fought providing them. The fifteen states which do not pay a relocation fee to persons, businesses, farms, or nonprofit organizations in the path of a highway are: Alaska, Arizona, Arkansas, Colorado, Delaware, Florida, Idaho, Kansas, Louisiana, Mississippi, Missouri, New Mexico, South Carolina, Texas, and Wyoming.

And as for "fair market" value payments to property owners who were losing their homes or buildings, Bureau officials, in 1967, admitted that fair-market prices had not always been offered to homeowners. State highway departments admitted they were offering below-market prices to allow for bargaining if owners balked at selling out. Since this raised a hue and cry, the 1968 legislation provides that property owners may receive $5000 more than fair-market value, which in turn implies that by making attractive offers, highway departments can buy off freeway opposition.

Although our highways are supposed to be safer than ever today because engineers are building them wider, controlling the access,

eliminating train crossings and intersections at grade level, building
in acceleration lanes and exit and entrance ramps, figures of motor
vehicle deaths show a steady upswing. In 1956, more than 39,000
persons were killed in motor vehicle accidents. In 1968, that annual
figure had topped 55,000 persons killed and 3,712,000 injured.
By comparison, 15,000 Americans were killed in the Vietnam War
in 1968. Your chances of getting killed by an auto accident in
1968 were almost four times greater than getting killed in the war.

One can argue that the American soldier was drafted for the war,
that it was not his free choice to go, while those persons killed in
auto accidents were exercising their free choice to move about. But
is this really so? How many transportation alternatives does the
average citizen have? We continue to pour billions into a highway
system which induces or forces people to use it at peril to their lives.
And even engineers are coming around to thinking that it is not
only the nut behind the wheel who causes accidents. Federal officials
have for several years been preaching that we have now about all
the capability we can reasonably expect from a human driver. They
will not go so far, however, as to suggest that the highway system
is operating about as well as can be expected. To do so would be to
admit that the system is deadly and was a mistake. For they know
there are other, safer and cheaper, means of transporting people
and goods.

In 1963, a year when 43,564 persons were killed in motor
vehicle accidents, BPR and state highway officials claimed that the
Interstate System would save approximately 8000 lives annually when
completed in 1972. By 1968, five years later, an additional 12,000
persons were being killed on the highways, 4000 more than the
8000 highway officials predicted would be saved upon completion of
the Interstate System on the new date, 1974. The Interstate System
will save more lives if state highway departments are forced to repair
the death traps the Blatnik watchdog committee continues to uncover.
Nevertheless, the number of deaths will continue to climb because
more people, given more highways, will use them. And most motoring

is done, anyway, on highways other than the Interstate System which, when it is completed, will handle only 20 percent of all traffic.

The total number of deaths of American soldiers in all wars in which we have participated from the Revolutionary War to the Vietnam War through 1968 was 1,120,000. Between 1900 and 1966 more than 1,600,000 persons were killed by motor vehicles in the United States, roughly half a million more than were killed in all of our wars. And the price tag for the slaughter on our highways in 1967 alone was $10 billion, just two thirds the $15 billion that went into all new road construction that year and one third the cost of the Vietnam War in 1968. But few voices were raised in protest. The public has been brainwashed into believing that our gigantic highway program is "progress." As Daniel Moynihan pointed out in 1960, "better schools, better hospitals, better roads" has become part of the liberal litany. That incantation, at least the part about better roads, has become a *must* in the lexicon of just about every politician in the country, and it stems directly from the hoopla attending passage of the 1956 Highway Act. It is almost amusing to note that the Act was hailed as the vehicle that would solve our transportation problems, cut the accident fatality rate, stimulate economic growth, and aid national defense. Better still, the money it would cost the American motorists or highway users to build the roads would be more than offset by the economic savings of driving on them. Yet thirteen years later, our cities are beset by worsening transportation, housing and environmental problems exacerbated by construction of urban expressways. Automobile traffic congestion is no longer possible to mask. Our accident rate has increased 50 percent, and anyone who witnessed the mass exodus of panicked suburbanites from the District of Columbia on the afternoon preceding the riots of April 5, 1968, and the attendant traffic jams on all bridges across the Potomac and every major arterial in the city, had living, stalled proof that in emergencies, the system cannot serve national defense. In fact, traffic was so jammed that freeway opponent Sam Abbot was overcome by what he termed a laughing jag as he watched the ensuing crush of people and vehicles crawling along local streets as people attempted to reach expressways and bridges. Fortunately, the military seem to have quietly abandoned the roads. A spokesman in the Military Traffic Management and Terminal Service calculated that 80 percent of military personnel passenger miles are traveled by air, the fastest and cheapest mode available, while short bus and rail trips make up the remainder. A very small amount of troop movement is conducted by military vehicles on highways, while 75 percent of military cargo, calculated on a tonnage basis, is shipped by rail, pipeline, water, and air. Only 25 percent moves over our roads. In an emergency, he pointed out, more troops could be moved by one engine pulling numerous cars on rails than by trucks.

Art Buchwald wrote a funny column early in 1968 about some Venusian scientists who landed a satellite on the eastern side of Manhattan. After taking some samples of the environment, the satellite returned to Venus and the scientists analyzed earthly conditions. They concluded that the earth was uninhabitable because it was covered with concrete and contained no oxygen. Nothing would grow there, they concluded, because the atmosphere was filled with carbon monoxide. The scientists from Venus commented that atmospheric conditions ruled out life on earth because no one could possibly breathe earth's air and survive.

They observed some metallic particles moving along specific paths which emitted gases, made noise, and, on occasion, crashed into each other. The Venusians forthwith decided to commit billions of dollars to attempt to land a manned flying saucer on earth because, they reasoned, if Venusians can learn to breathe in earth's atmosphere, they could live anywhere.

At about the same time Buchwald's column was appearing in newspapers around the country, an article appeared in the New York *Times* about Tokyo's air-pollution problem. The story reported that school children were wearing surgical masks to filter the air, that it had become commonplace for housewives to stop at their local pharmacy for a free lungful of pure bottled oxygen to counter the effects of a one-hour shopping trip through Tokyo streets, that clouds of automobile exhaust fumes were forcing traffic policemen indoors for oxygen treatment after a two-hour stint at major intersections. There was an account, too, of what was described as an enterprising coffee shop that had installed oxygen bottles at every table. The public outcry had, according to the story, moved officials to do something. They had promptly ordered the dispensation of free oxygen in one district of the city crossed by a superhighway!

In the summer of 1967, a Connecticut farmer complained that an entire field of spinach was mottled and unmarketable. A state agricultural specialist took one look and diagnosed, "automobile exhaust," in spite of the fact that the nearest big highway was miles away. To prove the point, New Haven's agricultural experimental station demonstrated the effects of exhaust on tobacco plants and petunias which were grown on high ground flanked by wooded hills. The plants were severely mottled. And the agricultural specialists didn't simulate the smog, it was right in the air. Much of the damage is done by ozone and other gases formed by the action of sunlight on exhaust fumes. Coupled with a temperature inversion, the smog gets trapped at the bottom where it acts upon the plants. A chart displayed by the station showed the rise in both gasoline consumption and peak traffic flow on the West Haven toll station of the Connecticut Turnpike coincided with the peak growing season. Both growing season peak and highest rate of travel fall during the summer vacation months of July and August. That's when the crops suffer.

Is Buchwald's column just a spoof? The air pollution division of Health, Education and Welfare estimates that the 142 million tons of air pollutants dumped into the air we breathe is costing the U.S. public $11 billion each year, and that 60 percent of those tons come out of auto exhausts. Beyond just the cost in terms of dollars, what are we supposed to do when there is no air left to breathe? If you believe there will always be air to breathe, you have not had the experience of living downtown and having to keep your children inside an air-conditioned house because the odor of gasoline fumes outdoors was overpowering.

An air-pollution study conducted by HEW's Public Health Service in 1964–65 in Washington, D.C., demonstrated too well the increase in pollutants that accompanies auto traffic. The nation's capital is particularly suitable for an auto exhaust pollutant study because there is little industry in the area to contribute to air pollution. It has been estimated that as much as 80 percent of Washington's air pollution stems from auto traffic alone. Auto pollution was calculated by multiplying the average number of miles traveled per vehicle in the area per day by a factor representing the amount of carbon monoxide released by one vehicle for one mile of travel. Such calculations show that 1150 tons of CO were released per day in 1964. But when the D.C. Highway Department's 1985 projected traffic forecast figures were substituted, the study revealed that 2170 tons would be emitted every day by 1985, an increase of 89 percent. However, since the city is expected to continue to expand, this amount will be distributed over a larger area so that the mean annual concentration in 1985 will be "just" 50 percent more than the amount it was in 1964. Even if the 1964 emissions can be reduced by 50 percent in 1985, levels at an inner city location will decline by only 15 percent of the 1964 level, the study revealed. Increased traffic growth beyond 1985 would wipe out that small gain. The study also compared the traffic density growth factors for Chicago and found them similar to those of D.C. Since most growth occurs in the outskirts of cities and accounts for a much larger area than for the downtown regions, "the more significant increase in the city's total emissions takes place in the outskirts and not in the downtown areas," the study concludes. Great news for fringe neighborhoods.

Since, as has been the case in D.C., traffic volumes rise to meet road capacity and fulfill predicted traffic volume increases when proposed freeways are constructed and do not meet future traffic projections where expressways are not built, one of the simplest and *cheapest* devices for controlling future inundation by pollutants would be the suspension of freeway construction in metropolitan areas.

Road maintenance is another expense. Maintenance of all roads has always been the responsibility and expense of the states, and they are feeling the pinch. The Highway Trust Fund cannot be spent on this item either. One BPR researcher estimated that it is costing the states a minimum of $10,000 per mile maintenance per year on the IS alone. And that represents the smallest mileage of our various systems. Since there will be 41,000 miles of Interstate System upon completion, the public will be paying $410 million each year for that. In 1965, we spent $3.021 billion on maintenance for all of our roads. DOT figures show that between 1966 and 1985 we will have spent a grand total of $100.6 billion for road maintenance alone!

In 1965, the total cost of administrative and miscellaneous needs of the highway program was $2.1 billion. The total for such expenses between 1966 and 1985 is expected to reach $49.5 billion. This money will be spent on highway safety programs, including highway patrol, driver training, etc., and interest and amortization costs of highway bonds. For these purposes there will be no federal aid. State and local governments must foot the bill, including nonusers as well as highway users.

Governor Rockefeller spoke frankly when he told New York State's AAA that he planned to amortize his 1967 $2.5 billion bond issue from the state's general fund. He said, "It is not my intention to finance the bond issue from highway user charges alone. It will be amortized from the state's general fund, and this means that all citizens of the state will share in the course of providing new, safer, and more efficient transportation facilities." His bond issue placed heavy emphasis on highway construction, when teeming New York and its sister cities across the state were already choked with automobile traffic and crying for public transit.

Although congressional committees, the automobile, trucking, petroleum, and other highway related interests continue to chant that we are getting a bargain for our highway taxes, BPR and DOT studies indicate that the public has literally been taken for a ride. To begin with, in 1965 the BPR requested all state highway departments to estimate their highway needs for the next twenty years, through 1985. They came up with a price tag of $294 billion. Of this amount, they estimated they would need $225.7 billion between

1973 and 1985. At the time the study was undertaken, it was believed the Interstate System would be completed by 1972. Their
estimate of future needs, then, was post-Interstate. Coincidentally,
their estimated $225.7 billion "need" matches the current and antic-
ipated annual expenditure of approximately $18 billion for the
then post-Interstate System thirteen-year period between 1973–85,
a total of $234 billion. Consequently, as Senator Randolph has
pointed out, so logically, there is no trust fund money available for
other modes of transportation, because future revenues will barely
cover future highway "needs." Which came first, highway revenue or
highway need?

Despite assurances from congressmen that our road program is a
bargain, the fact remains that no one has yet been able to compare
the economic input and output of our highways, for the simple reason that for all of the millions spent in the name of highway research,
no one has devised the capability for measuring highway output.
The assumption that highways are creating actual benefits remains
untested.

Nevertheless, we continue to support a $15-billion-a-year program.
Furthermore, the Department of Transportation reports that by
1976 it will be spending $4.5 billion annually to comply with the
Highway Safety Act. This estimate does not include hospital expenses nor the cost of installing additional safety equipment for
automobiles. For instance, it will cost $20 billion alone for such
equipment if all the steps being contemplated by safety experts are
implemented. This figure is derived from multiplying the $200 cost
estimate for proposed safety changes on each car times the 100 million
registered vehicles. None of this money will come from the Trust
Fund; it will come from your pocket, and it will be spent on "highway safety" when it is common knowledge that there are feasible
safer alternatives to automobile transportation for our urban areas.

Just how great a bargain our highway program is has been described in the Bureau's 1965 Highway Cost Allocation Study, a
367-page document which computed the dollar benefits accrued to
motorists during 1964 from our highways. The Bureau concluded
that in 1964 the motoring public and truckers saved $6.12 billion

in time, cost of operating vehicles, and savings in reduced accidents, as a result of improved highways. In other words, savings from fewer accidents than would have occurred had safer highways not been built. It is important to note, however, that BPR did not include the cost of actual auto accidents that year, which were $8.1 billion. While some economists wince at the thought of putting a price tag on a human life, the loss of real income to survivors of an auto accident victim can be a very real hardship. Ironically, as the system entices more users, who in turn become involved in more accidents, nudging the fatality rate higher each year, there are louder cries for more safety, resulting in still more money being invested in the system in the form of grants. For instance, in 1968 DOT spent $1.9 billion for such highway safety items as a $317,000-television-surveillance system for Detroit freeways in co-ordination with the use of helicopters and citizen band radios of the type often found in radio dispatched vehicles. Or the $130,000 grant to New York City to apply computer techniques in the deployment of ambulances. Washington received a paltry $15,000 to study possibilities of using helicopters to carry crash victims.

The 1965 BPR study estimates that in 1973, the motoring public and truckers will reap $20.318 billion in benefits, that is, in terms of savings of time, wear on vehicles, and gasoline. Again, they do not include the annual accident toll. But auto accidents in 1964 were costing $8.1 billion. Four years later, in 1968–69, the figure had jumped to $13 billion, an increase of 50 percent. Now, if accident tolls continue to mount at their present rate, as more people pour onto our roads and car registration continues to climb, we can expect that four years from 1969, accident costs are likely to increase 50 percent again, over the $13 billion, which will bring the figure close to $20 billion. When you tack on the $11-billion-annual air-pollution price tag, it becomes painfully clear that the federal-state highway program is a gigantic hoax on the public.

8. Transportation in the Urban Scene

"The body travels more easily than the mind, and until we have limbered up our imagination we continue to think as though we had stayed home."

—John Erskine, 1879–1951

There is no simple panacea, universally applicable to all of our major cities, that will solve our transportation problems. Each city needs, and indeed is entitled to, its own particular solution to its own problems. But in order to even begin to address ourselves to the transportation mess we have had created for us, we must use some imagination and change existing policies that only exacerbate our current dilemma.

Since it is the never ending flow of Highway Trust Fund money which has created the vast imbalance in our transportation situation, the federal Trust Fund and its counterparts in the states must be eliminated as an exclusive conduit of money for highways. Revenue should continue to be tapped from gasoline, tire, and oil sales taxes. But at both state and federal levels, the money should go into *general funds* so that highway boosters will, for the first time since 1956, have to *compete* for priorities, instead of being automatically funded.

The way things work now, the highway program is simply not subject to the same competitive pressures as other programs. Other government projects have to be authorized by the Congress or the state legislatures, and then after authorization, must go to the appropriations committees which cut and prune and allocate money from the general fund. Depending on events, the skill of the program advocates, and the pressures of public opinion, the Congress or state legislatures decide which items are most pressing and how much each will get.

For instance, our national space program began in 1959 with appropriations totaling a paltry $370 million. In 1960, it received $485 million. As momentum built for the program, the budget increased. By 1963, it was $3.6 billion, and in 1965, $5.1 billion. But a less enthusiastic Congress, concerned with inflationary pressures and, to at least some degree, the press of social problems, by 1969, provided $3.9 billion, a reduction and beginning of a leveling off.

Not our highway program, however. As the money pours into the Highway Trust Fund, in ever increasing amounts each year, the program expands—automatically. In 1957, the highway program received $1 billion in federal funds. From then on through 1965, the amount fluctuated at around $2 billion yearly. In 1966, it jumped to $3 billion, and by 1969, the program received $5 billion. Since money is authorized for several years in advance, the 1968 Highway Act was able to provide for a total of $21 billion for roads through 1974. The way it works is that the House and Senate Public Works committees simply agree on a bill to authorize expenditures to meet future revenues from the Trust Fund, and Congress passes the bill. The funding is beyond the purview of the Appropriations committees. This is "back-door financing."

With the highway user revenue back in the general treasury, where it was until 1956, *all* forms of transportation would be able to compete for money from the enlarged general fund. Then a state or community could request either a block grant from the Department of Transportation or appropriations for a specific project and have some real chance to plan and buy a system appropriate to its needs, rather than having to accept highways or nothing. Consider this absurd situation: Current plans by cities to consider rail rapid transit systems run head-on into the problem that the 1969 federal mass transit budget for the *entire* country was only $175 million, not even enough to provide adequate planning funds—a drop in the bucket compared to the billions of dollars that pour into the Highway Trust Fund exclusively for highway funding. Our interplanetary transportation system speeds ahead, however. We spent $25 billion to send two men to the moon and there is talk already of sending men to Mars at a cost of $40 billion.

Unfortunately, in the light of the Highway Trust Fund experience, there is a strong sentiment developing for establishment of a separate *mass transportation trust fund,* or, as others envisage it, the conversion of the Highway Trust Fund to mass transportation. As tempting a prospect as this seems, it would only create a new boondoggle. Trust funds are bad policy. However purely motivated their sponsors, such aggregations of money take on a life of their own. Should such a mass transportation trust fund be established, by whatever means, it is quite likely that every one of our urban areas would soon be covered with a complex of subway stations, whether they made any transportation sense or not.

If anything, our experience with the Highway Trust Fund shows that "planning" is guided by funding, not the other way around. Comprehensive planning, as incorporated in the 1962 Highway Act, simply meant planning more highways because there was no money available for alternatives. As desirable as it may be for many communities, rail mass transit is not necessarily the only other alternative to freeways. We should not be locked into any funding system that is exclusively dedicated to any single mode of transit.

Not surprisingly, Secretary of Transportation Volpe, a highway enthusiast and champion of the Highway Trust Fund, has endorsed the creation of a special trust fund for mass transit. He believes this will fend off enemies of the Highway Trust Fund. One proposed mass transit fund would derive from the 7 percent excise tax on either automobiles and automotive equipment (which at present goes into general federal revenues and is scheduled to expire in 1974) or cigarettes. As proposed by Congressman Wright Patman, Democrat of Texas, the $1.5 billion the auto tax now generates annually would be set aside for mass transit until 1970. At that time, the tax is scheduled to be reduced to 3 percent, providing only $700 million each year thereafter. This tax is being allowed to drop in 1970 from 7 to 3 percent at a time when the 10 percent income surtax is being extended. If Congressman Patman were to suggest increasing the excise tax from 7 percent to 10 percent, a mass transit fund could expect to receive $2 billion annually, instead of dropping to a mere $700 million annually after 1970 as it will under his proposed bill. Thus, even if a mass transit trust fund *were* a good idea, the way this one is being proposed suggests that it will start shrinking very early in its life.

Volpe's support for a transit fund derived from cigarette taxes is inconsistent with his argument that there can be no diversion of the Highway Trust Fund because it was collected from users specifically to build more roads. That kind of logic would dictate that cigarette taxes be devoted to promote better, safer cigarettes.

Other bills to establish mass transit funds are making the rounds of Congress, too. President Nixon sidetracked Secretary Volpe's trust fund concept with a twelve-year mass transit program of his own that would cost $10 billion. The money would come from annual appropriations and provide matching funds at the rate of two-thirds federal and one-third state. Critics of this proposal point out that there is no guarantee that this amount of money would actually be appropriated for mass transit, since transit would vie for priority along with all other interests while the highway program rolled along financed by its own trust fund.

The President's proposal was rejected by the fifty governors who, instead, endorsed a bill sponsored by Congressman Koch. His bill establishes a trust fund of $10 billion over the next four years which would be parceled out on the same 90–10 ratio as the federal highway program. The $10 billion would, like Volpe's proposal, derive from the auto excise tax.

Again, however, Koch's proposal does not get a handle on the Highway Trust Fund; it simply establishes still another trust fund, this one for mass transit. Since it can be argued that our national housing and education needs are as pressing as our transportation crisis, it would follow just as logically that we should establish trust funds from property taxes for public housing and introduce a tax per head on every child who attends public school. Trust funds are bad government.

Change can take place in other ways, too. Public officials must be persuaded that highways and rapid transit cannot meet all of our transportation needs. Transportation does more than move people and goods. It determines land use and affects the quality of our environment. For example, our auto orientation has led to the practice of using the playgrounds of inner-city schools for parking lots for teachers. This practice has been defended in Washington, D.C., by the school administration on grounds that parking is at a premium in downtown neighborhoods. Not a word on the need for play space for kids.

We also have to come to grips with air pollution. The California Senate already has done so by passing a bill, 26 to 5, serving notice on Detroit that it must develop an alternative to the internal combustion engine by 1975 or peddle its product elsewhere. And this occurred in the only state that makes mandatory an exhaust emission control device on every automobile. Where are the other states?

Public opinion must also play a stronger role in transportation planning than it has in the past. Organizations such as AASHO, which likes to take full credit for insisting back in 1954 that the Interstate System penetrate our cities instead of skirting them in the manner of the German autobahnen, must be made to understand that critics of highways are not fanatics, screwballs, Communists, or misinformed, but concerned citizens with a legitimate point of view. Those states with departments of transportation must respond to public opinion. Engineers cannot be allowed to impose their ill-conceived plans on the public. Of course, the flow of cash to these departments will define their future role.

The Department of Transportation in Washington has taken a few steps to strengthen the role of public opinion in highway planning. This agency made the first meaningful step toward effectively involving the public in highway building decisions when Lyndon Johnson's Secretary Boyd put into effect a regulation concerning public hearing procedures. Before the regulation, highway departments

simply posted a notice of a public hearing on alignment of a proposed highway. If the community liked the route selected, fine. If
not, complaints were duly recorded and duly ignored. Late in 1968,
the Department of Transportation circulated for comment a proposal that would provide for two separate public hearings on any
highway proposal. The first hearing would provide for comments
before the general route was selected. A second hearing would be
held after the highway was designed. The proposed regulation also
included an appeals procedure if critics still were not satisfied with
the highway plan and provided that the public would be permitted
to consider alternate methods of transportation. Volpe, at the time
President Nixon's Secretary-designate, said the regulation contained
"administrative obstacles" which could snarl highway construction
for years. Meanwhile, copies of the proposed regulation fanned out
across the country. Every governor, mayor, and highway department head received one, as well as other interested local politicians.
Freeway critics helped spread them into the hands of the public. The
result was that DOT lawyers experienced a rare phenomenon. Proponents of the regulation outnumbered opponents and some suggested taking the regulation even further. Usually, such federal regulations bring responses mainly from people who are against the
proposal, but in this instance, organizations and private citizens supported the regulation so enthusiastically that they took the time to
sit down and say so in writing. In general, governors and highway
department commissioners as well as big city mayors and representatives of the road-building industry and other highway lobby
groups were against the regulation, but they were clearly in the
minority.

Three days before leaving his post as Secretary of Transportation,
Boyd ordered the regulation to go into effect in modified form. The
two public hearings were retained but the appeals procedure and
the opportunity to consider alternatives to highways were knocked
out. They must be put back into the regulation. After taking office,
Volpe vowed to rewrite the rules and eliminate administrative obstacles to the highway program, a step which he has not yet taken,
at this writing. He later commented, "We have accepted the dual

hearings as left to us by our predecessors but we are not wedded to the idea. If we can find administrative shortcuts to speed up the process, we'll use them."

In an effort to speed up construction of inner city freeways, Volpe has appealed for what he calls "common sense" and compromise from those conservation and civic groups that oppose highways on grounds that they destroy homes and parklands. He points out that city highways can be designed to enhance the opportunities for replacement housing and to serve the total needs of a community. An old tune.

Mr. Nixon's Secretary of Housing and Urban Development, George Romney, has cited one such opportunity, a Michigan law which was passed while he was still governor. The law requires that local politicians appoint an advisory board to assist displaced persons find suitable housing before the Michigan Department of State Highways can proceed with highway construction. The law in no way actually creates any housing units, nor is any money provided for such housing. Therefore, it is possible that persons displaced from their homes by highway construction under this law may merely get at the head of the line in the waiting list for available housing, nosing out persons who are also being displaced because of school, police or fire station, or whatever construction. In cities where a housing shortage exists, no extra advisory services, aid in moving cash outlay, or priority in line will result in a net gain to the community in either social or physical terms. Such a policy offers advice only to persons displaced by highways; it is a sop.

Romney labeled the Michigan law "a marked change in the highway program" and in the next breath vowed his willingness "to go to the mat" with the federal highway program over the issue of housing.

In March 1969, Volpe said in a New York *Times* interview that he was mystified by attempts of critics to associate him with the "highway lobby." Ingenuously, he declared:

I don't know who the "highway lobby" could be except the 205 million Americans who want to travel more efficiently than they do today. The average American spends 13 percent of his working day behind the wheel of a car, getting to and from work. He wants an improvement, and that's what highways can provide.

Volpe implies that improving highways will improve transportation. But the fact is that trip time remains fairly constant for the average commuter and improved highways only make it possible for people to move farther away from their place of employment.

Volpe revealed his bias toward the highway tong when he appointed forty-year-Bureau-of-Public-Roads careerman Frank Turner as Federal Highway Administrator. "Some people suggested that I appoint a city planner or a psychologist to the Highway Administration. But you don't go to a doctor with a legal problem, and I needed an experienced man to run our massive highway program," he explained. Yet Volpe contradicted himself in choosing a new chief for the Urban Mass Transportation Administration. He chose Carlos Villarreal, a sales executive in an aerospace corporation. Volpe explained his choice: "He's not a transit man and that was deliberate. I wanted someone who wasn't wedded to old concepts but someone who could think fresh and was familiar with technological research."

Along with administrative changes which would occur as a result of removing the funding impetus for the program, it would be possible to initiate immediate and practical steps to salvage our urban areas. This calls for rethinking the whole transportation picture. Cities in Europe provide us with some excellent guidelines. For instance, the downtown shopping and business centers of our major cities are plagued by the problem of both pedestrians and vehicles all mixed together and getting in each other's way. We can stop mixing this traffic very easily. Venice is an excellent example of a city that maintains pedestrian traffic completely separate from vehicles, which operate on the canals. This is not to suggest that we flood streets for canals, but that we remove vehicles from our cities' business and shopping cores so that people could conduct their functions unimpeded by the constant interruptions and dangers to life, limb, and breath of automobiles, trucks, and buses, all vying for the same space at the same time. Truck deliveries could be made during hours when the streets are closed to pedestrian traffic, mainly in the early and late hours of the day. Or, as in Rome, shops could close down for several hours during the afternoon, deliveries could be made, and pedestrian traffic welcomed afterward.

New York City has initiated just such a plan on narrow Nassau Street in the midst of the financial district of Lower Manhattan. Between 11 A.M. and 2 P.M., the street is closed to all vehicular traffic on Nassau's five blocks between Spruce Street and Maiden Lane. An estimated 27,000 pedestrians jam the "instant pedestrian shopping mall" daily as they venture out to eat, shop for discount drugs, television sets, dresses and ties, and visit doctors and dry cleaners in shops and offices in the buildings clustered along the street. The shop owners themselves have hailed the ban on traffic as "good for business."

The carless urban street is a first step toward revitalizing transportation in our urban centers. Entire central business districts will soon follow suit, with vehicular traffic in the form of buses and taxis dropping passengers at some peripheral point of a circumscribed pedestrian way that is close to downtown. Passengers will alight within a short walking distance from their destinations.

Furthermore, we must stop freeway construction in our cities and consider demolishing some of them. The old Whitehurst Freeway along the Georgetown waterfront in Washington, D.C., is scheduled by the D.C. Highway Department for the wrecking ball. Clearly, San Francisco's dangling Golden Gate Freeway at the Embarcadero should go. Others will soon prove, if they have not already, that they were mistakes and have become a burden, rather than a relief to the commuter and his community.

Each community should be able to exercise control over the number of automobiles it is willing to accommodate.

This is not such a difficult idea to implement. In December 1968, Washington's National Capital Planning Commission decreed that "a policy that seeks to limit the flow of automobiles into the heart of the city is a practical and realistic approach to transportation planning. The commission would go so far as to say that through no other approach can it meet its basic planning responsibilities." The members of the commission went on to declare that freeways cause *more* problems, not less.

In September 1969, officials at Yosemite National Park introduced a tramway bus service in Mariposa Grove and banned automobiles from entering that magnificent area in an effort to keep it from being ruined by smog and traffic jams. Park officials said cars also might be prohibited from entering other areas of the park, where exhaust fumes from a million automobiles often leave an urban-like haze over Yosemite's centurial redwoods.

Surely if the need to ban automobiles in parkland can be recognized and dealt with intelligently, civilized urban man can respond in kind. Automobiles can be banned from specific areas of cities and limited in other areas.

Limitations on autos could be accomplished in many ways: Rationing parking spaces and hiking the price to discourage commuters from bringing their cars downtown are two obvious approaches. It would be interesting to find out how many persons would be willing to pay $7 per hour to park their cars. And if curb parking was eliminated, it would act as a further check on bringing cars into the city and make more obvious the true out-of-pocket costs of operating the vehicle, since the driver would always be forced to pay dearly for parking in a garage. Also, with parked cars off the streets, those emergency and public transit vehicles which must use the streets would be able to do so more efficiently.

Another method of limiting the number of autos is simply to stop building the highways that tempt their use.

As a matter of fact, much more could be done to improve transportation conditions than by spending billions for more freeways: Making transit travel a few cents cheaper and automobile travel a few cents more expensive. For instance, a "Washington Area 1980 Rail Rapid Transit Patronage Forecast," completed by Alan M. Voorhees and Associates in July 1967, demonstrated that increasing the cost of downtown parking by eight cents per day would increase the proportion of bus riders by three percent. Likewise, a decrease of two cents per bus token would do the same. If this approach were applied over the entire Washington metropolitan area, each percentage point of increase in transit ridership would fill many buses, and each additional rush-hour bus would remove forty automobiles from the peak load on our highways.

There is also a hidden culprit in our transportation picture. It is the subsidy supplied by employers to their employees. Both private firms and government agencies typically provide free parking for their highly paid executives, but few, if any, give free bus tokens to a stenographer or file clerk. To make matters worse, a private firm can write off the expense of providing such parking as a business expense, while the employee receives a payment in kind, for which he pays no tax, since it does not appear on his pay check as income.

Another device to cut down on the use of cars would be steep bridge tolls, especially during peak hours in lanes both entering and leaving the city, so that drivers would face two stiff tolls for the right to drive an automobile into a city. Or double ramps could be built at expressway entrances: One ramp would absorb automobiles, the other ramp could be reserved for express buses in a priority or head-of-the-line merge. As these vehicles carrying many passengers speed away on the expressway, the automobiles would wait in line on their ramp to take their turn. This kind of priority is not new. Already, at some of our biggest and busiest airports, the number of flights per hour is being rationed to reduce congestion. At Kennedy Airport, a $25-minimum landing fee has been imposed on private planes that land during the airlines' peak travel periods. This is simply another way of discouraging planes with one or two passengers from landing ahead of "mass-transit" planes with many passengers. The same could be done with automobiles.

Such measures would not reduce the number of people who enter downtown every day. Rather, they would tend only to reduce the number of automobiles that do so. For the past thirty years, the number of persons entering the central business district of our major cities has remained constant. Interestingly enough, the number of automobiles entering the same areas has steadily *risen* over the same period of time. It is cars more than people that are clogging the cities.

Hans Blumenfield, a noted planner, has examined the growth patterns of our cities and explains the phenomenon this way: There are four types of land use in our metropolitan areas, central business, industrial, residential, and open. Within a metropolitan area, the "original city" remains the core. Main transportation lines are oriented to this area and all those functions which require "mutual contact" concentrate here, usually in office buildings. In addition, this center attracts all those functions which serve the entire area. These two basic functions, mutual contact plus service to the entire area, in turn attract other service activities such as restaurants, parking facilities, etc.

The crush to get into this center creates a competition for space both within the core and on the transportation facilities leading to the core. This in turn leads to a displacement from the center of all those uses which require a lot of space and can function elsewhere, such as warehouses, manufacturing, consumer services, and residences. As the population spreads out, sectors beyond the core city begin to accommodate enough population and purchasing power to support "second order" services of their own, notably retail, consumer, and some business services. As growth continues, the quality of this second order moves up, leaving a narrow range of "highest order" in the center. Similarly, all second order routine office functions also move out, leaving only the highest order contact functions in the center. Since our metropolitan centers continue to grow, the highest order functions continue to grow and are even augmented by others of still higher order that exist as the size of the total market increases. Therefore, the center is constantly undergoing a continuous process of selective adaptation to these highest order and second order functions. Surprisingly, this relatively constant process of selectivity produces a stable number of persons entering the central area. It seems ironic that while contact is the lifeblood of the center city and concentration and pedestrian movement are its most essential requirements, our public policies have had the effect of interfering with all of these basic relationships.

That is, we build facilities that encourage increased vehicular traffic. Blumenfield has eloquently commented on this practice in a paper entitled "Urban and Social-Economic Development," which he presented to the First Canadian Urban Transportation Conference in Toronto in 1968.

> Traffic expands up to the limits of available facilities—but not beyond. The centers of big cities may always be choked, but they are never choked to death.

Since traffic demand increased with the supply of facilities, the traffic problem will never be "solved" in the sense that all will be satisfied, he added.

Our city freeways should be utilized by essential traffic only, trucks, buses, taxis, and those automobiles essential for shopping and business. All other travel should be provided by public transportation, preferably free. There is nothing new or novel about free transportation. Everyone uses it when he steps into an elevator for a vertical ride. There is no charge for this service; the owner of the building provides it for everyone's use; he has to.

With free, subsidized transit, everyone who benefits from the service pays for it. This is because everyone would benefit from transit. (Or spend the money earmarked for subsidy to overhaul and improve the system instead.) The car owner would benefit when his neighbor leaves his car at home and takes the subway or bus, making fewer demands upon existing highways. After all, the more people who drive downtown, the quicker congestion occurs. On the other hand, most people don't want to drive downtown and don't. So why should they pay? For the same reason everyone pays for a park or playground. Not everyone uses them, but everyone pays for them.

Speed would be served, too, by freedom from fares. Passengers could board streetcars or buses at more than one door, reducing running time. The percentage of passengers would increase, possibly up to 40 percent or more, half of whom would be persons who formerly drove automobiles, thus reducing auto congestion. This reduced traffic would in turn mean less money for roads, parking facilities, and maintenance.

Blumenfield points out that in 1961 it was costing Torontonians $40 million a year in fares to operate the public transit system. If fares were abolished, he calculated, the cost of running the system would be the same—but paid for with general revenue—and Torontonians could get 400 million rides a year, instead of the present 300 million. The actual cost per ride would drop from 15 cents to 10 cents per capita.

Strange as it may seem, downtown residents do not have a great transportation problem. They are near enough to the central core to shop, near enough to their schools to walk, near enough to the grocery store to purchase food, and even close enough in to reach a museum, theater, or library in a relatively short amount of time. It is the suburban commuter who really faces problems and causes them when he hits the city line with his automobile. But it is not his fault, nor is he the real culprit who is causing the resentment and anger of city residents who are being inundated by automobiles. Both are victims of sprawl. As Hans Blumenfield has pointed out, a metropolitan area extends as far as daily commuting is possible and no farther. In most cases, the area embraced by a metropolis has a radius represented by a travel time of forty minutes in the principal vehicle of transportation, either train or auto, or about forty-five minutes from door to door. As speed of the vehicle is improved, the extent of the metropolitan area can expand. In most metropolitan areas the average travel time to work is half an hour. Only 15 percent of the workers spend more than forty-five minutes traveling to work.

This, of course, was not always so. Our earliest cities were limited by internal restrictions. Travel within the city was by hoof or foot. This situation limited cities to a radius of only about three miles from the center. In the absence of elevators, the city was also limited in terms of vertical expansion. The only possible growth was interstitial, by covering every available square inch with residences, factories, shops, and offices, all crowded around the center. Naturally, the price of city land became steep and the shape of the city was circular.

Then long-distance transportation by steamship and railroad and communication by the electric telegraph made it possible for cities to draw on large regions and grow to populations of millions. The elevator and development of the steel frame nurtured vertical growth in the form of skyscrapers. Then, streetcars, bus lines, and railroad stations began reaching out into suburban areas, creating ribbons of development along their routes, surrounded by wide open spaces. When the automobile made it possible to fill up the interstices or open spaces, we were back to the circular form of the foot-and-hoof city. The structured pattern of development and open land, which had begun to emerge in the railroad and streetcar era, was submerged in universal sprawl. Ironically, Blumenfeld points out, people moved to the suburbs to have the city nearby on one side and the country on the other. But as more and more people did the same thing, the ring of suburbs widened, the country moved farther away and suburban growth became self-defeating.

Anyone who has tried to drive to a suburban shopping center on a Saturday knows that highways and automobiles cannot continue to be the only transportation mode available for suburban communities. Even more, the trip to the shopping center reveals that the highway engineers, the supposed experts, have not properly planned those expressways and beltways they have built. Everyone is trying to use the facility at the same time and the only governing mechanism is congestion. We do not need any more radial freeways from the center city to suburban communities. Efficient public transit can serve the commuting public far better. Because traffic is growing faster among the suburban communities than between the central city and its surrounding communities, the suburbanites need a few strategically placed expressways, particularly beltways, to connect them with each other in a more efficient manner than they now do. Shopping centers must also "thicken up" so that each can offer the surrounding residents enough second order services so fewer trips will be necessary. Bus and jitney service, moving beltways for pedestrians, all of these services could be installed now to ease the load of the suburbanite who spends so much time just trying to get somewhere.

We must stop planning for the impossible goal of congestion-free highways, which only result in still more highways to serve ever increasing traffic volumes. We will have smaller traffic volumes if we concentrate on *limited* highway systems. Now, and in the future, proposals for new highways must be supported by data showing traffic volumes and degrees of congestion that will occur under various combinations of public and private transportation investments. Such presentations would show more clearly the amount of traffic which would be *induced* by each additional highway. Armed with these facts, each community can then decide how it wishes to proceed. If a community decides it really wants more freeways and automobiles, fine. If it votes to invest in public transportation as the main common carrier, then outsiders who visit the community will simply convert to whatever system is available. Surely we have enough streets and highways now to accommodate the trips, for pleasure or business, that absolutely must be made by private vehicle. As to surface-bus transit, the public is entitled to well-designed and comfortable carriers. Other countries have comfortable buses that can even accommodate baby carriages and have eliminated steep steps, something which General Motors apparently considered impossible, judging from the line of buses they have continued to crank out over the years.

As to subway systems, there are innumerable technologically feasible improvements. The main problem subways face, more so than any other commuter service, is the fact that as long as highways are indiscriminately provided, people will use cars and roads no matter how attractively designed the trains are—until congestion becomes intolerable. And don't be fooled by the kind of theory peddled by "experts" at our universities who state that cities must have populations of at least 1.5 million in order to support a subway system. Not if that is the *main* carrier, they don't. If we discourage automobile use, public transit will revive and improve. Many European cities boast of excellent public transportation subway-oriented systems, particularly Moscow, Paris, and London.

Here, on the other hand, good old American technology dictates that we pay lip service to attempts to provide transit while at the same time we provide every highway the Trust Fund can finance—and label such efforts, "balanced transportation."

Colin Buchanan, noted British town planner, made some interesting observations back in 1962 about the automotive age in America, particularly as it pertains to suburban and residential areas. He labeled one aspect of the negative effect of proliferation of automobiles as "visual intrusion." He pointed out that in the United States, where so much has been done to create beautifully landscaped residential areas, the cars stand out all over the place and are accepted as part of the scene. Disused garages are converted to playrooms. Indifference to visual intrusion has led to curb parking, with its attendant maintenance and repairs, derelict cars, street garbage and litter, which cannot be easily swept away, oil stains, and grease. Open parking lots, damaged curbs, broken railings, and signs everywhere don't add anything pleasant either. "There is nothing . . . in the experience of the United States to suggest that frank acceptance of the visual impact of the motor vehicle is leading to the emergence of any new kind of brilliant, lively urban townscape. On the contrary, it is producing unrelieved ugliness on a great scale," he says.

As for the concept of dispersal of a city, Buchanan noted that Los Angeles is an example of a city that planned for dispersal and that "dispersal taken beyond a certain point complicates the transport situation by positively generating the need for vehicular movement."

Our future development must include new towns, too, connected to the central city by fast public transportation for those persons who must enter the central city, although, again, that number will remain relatively constant. The rail line can also serve to connect new towns with other suburban communities so that exchange among them can occur without more radial highways and sprawl.

If you think all new town and suburban residents are "wedded" to their automobiles, visit Reston, Virginia, a "new town" outside Washington, D.C. Several businessmen and government employees, who were driving the twenty miles between D.C. and Reston every day, chartered an express bus early in 1968 to make the round trip from Reston in the morning and return in the evening, for two dollars. Soon the bus was filled with thirty satisfied commuters daily. One year later, demand for the service had grown and the residents had four buses operating, providing greater flexibility for passengers. Now Gulf-Reston Incorporated (Gulf Oil is a principal investor in the enterprise), which is managing Reston development, features the service in its real estate ads as a big plus for choosing to live in the new town. The fact that the service became a success under the guidance of private citizens for their own convenience demonstrates that the public is not being offered the kinds of services it will use if they are made available. It also means that those people who preach that everyone wants to drive an automobile everywhere are wrong. Also, the bus service is not using any new expressway to get to D.C. either. It is running on the same old route on which the passengers used to drive their own automobiles. But now instead of driving a car, these commuters spend their time reading and relaxing.

In addition to discouraging private automobiles and beefing up public transit, in whatever form, we could explore some new variations on known modes of transportation. One such variation is the Dynamically-Actuated Road Transit, or DART for short. The system can offer door-to-door limousine pickup service, or it could act more like a bus service within a particular area. In the first instance, the vehicle might carry a group of passengers headed for approximately the same destination at the same time. The fleet could operate somewhat like a car pool but with the advantage of always being available. It is reasonable to assume that the highest level of door-to-door service would cost no more than a taxi, while its lowest level of buslike service would cost no less than that of a bus system. During peak hours, the DART system could function as a collector of passengers in low-density neighborhoods that would deliver them to a high-speed rail station for the trip downtown or wherever. Because DART is capable of bringing people from a wide area to a single point, there would be need for fewer stations for the rail line, thus enhancing speed of the rail line.

Another obvious service that is needed in many cities is a direct rail line to airports. A study of major airports at San Francisco, Boston, New York, and Detroit by Wilbur Smith and Associates revealed that airport parking lots contained more cars than airline passengers in both Boston and San Francisco. This is so because a large number of people work at the airport and many of them drive automobiles to work. In New York, however, most people used public transportation to get to and from the airport. In Detroit, 67 percent of passengers arrived by private vehicle. Therefore, not surprisingly, Wilbur Smith researchers concluded erroneously that when new airports are planned, enough more land should be purchased to accommodate high capacity freeways and parking lots to serve airport passengers. They come to this conclusion despite the fact that they noted carefully that the Boeing Company predicts 102 daily departures of its 747 jumbojet aircraft alone from Kennedy Airport by 1971. This averages out to approximately 5000 passengers for any single peak hour! If such numbers of airport travelers used private automobiles to get to and from the airport, our parking lots at the airports would be so large and far from the terminal that it would be necessary to provide transportation between the parking lots and terminal.

The new high-speed metroliner train between Washington and New York demonstrates not only that people are still willing to use "old" methods of transportation if they are modernized, but also that time saved by flying is offset by time lost in inefficient ground transportation between airports and final destinations. The train passenger who boards the train in downtown Washington steps off it in midtown New York in two and one-half hours. These days, the same trip by air takes about the same time. Presumably, many people like the convenience of railroad-station-to-railroad-station delivery because Penn Central has put a second train on the line, and agents advise passengers to book a week in advance, if possible, to assure a seat. The really meaningful test will occur when high-speed trains run as frequently as flights between Washington and New York, offering passengers a real choice. Currently, the train passenger must plan his trip well in advance, since there are only two trains daily, while the airplane passenger can catch any of the numerous flights, almost like hailing a taxi.

There are many other alternatives to the private car. Given some fair competition, that is by curtailing automobile use, private enterprise and DOT subsidies could offer the public an array of services. What is required is a change in the kind of thinking that has dominated transportation research. Alexander Ganz, lecturer in MIT's Department of City and Regional Planning, recently demonstrated how the very thought processes of the "experts" need a radical change.

In an article in MIT *Technology Review,* January 1969, Ganz estimated that by 1985 possibly one fifth of all American households will have an income of less than $4000 a year and, therefore, be unable to purchase an automobile. He allows that our public transportation system may prove inadequate for this group of Americans. What to do? He says we "tend" to assume that massive subsidies will bolster our sagging public transport, while "recent studies now suggest that subsidizing the household may be a better solution than subsidizing the transport system, because public choice suggests continuing and indeed rising resistance to the use of public transportation systems." From this trend, Ganz anticipates that the future demand for freeways will necessitate doubling our present urban freeway mileage. In other words, supply automobiles for low-income families and build freeways for their use. Ganz's article is based on a study completed during 1968 for MIT's Project Transport, with financial support from a General Motors Corporation grant for highway transportation research.

It is important—and astonishing—to note that Ganz believes that the public has exercised some choice in determining its transportation mode. This argument has as much merit as the one that states that automobiles cannot be banned from our cities because our country was founded on the belief that every American has the right to go wherever he pleases, whenever and however. But at someone else's expense? How much longer can we tolerate what has been done to our cities in the name of automobiles? No other society has so exploited its natural resources and allowed its environment to become so cluttered, polluted, and ugly.

Greed and stupidity have contributed to this tragedy. The argument has been made time and time again that we cannot curtail automobile use because our economy depends so heavily on the automobile industry. We are told that we cannot afford to throw millions out of work, destroy the big auto companies that are pillars of our American way of life. Yet Walter Reuther for several years has pleaded to deaf ears that the auto industry must begin a program of diversifying. The industry has taken some small steps toward doing so. They will not do so on a broad scale until forced. Ford Motor Company or General Motors and all the rest can be depended upon to act in the best interests of the auto industry, as will all the highway groups. Must the public also act in the best interest of the industry? Public Works Committee hearings are replete with pleas from various quarters that contractors are working at only 35 or 60 or some percentage of capacity, as if each of us is personally responsible for a comfortable livelihood for people who —in their ignorance—are paving us all over.

The people who clamor on Capitol Hill for more funds to finance their grandiose road schemes at present have some very practical advantages over the average citizen. For one thing, they have the ear of public officials who commingle in private organizations such as the ARBA, AGC, and the Road Gang, and who have performed their official public functions in virtual seclusion, shielded from scrutiny. Then, too, highway promoting organizations are allowed to treat their lobbying activities as business expenses. Members of the Emergency Committee on the Transportation Crisis in Washington and their counterparts across the land enjoy no such advantages, although they spend a great deal of time fighting to promote and protect the public interest. These groups of private citizens spend time and energy and money because the Congress has failed to curb the highway interests, and because the public is not aware of the nature of our transportation dilemma.

Few congressmen and senators will take a hard line against high-

ways without an outcry from their constituents to support them.
The attitude of Senator Tydings of Maryland is typical of the
thinking that pervades the minds of too many of our legislators.
In July 1967, he wrote a complaining constituent:

> We must recognize the fact that for all practical purposes the industries
> and interests constituting what is commonly known as "the highway
> lobby" have sufficient political influence to prevent any diversion of
> the highway trust fund before the completion of the present interstate
> highway program.

One can only ask the senator just who allowed the lobby to become so
powerful, because the Congress itself can take steps to control the
influence of the highway lobby. They include such measures as
requiring full financial disclosures of themselves and all those who
try to influence legislation. Strict conflict-of-interest laws must be
formulated which cover both legislators and administrators to avoid
the kinds of commingling of interests between public officials and
representatives of private interests so prevalent in such organizations as ARBA and the Road Gang.

In this manner, highway boosters in both private industry and
public offices will no longer be able to mislead the public, a feat
which they managed to accomplish with President Eisenhower at
the time he endorsed the Interstate System in the mid-fifties. This
was revealed in 1959 at a White House meeting at which Washington planners presented their proposed regional transportation
plan for the city to the President.

After perusing the plan, which contemplated extending numerous
interstate freeways into the heart of the District of Columbia,
particularly I-95, President Eisenhower commented that he never
thought when highway advocates proposed the interstate program to
him that freeways would be extended into the centers of cities.
He said he understood that the Interstate System would connect
to the cities but not enter them.

One of the planners who was present at the 1959 meeting recalls
that the President also commented at that time about the heavy

commuter traffic he observed during his drives to suburban Maryland's Burning Tree Club for a game of golf. Mr. Eisenhower noted that a large number of automobiles was entering the city, but that most of these carried only one person. He suggested that since these automobiles clog streets and demand precious space for parking it might be feasible to limit the number of automobiles entering the city.

President Eisenhower's doubts and reservations about our highway program were voiced many years ago. They are even more valid today.

AASHO American Association of State Highway Officials; consists of heads and other members of the fifty state and District of Columbia and Puerto Rico highway departments.

AGC Associated General Contractors; 8416 builders and highway contractors.

AMA Automobile Manufacturers Association; consists of representatives of the automobile industry and bus and truck manufacturers.

ARBA American Road Builders Association; represents 5300 highway contractors, manufacturers, and distributors of highway construction equipment, investment bankers, materials producers and suppliers, faculty members and students of engineering schools, state and federal officials, and members of the Congress.

ASF Automotive Safety Foundation; formerly an arm of the Automobile Manufacturers Association, ASF is supported by the automobile industry, petroleum, asphalt, cement, and rubber interests.

ATA American Trucking Associations; sixty-four organizations representing the fifty state trucking associations plus the District of Columbia and thirteen "conferences," whose purpose is to promote bigger and more highways.

HRB Highway Research Board; a nongovernmental organization consisting of public officials, state highway officials, auto manufacturers, and representatives of engineering firms, petroleum, and steel interests.

NHUC National Highway Users Conference; 3000 private member groups dedicated to promoting more highways.

1916   Established federal participation in highway construction and instructed participating states to organize highway departments.

1921   States were instructed to formulate a planned system of highways.

1944   Funds were designated for the primary, secondary, and urban programs for the first time, and the 40,000-mile interregional highway system was designated.

1956   The Highway Trust Fund was established by a special revenue act. The Interstate System was launched.

1962   Urban areas were required to establish comprehensive transportation plans by 1965. State highway departments were invited to participate in relocation advisory assistance programs.

1966   A specific clause was added to the regular Highway Act to the effect that no trust funds could be used for beautification, i.e., for controlling outdoor advertising, screening junkyards, or scenic enhancement.
Legislation established traffic and motor vehicle safety programs, also not to be funded from the Highway Trust Fund.

1968   An additional 1500 miles were added to the Interstate System, freeways were ordered to be constructed in the District of Columbia, the Secretary of Transportation's authority over parkland was changed, state highway departments were authorized to offer as much as $5000 above appraised value to homeowners displaced by highway construction, and funds were authorized for fringe parking facilities.

Chapter 1

"Interregional Highways," message from the President of the United States transmitting a report of the National Interregional Highway Committee outlining and recommending a National System of Interregional Highways. January 12, 1944.
Federal Laws, Regulations and Other Material Relating to Highways, through December 1965, U. S. Department of Commerce.
"Highways and Human Values," Bureau of Public Roads report for fiscal year 1966, United States Department of Commerce.
1967 Automobile Facts and Figures, Automobile Manufacturers Association, Detroit.
The Story of Gasoline, Ethyl Corporation, 1964, New York City.
The Highway Transportation Story in Facts, 1961, National Highway Users Conference, Washington, D.C.
"Premium Special Bus Service," an Interim Summary report, September 1966, Department of Housing and Urban Development.
"Looking Ahead," June 1967, vol. 15, no. 5, National Planning Association, Washington, D.C.
Zisman, S. B., *Urban Open Space,* Transactions of the 31st North American Wildlife and Natural Resources Conference, March 1966, Wildlife Management Institute, Washington, D.C.

Chapter 2

AASHO 1964 Golden Book, American Association of State Highway Officials, Washington, D.C.
Senate Public Works Committee Roads Subcommittee Hearings, February, May 1955.
Clay Committee Hearings, October 7–8, 1954, Bureau of Public Roads library, Washington, D.C.

"Clay Committee Report," January 11, 1955, Bureau of Public Roads library, Washington, D.C.

House Public Works Committee Roads Subcommittee Hearings, March 9, 1955.

"Proceedings of the Governors Conference," 1954, Bureau of Public Roads library, Washington, D.C.

Chapter 3

Seneca Nation of Indians v. U.S. of America, 338 F 2nd 55 (2nd Cir. 1964), Cert. Denied 380 U.S. 952 (1965).

Federation of Civic Associations et al v. Thomas Airis et al 391 F 2nd 478 (D.C. Cir. 1968).

"A Review of Transportation Planning in New Orleans," a report to the Stern Family Fund, Arthur D. Little, Inc., April 1967.

Deposition of Brigadier General Charles M. Duke, January 3, 1967, Covington & Burling, Washington, D.C.

New York *Times* 1952–69.

Chapter 4

American Road Builder, January 1957–December 1968, American Road Builders Association, Washington, D.C.

Highway Officials and Engineers, a directory of personnel, as of June 1968. ARBA, Washington, D.C.

How an AGC Contractor Benefits from His Membership in the Associated General Contractors of America, Associated General Contractors, Washington, D.C.

Organization and Work of the AGC, AGC, Washington, D.C.

What Is the National Highway Users Conference? National Highway Users Conference, Washington, D.C.

"National Organization of the Trucking Industry in the United States," American Trucking Association, Inc., Washington, D.C.

American Trucking Trends, 1967, American Trucking Association, Inc., Washington, D.C.

"Major Highway Corridors of North America," Portland Cement Association, Washington, D.C.

Highway Safety With Asphalt Pavement, Asphalt Institute, December 1966, College Park, Md.

The Automotive Safety Foundation, What Is It? How Does It Operate? Automotive Safety Foundation, Washington, D.C.

Urban Freeway Development in Twenty Major Cities, Automotive Safety Foundation, Washington, D.C.

The Highway Research Board, What It Is and What It Does, National Research Council, National Academy of Sciences, National Academy of Engineering, Washington, D.C.

"Automobile Manufacturers Association Report of Activities to the Fifty-fifth Annual Meeting of Members," AMA, Detroit.

Chapter 5

American Association of State Highway Officials Constitution, By-laws and Standing Committee Organization, 1966, AASHO, Washington, D.C.

1967 AASHO Reference Book of Member Department Personnel and Committees, AASHO, Washington, D.C.

Coles, Flournoy, "Highway Development and Human Relations," Fisk University, Nashville, Tenn.

"Audit Report on District 10 Babylon, Department of Public Works, New York State, 1961–1963," New York State Department of Audit and Control, Albany, N.Y.

"National Survey of Transportation Attitudes and Behavior, Phase I Summary Report," Highway Research Program Report 49, Highway Research Board, Washington, D.C.

Study of Certain Future Highway Needs, Hearing before the Committee on Public Works, House of Representatives, November 1963.

"A Preliminary Presentation of the American Association of State Highway Officials Special Committee for Planning a Continuing Federal-Aid Highway Program," Senate Roads Subcommittee, June 5, 1967.

Preliminary Report of AASHO on Federal-Aid Highway Needs After 1972, Hearing before the Committee on Public Works, House of Representatives, June 7, 1967.

Chapter 6

"Highways and Urban Development," report on the Second National Conference, Williamsburg, Va., AASHO, December 1965, Washington, D.C.

"Summary of Activities of the Special Subcommittee on the Federal-Aid Highway Program," House Committee on Public Works, 1966.

"Problems Associated With Location and Design of Segments of the Interstate Highway System in Major Metropolitan Areas," by the Comptroller General of the United States, August 1967.

Urban Highways, Part I, Hearings before the subcommittee on roads of the Senate Public Works Committee, November 1967.

Urban Highways, Part II, Hearings before the subcommittee on roads of the Senate Public Works Committee, May 1968.

Federal-Aid Highway Act of 1968, Hearings before the subcommittee on roads of the Senate Public Works Committee, June 1968.

Federal-Aid Highway Act of 1968, Hearings before the subcommittee on roads of the House Public Works Committee, February, May, June 1968.

"Federal-Aid Highway Act of 1968, Report #1340," United States Senate, June 28, 1968.

"Federal-Aid Highway Act of 1968, Report #1584," United States House of Representatives, June 25, 1968.

"Federal-Aid Highway Act of 1968, Conference Report #1799," United States House of Representatives, July 25, 1968.

Chapter 7

Bain, Henry, Jr., "Transportation in the Comprehensive Plan," a report to the National Capital Planning Commission, December 21, 1965.

————, "What Should Washington's New Government Do About the Transportation Problem?" December 1967. Washington Center for Metropolitan Studies, Washington, D.C.

Craig, Peter S., *Freeways and Our City,* a handbook on Transportation Facts, National Capital Region, 1965.

Downs, Anthony, "The Law of Peak Hour Expressway Congestion," *Traffic Quarterly,* July 1962.

Kuhn, Tillo, *Public Enterprise Economics and Transport Problems,* University of California at Berkeley, 1962.

Meyer, J. R., Kain, J. F., Wohl, M., *The Urban Transportation Problem,* Harvard University Press, 1965, Cambridge, Mass.

"Cost of Operating an Automobile," Department of Transportation, November 1968.

"Transportation Survey and Plan for the Central Area of Washington,

D.C.," J. E. Greiner Company and DeLeuw Cather Associates, 1944, District of Columbia Highway Department.

"Transportation Plans for Washington," J. E. Greiner Company and DeLeuw Cather Associates, 1946, District of Columbia Highway Department.

"Transportation Planning in the District of Columbia, 1955–1965," a review and critique, Arthur D. Little, Inc., March 1966, Cambridge, Mass.

"Engineering Analysis and Recommendations on Alternative Proposals for the District of Columbia Comprehensive Transportation Plan," Department of Highways and Traffic, District of Columbia, November 1968.

"Need for the Lower Manhattan Expressway," Madigan-Hyland, Inc., New York, July 1964.

"The Lower Manhattan Expressway Project," Madigan-Hyland, Inc., New York, July 1966.

"Relocation: Unequal Treatment of People and Businesses Displaced by Governments," Advisory Commission on Intergovernmental Relations, January 1965.

"Highway Relocation Assistance Study," House Public Works Committee, July 1967.

"Supplementary Report of the Highway Cost Allocation Study," House Document #124, March 24, 1965.

"1968 National Highway Needs Report," House Committee on Public Works, February 1968.

Chapter 8

Blumenfield, Hans, *The Modern Metropolis,* M.I.T. Press, 1966.

"Urban and Social-Economic Development," First Canadian Urban Transportation Conference, Ottawa, 1969.

Buchanan, Colin, *Traffic in Towns,* Her Majesty's Stationery Office, 1963.

Middleton, J. T., and Ott, Wayne, "Air Pollution and Transportation," *Traffic Quarterly,* April 1968.

"Elements of the Comprehensive Plan for the National Capital," Goals for the National Capital General Land Use Objectives, December 11, 1968. National Capital Planning Commission.

"Politics and Principles for a Transportation System for the Nation's

Capital," approved by the National Capital Planning Commission, December 11, 1968.

"Supplement to the 1968 National Highway Needs Report," House Public Works Committee, February 1968.

"Calculating Future Carbon Monoxide Emissions and Concentrations from Urban Traffic Data," United States Department of Health, Education and Welfare, Public Health Service, June 1967.

318   *Index*

Turnpike companies, and roads of stagecoach era, 22
Tydings, Joseph, 298

Udall, Stewart L., 65, 66, 71–72, 79, 88
Urban America, representative of, at 1968 hearings of Senate roads subcommittee, 192, 193–94
Urban expressways: effects of, 4–6; opposition of public to construction of, 6, 54; and 1956 Federal Highway Act, 9; high cost of, 47; securing right-of-way for, 48; and 1962 Highway Act, 130, 303; ARBA advocacy of construction of, 131; criticism of, and Senate committee hearings on, 135; OCA's report on, 146; types of construction of, 148; and urban renewal, 148; federal government beefing up of, with more money, 209; Volpe's attitude toward speeding up construction of, 283
Urban Freeway Development in Twenty Major Cities, of ASF, 148
Urban Mass Transportation Administration, 284
"Urban and Social-Economic Development" (Blumenfield), 289
Urban "sprawl," 2, 209

Venice, traffic in, 284
Verrazano-Narrows Bridge from Staten Island to Brooklyn, 261–63
Villarreal, Carlos, 284
Virginia, saving of landmark in, 87–88
"Voice of the Highway Industry, The." *See American Road Builder,* of ARBA
Volpe, John A., 54, 57, 58, 72, 109, 138, 165, 209, 219, 279, 280, 282, 283–84

Wagner, Robert, 59, 60, 61
Walsh, Joseph P., 33
Warren, Audrey, 218, 224
Washington, D.C., freeway building in, 18–20, 91, 92–109, 242, 257; citizen opposition to program, 19, 93–96, 99, 101–2, 103–4, 108, 109, 251; attitude of Washington press toward, 93, 100, 102, 107–8, 256; hearings on proposed legislation, 102–7; legislation for, incorporated in 1968 Federal Highway Act, 107, 175, 221
Washington, Walter, 99, 101, 107, 108, 222
Watts district of Los Angeles, isolation of, by freeway construction, 5
Weeks, Sinclair, 40, 44, 52
We'll Take the High Road, movie of ARBA, 118–19, 120
Westchester County, New York, and controversies over highway building in, 73–79
Western Highway Institute, of ATA, 241
White, Donald O., 114
Whitton, Rex, 39, 41, 48–49, 76, 77–78, 113, 114, 131, 153, 167, 198–201, 205
Wilderness Society, representative of, at hearings of House Public Works Committee, 49
Wildlife sanctuaries, and highway building, 49, 74, 75, 76, 77, 78
Williamsburg Conference (1965), on urban highway building, 200, 203
Wilson, Woodrow, 23
Winfrey, Robley, 235–36, 241
Wirth, Harold E., 100, 102
Wiseman, S. E., 39–40
Wolff, Jerome, 91, 264–65
Womack, J. C., 89, 114
Wrenn, Raymond F., 115
Wright, Jim, 49

THE NATIONAL SYSTEM OF
STATUS OF IMPRO

INTERSTATE

TOTAL

42,500

MILES